Myth and History

THEMES IN RELIGIOUS STUDIES SERIES

Series Editors: Jean Holm, with John Bowker

Other titles

Worship
Making Moral Decisions
Attitudes to Nature
Human Nature and Destiny
Picturing God
Rites of Passage
Women in Religion
Sacred Writings
Sacred Place

Myth and History

Edited by

Jean Holm

with John Bowker

PINTER
PUBLISHERS
LONDON, NEW YORK

Distributed exclusively in the United States and Canada by St. Martin's Press

Pinter Publishers Ltd.
25 Floral Street, London WC2E 9DS, United Kingdom

First published in 1994

Distributed exclusively in the USA and Canada by St. Martin's Press, Inc., Room 400, 175 Fifth Avenue, New York, NY 10010, USA

British Library Cataloguing in Publication Data

A CIP catalogue record for this book is available from the British Library

ISBN 1 85567 098 4 (hb)
ISBN 1 85567 099 2 (pb)

Library of Congress Cataloging in Publication Data

A CIP catalog record for this book is available from the Library of Congress

Typeset by Mayhew Typesetting, Rhayader, Powys
Printed and bound in Great Britain by Biddles Ltd., Guildford and King's Lynn

Contents

Series Preface

The person who knows only one religion does not know any religion. This rather startling claim was made in 1873, by Friedrich Max Müller, in his book, *Introduction to the Science of Religion*. He was applying to religion a saying of the poet Goethe: 'He who knows one language, knows none.'

In many ways this series illustrates Max Müller's claim. The diversity among the religious traditions represented in each of the volumes shows how mistaken are those people who assume that the pattern of belief and practice in their own religion is reflected equally in other religions. It is, of course, possible to do a cross-cultural study of the ways in which religions tackle particular issues, such as those which form the titles of the ten books in this series, but it soon becomes obvious that something which is central in one religion may be much less important in another. To take just three examples: the contrast between Islam's and Sikhism's attitudes to pilgrimage, in *Sacred Place*; the whole spectrum of positions on the authority of scriptures illustrated in *Sacred Writings*; and the problem which the titles, *Picturing God* and *Worship*, created for the contributor on Buddhism.

The series offers an introduction to the ways in which the themes are approached within eight religious traditions. Some of the themes relate particularly to the faith and practice of individuals and religious communities (*Picturing God, Worship, Rites of Passage, Sacred Writings, Myth and History, Sacred Place*); others have much wider implications, for society in general as well as for the religious communities themselves (*Attitudes to Nature, Making Moral Decisions, Human Nature and Destiny, Women in Religion*). This distinction, however, is not clear-cut. For instance, the 'sacred places' of Ayodhya and Jerusalem have figured in situations of national and international conflict, and some countries have passed laws regulating, or even banning, religious worship.

Stereotypes of the beliefs and practices of religions are so widespread that a real effort, of both study and imagination, is needed in order to discover what a religion looks – and feels – like to its adherents. We have to bracket out, temporarily, our own beliefs and presuppositions, and 'listen in' to a religion's account of what *it* regards as significant. This is not a straightforward task, and readers of the books in this series will encounter a number of the issues that characterise the study of religions, and that have to be taken into account in any serious attempt to get behind a factual description of a religion to an understanding of the real meaning of the words and actions for its adherents.

First, the problem of language. Islam's insistence that the Arabic of the Qur'ān cannot be 'translated' reflects the impossibility of finding in another language an exact equivalent of many of the most important terms in a religion. The very word, Islam, means something much more positive to a Muslim than is suggested in English by 'submission'. Similarly, it can be misleading to use 'incarnation' for *avatāra* in Hinduism, or 'suffering' for *dukkha* in Buddhism, or 'law' for Torah in Judaism, or 'gods' for *kami* in Shinto, or 'heaven' for *T'ien* in Taoism, or 'name' for *Nām* in Sikhism.

Next, the problem of defining – drawing a line round – a religion. Religions don't exist in a vacuum; they are influenced by the social and cultural context in which they are set. This can affect what they strenuously reject as well as what they may absorb into their pattern of belief and practice. And such influence is continuous, from a religion's origins (even though we may have no records from that period), through significant historical developments (which sometimes lead to the rise of new movements or sects), to its contemporary situation, especially when a religion is transplanted into a different region. For example, anyone who has studied Hinduism in India will be quite unprepared for the form of Hinduism they will meet in the island of Bali.

Even speaking of a 'religion' may be problematic. The term, 'Hinduism', for example, was invented by western scholars, and would not be recognised or understood by most 'Hindus'. A different example is provided by the religious situation in Japan, and the consequent debate among scholars as to whether they should speak of Japanese 'religion' or Japanese 'religions'.

Finally, it can be misleading to encounter only one aspect of a religion's teaching. The themes in this series are part of a whole interrelated network of beliefs and practices within each religious tradition, and need to be seen in this wider context. The reading lists at the end of each chapter point readers to general studies of the religions as well as to books which are helpful for further reading on the themes themselves.

Jean Holm
November 1993

List of contributors

Jean Holm (EDITOR) was formerly Principal Lecturer in Religious Studies at Homerton College, Cambridge, teaching mainly Judaism and Hinduism. Her interests include relationships between religions; the relationship of culture to religion; and the way in which children are nurtured within a different cultural context. Her publications include *Teaching Religion in School* (OUP, 1975), *The Study of Religions* (Sheldon, 1977), *Growing up in Judaism* (Longman, 1990), *Growing up in Christianity*, with Romie Ridley (Longman, 1990), and *A Keyguide to Sources of Information on World Religions* (Mansell, 1991). She has edited three previous series: *Issues in Religious Studies*, with Peter Baelz (Sheldon); *Anselm Books*, with Peter Baelz (Lutterworth); and *Growing up in a Religion* (Longman).

John Bowker (EDITOR) was Professor of Religious Studies in Lancaster University, before returning to Cambridge to become Dean and Fellow of Trinity College. He is at present Professor of Divinity at Gresham College in London, and Adjunct Professor at the University of Pennsylvania and at the State University of North Carolina. He is particularly interested in anthropological and sociological approaches to the study of religions. He has done a number of programmes for the BBC, including the *Worlds of Faith* series, and a series on Islam and Hinduism for the World Service. He is the author of many books in the field of Religious Studies, including *The Meanings of Death* (Cambridge University Press, 1991), which was awarded the biennial Harper Collins religious book prize in 1993, in the academic section.

Christopher Lamb is Lecturer in Indian Religions in the School of Philosophy and Religious Studies, Middlesex University. His research is in the Tibetan religious biography, the *rnam-thar*, which he is pursuing at the School of Oriental and African Studies (SOAS), University of London. At present he is engaged in introducing the new computer technology into the teaching of traditional Humanities subjects. He has recently co-operated on a project, 'Animated Graphics in Industry', funded jointly by the Department of Education and Science and industrial partners, to produce, as a means of teaching Buddhist cosmology, a hypermedia version of the Tibetan game of *Rebirth*, invented in the early thirteenth century by the Sa-skya *pandita*, and he has also received external funding for two years to author a hypermedia package on Hindu polytheism. A longer-term project in view is a collaborative venture, *The Cathedral as Text*, which will use the structure of the medieval cathedral as its graphical metaphor, providing a hypertext resource for medieval studies, art history and religious studies.

Douglas Davies is Professor of Religious Studies in the Department of Theology at the University of Nottingham, where he specialises in teaching the social anthropology of religion. He trained both in theology and social anthropology and his research continues to relate to both disciplines. His interest in theoretical and historical aspects of religious studies is represented in a major study of the sociology of knowledge and religion, published as *Meaning and Salvation in Religious Studies* (Brill, 1984), and in a historical volume, *Frank Byron Jevons 1858–1936, An Evolutionary Realist* (Edwin Mellen Press, 1991). He is also very much concerned with practical aspects of religious behaviour and is a leading British scholar of Mormonism and, in addition to various articles, is author of *Mormon Spirituality* (Nottingham and Utah University Press, 1987). He was joint Director of the Rural Church Project, involving one of the largest sociological studies of religion in Britain, published as *Church and Religion in Rural Britain* (with C. Watkins and M. Winter, T. & T. Clark, 1991). As Director of the Cremation Research Project he is conducting basic work on Cremation in Britain and Europe and has already produced some results in *Cremation Today and Tomorrow* (Grove Books, 1990).

Jacqueline Suthren Hirst is Lecturer in Comparative Religion at the University of Manchester where she teaches in Indian religions. Until recently, she was Senior Lecturer in Religious Studies at Homerton

College, Cambridge, training primary and secondary teachers. Dr Hirst's research is in the Vedāntin traditions, specialising in the thought of Śaṃkara, the famous Advaitin commentator. She is also interested in attitudes to Religious Education among Hindus in Britain. She has written articles on Śaṃkara's thought for the *Journal of Indian Philosophy* and for a collection edited by Karel Werner entitled *Love Divine: Studies in Bhakti and Devotional Mysticism* (Curzon Press, 1993). She has also written books and articles for pupils and teachers on teaching about Hindu traditions, including *Growing Up in Hinduism* (Longman, 1990) with Geeta Pandey. She is currently working on a book on Śaṃkara's method suitable for undergraduate studies.

Martin Forward is Secretary of the Methodist Church's Committee for Relations with People of Other Faiths, and a Consultant to the Council of Churches for Britain and Ireland's Commission for Inter-Faith relations. He used to work in the Henry Martyn Institute for Islamic Studies, Hyderabad, India. Martin Forward has taught an introductory course on Islam at Leicester University, and now teaches courses on Islam at Leicester University.

Sybil Sheridan is a rabbi and a Lecturer at the Leo Baeck College and the Muslim College, London. She also arranges workshops and seminars on Judaism at Leo Baeck College for Christian theology students and recent ordinands. She is author of *Stories from the Jewish World* (Macdonald, 1987) and contributed two chapters to *Creating the Old Testament* (ed. Stephen Bigger, Basil Blackwell, 1989). Rabbi Sheridan is currently editing a series of texts on women's issues in rabbinic literature and is conducting research on the Song of Songs.

Beryl Dhanjal is a Lecturer at Ealing Tertiary College. She works on the programme for teaching ESOL (English to Speakers of Other Languages) and has special responsibility for developing community links, working mainly with people from the new commonwealth and with refugees. She studied Panjabi at the School of African and Oriental Studies, University of London. She has lectured at St Mary's College, Strawberry Hill, and the West London Institute of Higher Education, and has worked in adult education. She has written and translated many books, and particularly enjoys writing books for children and young people – she has written bi-lingual English/Panjabi books for children.

Xinzhong Yao is Lecturer in Chinese Religion and Ethics, St David's University College, University of Wales, Lampeter. His research interests include philosophy, ethics and religion; he is currently focusing on comparative philosophy and comparative religion. Dr Yao is author of *On Moral Activity* (People's University Press, Beijing, 1990), *Ethics and Social Problems* (City Economic Press, Beijing, 1989), co-author of *Comparative Studies on Human Nature* (Tienjin People's Press, Tienjin, 1988), co-editor of *Applying Ethics* (Jilin People's Press, Changchun, 1994), and main translator of Charles L. Stevenson's *Ethics and Language* (Social Sciences of China Press, Beijing, 1991). He is a member of the Chinese National Association of Ethics and Deputy Director of the Institute of Ethics, the People's University of China, Beijing.

Ian Reader is Senior lecturer in Japanese Studies at the University of Stirling, Scotland. He has spent several years in Japan travelling, teaching at Japanese universities and researching into contemporary Japanese religion. His major research interest is in the study of pilgrimage, and he is currently working on a volume on pilgrimage in Japan. Dr Reader is author of *Religion in Contemporary Japan* (Macmillan, 1991), and editor (with Tony Walter) of *Pilgrimage in Popular Culture* (Macmillan, 1993). He has also published numerous articles in journals and collected editions on Buddhism, Japanese religion, pilgrimage and Japanese popular culture, and is a member of the Editorial Advisory Board of the *Japanese Journal of Religious Studies*.

Introduction: Raising the Issues

Douglas Davies

Myth and history both involve ideas about time expressed through significant events and possessing an important bearing upon life. Myth and history reflect a characteristic search for meaning which is typically human and which, in life at large, takes many forms from science to poetry.

By such means the world is made less strange, and a degree of order and certainty is brought to what otherwise might be seen as chaotic and dangerous. Just as science has recently come to give an account of the natural world, so history has, for many nations, provided an account of their social world. Myth too has a similar explanatory power. This is obvious in preliterate cultures where myths are recited as part of the ritual way of life, providing an account of how things came to be and why certain values of life are important. But myth continues to be influential in literate cultures too where ancient myths form part of sacred scriptures and are subjected to changing interpretations as time goes on. So, for example, the Genesis creation narratives – strongly mythical in themselves – are now interpreted by many Christians in the light of the theory of evolution. This leads either to a greater emphasis upon the mythical quality of those texts or else to strong affirmation of their 'scientific' value. In other words, once the biological theory of evolution entered our cultural world, other forms of explanation could not be left untouched. In this way myths are open to changed interpretation as time and social circumstances change.

Defining myth

From the perspective of religious studies it is easy to define myth as stories which enshrine religious and social ideals expressed through the activities of divine, human or animal figures within an environment where astonishing things may take place. Myths occur in practically all societies and express what has been called the mythopoeic or myth-making capacity of the human imagination, an important concern for religious studies.

The problem of defining myth comes when the truths held by particular religions are enshrined in narratives which the devotees may believe actually occurred. In other words there is an argument over whether something is a myth, taking place in the imagination, or is history, having actually occurred in the world.

The approach to this myth–history problem varies from one religious tradition to another and, because of this, each of the following chapters takes its own course in dealing with the topic, each is an example of the problem of relating mythical truth to historical truth. Accordingly, each sheds light on the uses to which the very idea of both myth and history has been put by their respective tradition.

The chapter on Hinduism, for example, shows how western a distinction this divide between myth and history is, and how it changes when brought into the Indian religious tradition. The case of Shinto is another good example of indigenous meanings, with the Japanese characters used to write the word *shinwa*, or myth, being composed of two ideograms, one for the word *kami* or deity and other for *wa* or story. These myths are, then, stories about the gods, but they have the local purpose of underpinning the imperial rule and political organisation of the nation. This element of power underlying myths and certain kinds of history appears in many religious traditions as also, for example, in Islam.

The distinction between myth and history has become an increasing problem for western societies throughout the nineteenth and twentieth centuries as scholars have become increasingly aware of the ways in which actual events can be interpreted to produce different meanings for different people. Some, like the anthropologist, Claude Lévi-Strauss, whose work on myth has been especially extensive, see history as coming to function as myth in modern societies (1978), while others such as the historian of religion, Mircea Eliade, see the growth of fantasy film as another outburst of the human myth-making capacity (1968). Scientists themselves, especially physicists with their theories of the origin and end of the universe, and biologists with their accounts of the chemicals at the heart of all genes, have contributed to the idea of science as a kind of mythology of the meaning of life. The growth of fantasy games and the increasing potential of virtual reality all raise the question of the divide between mythical ideas and events which take place in the 'real' world.

For each religion there is an additional problem over myth and history, and it concerns differences between people over the distinction between the literal fact of things and the metaphorical interpretation of things. This depends upon the kind of education people have received as well, perhaps, as on the kind of people they are. For some it is easy to accept the metaphorical meaning of a myth, knowing full well that the story of the myth never 'actually happened', while others find this approach quite impossible and tend to say that something is either true or false (Cox 1984).

This distinction between literalists and those given to metaphor is also tied up with conservative and liberal interpretations of religious belief across many religions; it is a basic issue within religious fundamentalism and the identity which people gain from their religion. It becomes important as far as some of the additional traditions of religions are concerned as, for example, in Judaism, Islam and Sikhism.

The fundamental question of myth and history tends to emerge in the broad religious tradition of Judaism, Christianity and Islam, where the firm belief that God has revealed truth into the world at specific points in history itself comes to be the prime issue. Are these accounts, which reckon to be historical, actually non-historical myth? Or, perhaps, are they a special kind of myth which has had an historical dimension added to it, rather like the writings of C.S. Lewis which tended to see Christianity as a myth that happened also to be historically true? This is discussed clearly in the chapters on Christianity and Islam.

Texts and history

For millennia, the stories lying at the heart of myths gave people a picture of reality, and allowed them to interpret the complexity of life. Myths told of the origin of the world, of men and women in their dealings with supernatural beings and powers, of the source of good and evil, and of the institutions of society. Sometimes they also spoke of the future, as instanced in particular in Hinduism's looking for the coming of Kalkin, the tenth *avatāra* of Viṣṇu, and Buddhism's looking for Maitreya, the Buddha-to-come. The concern with issues of good and evil, and life after death, is also shown in the companion volume, *Human Nature and Destiny*, in this series.

Myths show how imaginative people can be as they reflect upon existence. Before the invention of writing, and even in some of today's literate cultures, as seen in Hinduism, myths exist as part of an oral tradition and often exhibit a considerable variation of content and presentation; once written texts come to exist, myths can easily turn into a more formal statement of belief (Goody 1986).

Conventions in myth

Myths are patterned in different ways from culture to culture. In some traditional societies animals play an important part as they give voice to fundamental values. In Buddhism, mythology defines whole realms of the supernatural world in what is a kind of mythological geography, one that is represented in the art and architecture of some temples.

In other religions, distinct human figures come to the fore. This is particularly clear in the chapter on Judaism where individuals are set in a growing relationship with God over time. In fact, Judaism gives the clearest possible example of history as the medium of divine revelation. The festivals celebrated are all focused on particular moments in the history of the people of Israel when God is believed to have acted in some way. This close link between history and the nation of Israel forges the very sense of identity of people in this tradition. Here there is a theology both of time and of place, of God's revelation through political events until a promised land is received.

The Judaism chapter is also important for showing not only that theological interpretations have been laid upon some preceding festivals, turning mythological phenomena into history, but also that some historical events come to be viewed mythologically. And basic to both is narrative, an important kind of narrative which tells stories in ways which include the present-day listener as a person with a living interest in what happened then. This continues to be true in India where even the televising of the great epics has attracted an audience adopting more of an attitude of piety towards the programmes than that of mere consumers of entertainment. The values and beliefs of a religion come to be encountered through such narratives and, in a sense, become timeless as far as the religious believer is concerned.

Chinese religious traditions are shown to be mixed in their attitudes, with myth playing a subsidiary part in Confucianism compared with Taoism. That chapter makes use of the important distinction between 'myth in history' and 'myth about history'.

Explanation

Part of the explanation provided by myths covers the creation and existence of the world while also explaining human nature with all its potential and problems (something that is dealt with in greater detail in the companion volumes on *Attitudes to Nature* and *Human Nature and Destiny*). In Judaism, the Genesis creation stories are shown to have links with earlier creation myths which were transformed in the process. These depict God as the sole ruler of all and give special attention to the Jews, as is clear with the first part of the Judaism chapter focusing on particular individuals who may or may not have been actual historical figures. Explanations of religious identity can be taken further when the narratives lying behind them, be they historical or mythological, become the basis for rituals conducted today, as in the case of the narratives of the Exodus of Jews from Egypt, now enshrined in the *seder* rite performed in Jewish homes.

History

History itself involves the human imagination reflecting on events and on patterns of cause and effect. Few cultures see these events as neutral activities or mere accidents. The Indian religious traditions believe that the *karma* of individuals influences their successive incarnations in a world which itself passes through major phases, with various levels of moral benefit. These religiously defined ages in the Indian traditions resemble the Judaeo–Christian classification of time in terms of various dispensations when divine activity varies in its purpose. The belief that ideas of history vary between the linear approach of the Judaeo–Christian–Islamic traditions and the cyclical view of the Indian traditions is explored in several chapters, and shown not to be as simple a concept as sometimes it is made out to be. The important fact is that history is not a single idea but is, itself, a construct of particular cultures.

The future

Religions which have an historical interest in the past tend, also, to have a clear sense of the future. Theologies describing the creation of a real world are associated with the end of that world or its future restoration. The Jewish case shows this as the Genesis accounts of creation lead into the words of the prophets about a future day of the Lord and the Lord's anointed, when the world will be ruled in a just way. The chapter on Judaism shows how Hasidic Jews today believe that the future Messiah has come and awaits full belief and revelation to the world at large. Similarly, the chapter on Japanese religion shows how the past is constructed to provide a basis for present-day life with its future goals, all for the sake of the nation.

This volume, with its emphasis falling largely in the past, needs to be studied alongside the other volume in this series on *Human Nature and Destiny*. That volume also deals with myths of human significance but takes them into the future whereas this volume stresses the past. Both are obviously radical complements to each other for a full picture of humanity's self reflection.

Persons and mythical figures

Values and beliefs of religions are expressed in different ways. Judaism's account of history in this book is conducted almost entirely by referring to particular figures in the Jewish Bible, from Adam to Elijah. This personifying of history enables the narrative to flow from purely mythological material through to historical literature, all under the same theological interpretation. So, too, in the discussion of Chinese cultural heroes.

History changes

People today approach history in many different ways. Some see it as providing an anchorage in the past for our contemporary living, while others see history as no longer a useful category of thought. This is discussed at length in the chapters on Christianity and Islam. One of these debates is focused in Francis Fukuyama's provocative study *The End of History and the Last Man* (1992) where history is associated with a hope and a drive for the future which gets lost or dies as modern people live comfortable lives devoid of ultimate explanations from history or myth and, accordingly, devoid of a sense of a future to be fulfilled.

Throughout the following chapters it is important to appreciate that each religion and culture deals with history and myth within particular contexts. Some of these may be academic contexts, but they are often religious contexts of worship which stimulate people to encounter ideas of the past, be they imaginary or not, in emotional as well as intellectual ways. It is only by appreciating this dynamic appropriation of the past that we can see how radically both myth and history enter into human faith and identity.

FURTHER READING

Cox, H. (1984) *Religion in the Secular City*, New York, Simon and Schuster.

Eliade, M. (1968) *Myths, Dreams, and Mysteries*, New York, Fontana.

Fukuyama, F. (1992) *The End of History and the Last Man*, London, Penguin.

Goody, J. (1986) *The Logic of Writing and The Organization of Society*, Cambridge, Cambridge University Press.

Lévi-Strauss, C. (1978) *Myth and Meaning*, London, Routledge & Kegan Paul.

Tonkin, E., McDonald, M. and Chapman, M. (eds) (1989) *History and Ethnicity*, London, Routledge.

1. Buddhism

Christopher Lamb

The Buddhist idea of time and history (which may be taken to include the whole period of Indian philosophical speculation from before Buddhism to post-Buddhist Hinduism) has generally been characterised as cyclic, in opposition to the Judaeo–Christian view that historical time is a unique linear process with a beginning and an end. The cyclic cosmos runs according to the so-called law of *karma*, meaning 'action' or 'cause and effect', whereas the linear cosmos is ruled according to the ordinances of a supreme Being, and, specifically, one who acts in history and who made everything that is. On the other hand, Buddhism has no creator-god theory, but might be said to attribute the role of creator to impersonal *karma*, since it is *karma* that keeps the processes of the phenomenal world (*saṃsāra*) in operation. It is sometimes said that history is about causation, but this is predicated on the notion of individuals or selves as agents of causation, not in any impersonal sense that robs history of significance (the ancient Indians had no sense of it). Both cultures put causation as fundamental, but the crucial difference between them lies in the way they view the self. In Buddhism the notion of self arises from fundamental ignorance, *avidyā*.

The Japanese philosopher, Keiji Nishitani (1982: 168–217), points out that the Buddhist conception of time is not entirely cyclical but is, after all, radically actual. He agrees with the historian Arnold Toynbee that a linear view of history has carried a positive value in that it has allowed human beings a sense that they can take control of their own destiny, but, on the negative side, has encouraged self-centredness. This has always been considered sinful, rooted in the *mythos* of original disobedience, and so on, resulting in separation from God. Further, notions such as 'chosen people', and 'the elect' are affirmed not only by the ideological point of departure, but are actually structural, giving rise to racism and nationalism.

However, he goes on to argue that, in fact, all religions at the level of *mythos* share the view of time as recurrent and ahistorical. For example, in the world of nature, seasonal cycles and astronomical time return to their starting point; the liturgical year is a recurring annual celebration of single historical events. (We note that the Mass is the continual offering of the sacrifice of Calvary throughout time; Christmas is not only the adaptation of the *mythos* of fertility cycles occurring at the winter solstice to the Incarnation of God in history, but it also celebrates the ahistorical generation of the Son from the Father at the heart of the Trinity.) In another sense, all religion is located in the field of history, and Nishitani reminds us of Kant's observation that evil is the start of history, so even if Buddhism has been more concerned with suffering than evil, within it salvation is an historic event.

Cosmology

In the early days of Buddhism, speculations about the origin and nature of the universe were discouraged because their existence was only a refraction of mental processes. Only the enlightened mind could perceive the ultimate nature of things: 'All the phenomena of existence have mind as their precursor, mind as their supreme leader, and of mind are they made' (*Dhammapada* I, 1; trans. H. Kaviratna (1980) Pasadena, Theosophical University Press). Nevertheless the *Abhidhamma* reveals that cosmological questions, such as the origin, arrangement and end of the universe, were addressed. The fullest and most systematic account is given in Vasubandhu's *Abhidharmakośa*. This massive compendium of doctrinal and commentarial material is based on earlier Sarvāstivādin *Abhidharma* treatises and is the most highly systematised account of Buddhist doctrine in the pre-Mahāyāna phase. The cosmological questions discussed concerned not only the universe as a receptacle, *bhājanaloka*, for living beings, but also the beings and their distribution within it.

The most ancient view of the universe is that it consists of a single system, a disc surrounded by a ring of iron mountains, *cakravāla*, and with a concentric series of golden mountains which rise from the surface of the earth. In the central ring rises the great Mount Meru, also known as Sumeru. There is a tradition observed by Northern

Buddhists, Hindus, Jains and Bon-pos that Mount Kailas in western Tibet is identifiable with Mount Meru, the vertical axis and navel of the world. The system is also called *trailokyadhātu*, The Triple World (see Diagram 1.1). The triple nature of the world refers to the three degrees of refinement in which conscious existence can take place.

LEVEL ONE

This is the realm of desire, *kāmadhātu*, which includes, on the one hand, the destinies of woe, hells, abodes of animals, ghost-realms, and anti-god-realms, and on the other hand, the abodes of humankind and the realms of the gods of desire; two classes of these gods dwell on terraces on the slopes of Meru leading up to Indra or Śakra, who dwells on the summit in the second heaven. *Tuṣita* heaven, the abode of the Buddha-to-come, is the fourth heaven.

Buddhist zoology

Beings exist throughout the five *gati*s (destinies): two of these are good and three bad. The human realm is a good destiny because only from there can enlightenment be attained. The gods are also considered fortunate because they have been born in one of several sub-*gati*s due to merit accrued in previous lives. Such merit, though, is only a finite resource. There are three classes of gods distributed throughout the three *dhātu*s (realms):

1. Four completely disembodied classes of gods in the formless realm, their existence sustained solely by their rebirth. In the infinity of space and consciousness they are neither conscious nor unconscious. The *Abhidharmakośa* says that highly realised persons might get powers to perceive them, but only in a form that is humanly perceivable.
2. Sixteen kinds in sixteen places in the realm of form.
3. Six kinds in six places in the realm of desire.

The three evil destinies include the animals, whose realm overlaps with the human, the hungry ghosts, who are to be found throughout the human realm but also in the realm of *Yama*, below Meru (not

Diagram 1.1 The Triple World

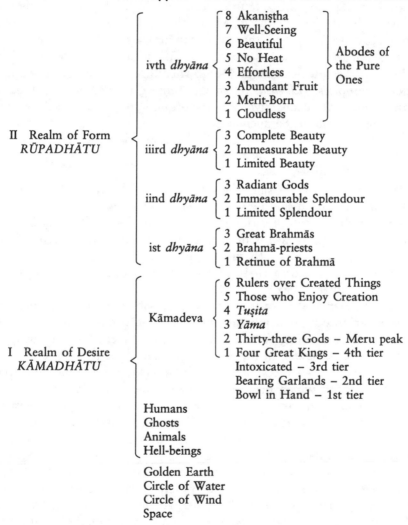

- III Realm of Non-Form *ĀRŪPYADHĀTU*
  - iv. Neither Consciousness nor Unconsciousness
  - iii. Realm of Nothingness
  - ii. Infinity of Intellect
  - i. Infinity of Space

NO ABODES ABOVE AKANIṢṬHA – RECEPTACLE-WORLD ENDS HERE

- II Realm of Form *RŪPADHĀTU*
  - ivth *dhyāna*
    - Abodes of the Pure Ones:
      - 8 Akaniṣṭha
      - 7 Well-Seeing
      - 6 Beautiful
      - 5 No Heat
      - 4 Effortless
      - 3 Abundant Fruit
      - 2 Merit-Born
      - 1 Cloudless
  - iiird *dhyāna*
    - 3 Complete Beauty
    - 2 Immeasurable Beauty
    - 1 Limited Beauty
  - iind *dhyāna*
    - 3 Radiant Gods
    - 2 Immeasurable Splendour
    - 1 Limited Splendour
  - ist *dhyāna*
    - 3 Great Brahmās
    - 2 Brahmā-priests
    - 1 Retinue of Brahmā
- I Realm of Desire *KĀMADHĀTU*
  - Kāmadeva
    - 6 Rulers over Created Things
    - 5 Those who Enjoy Creation
    - 4 *Tuṣita*
    - 3 *Yāma*
    - 2 Thirty-three Gods – Meru peak
    - 1 Four Great Kings – 4th tier
      - Intoxicated – 3rd tier
      - Bearing Garlands – 2nd tier
      - Bowl in Hand – 1st tier
  - Humans
  - Ghosts
  - Animals
  - Hell-beings

Golden Earth
Circle of Water
Circle of Wind
Space

(Adapted from Kloetzli (1983: 33–9)

the same as *Yāma*, one of the six kinds of gods of desire), and, third, the hells, eight of which are hot and eight cold.

There seems to be no clearly assigned place for the *asuras*, anti-gods. In the Tibetan pictures of the Wheel of Life, the *asuras* occupy a sixth *gati* between humans and ghosts, but commentators on the *Abhidharma* do not give them their own *gati*. Some of these also consider that they are able to intermarry with both gods and ghosts. They inhabit the caverns of Mount Meru below sea-level, in four great towns. From there they go out to attack the 'Thirty-three gods' of Mount Meru. This has given rise to the mistaken notion that they dwell at the fourth stage of Meru. There are other assorted beings, genii, vampires, (*rākṣasas*), serpents (*nāgas*), divine birds (*garuḍas*), and divine musicians (*gandharvas*), found in various realms, but their role seems to be ancillary.

Buddhist geography

The axial mountain is said to go up to the height of 84,000 *yojanas*. A *yojana* has been said by some commentators to represent as much as nine miles, in which case the height of Meru would go beyond the stratosphere. Each face is of a different material; the eastern face is silver or crystal, the southern is sapphire or lapis lazuli, the western is ruby and the northern is golden. The sun and moon have their orbits round the peak.

The human realms overlap, of course, with the animal realms. In the exterior ocean facing the four sides of Mount Meru are the islands or continents, *dvīpas*, inhabited by different kinds of people. Thus in *Pūrvavideha*, in the east, people live to be two hundred and fifty years old. To the south lies *Jambudvīpa*, Rose-apple land, the known world, which originally probably meant India, the land of the *buddhas*. Humans live no more than one hundred years here at this point in the *kalpa* or aeon, and are shaped like their continent. This is not the only correspondence between physiological and cosmic structures, and there seems to be a very ancient precedent for it. The Jains viewed the cosmos as a Great Person or Being, *mahāpuruṣa*, and later tantric practice drew correspondences between physiology and the cosmos. To the west is *Aparagodāna*, Western pasturage, where people live to be five hundred years old. In the north lies *Uttarakuru*, Northern *Kuru*. There are no villages or towns here but people live for two thousand years.

LEVEL TWO

This is the realm of form, *rūpadhātu*, rising in seventeen heavens, known collectively as *brahmāloka*. These levels are also grouped into four stages of meditation, *dhyānas*. The states of meditation through which the Buddha passed on the night of his enlightenment are linked to a series of meditation realms in the structure of the world system. It is not simply a piece of pre-scientific speculation but is a diagram of meditation practice. It is generally thought that the god Brahmā lives at the second of the *brahmālokas* in Brahmā-*purohita* heaven, and at the top of the *brahmālokas*, at the seventeenth level, is Akaniṣṭha, the place of *nirvāṇa* 'with remainder' (i.e., while the subject is still alive).

LEVEL THREE

This is the realm of non-form, *ārūpyadhātu*, rising as the four infinities. These are not places but trance-states, described respectively as:

1. The realm of the infinity of space.
2. The realm of the infinity of intellect.
3. The realm of nothingness.
4. The realm of neither consciousness nor not-consciousness.

The orthodox sources do not consider this part of the receptacle-world, *bhājanloka*, since the beings here are immaterial and therefore nowhere.

Cosmology of thousands

The triple-tiered world, *trailokyadhātu*, of the *cakravāla*, is possibly the most ancient Buddhist idea of the cosmos, but even in the oldest scriptures there is an indication that the early Buddhists had a conception of an infinite number of universes. If not infinite, the number was huge beyond imagining. The early cosmologists had no scientific means of establishing a mathematical basis for their models, so their dreams of the vastness of space could only be expressed in vast numbers; the same applies to numbers of world-systems.

Later, in the speculations of the *asaṃkhyeya* (innumerable) cosmology, *buddhas* are as numerous as the sands of the Ganges. Time was conceived in terms of the endless rotations of enormously long cycles, *kalpas*, each of which was divided into ages known as *yugas*. The *Lotus Sūtra* gives a *buddha*'s life-span as follows:

> If these world-spheres, whether an atom was deposited in them or not, were all reduced to atoms, and if each atom were a kalpa, the time since my achievement of Buddhahood would exceed even this. For a hundred thousand myriads of millions of nayutas of asaṁkhyeyakalpas I have been constantly dwelling on this Sahā world-sphere, preaching the Dharma, teaching and converting; also elsewhere, in a hundred thousand myriads of millions of nayutas of asaṁkhyeyas of realms [I have been] guiding and benefiting the beings.
>
> (Chapter 16, 'The Life-span of the Thus Come One'; trans. Leon Hurvitz (1976) New York, Columbia University Press, p. 238)

Louis de la Vallée Poussin (1911: 137) places the multiplication of world-systems in three steps:

1. A system of a thousand universes, 'small chiliocosm'.
2. A system of a million universes, a thousand 'small chiliocosms'; this is the 'middle chiliocosm'.
3. A system of a thousand million universes, 'great chiliocosm', or 'three-thousandth great-thousandth universe'.

Cosmology of innumerables

The *Mahāvastu* and *sūtras* of the Mahāyāna treat the *buddha* lands or *buddha* fields as innumerable (*asaṃkhyeya*). The *Mahāvastu* (I, 55) says it requires a hundred thousand *kalpas* to win enlightenment, and later (I, 59) says that for immeasurable incalculable *kalpas* and under a countless number of *tathāgatas*, *arahants* and perfect *buddhas*, those who seek perfect enlightenment in the future go on acquiring the roots of virtue. In the *Lotus Sūtra* (Chapter 11, 'Apparition of the Jewelled Stūpa', trans. Hurvitz, p. 187) we find:

> At that time, Śākyamunibuddha's emanations in the eastern quarter, Buddhas of lands equal in number to the sands of a hundred thousand

myriads of millions of Ganges rivers, each Buddha preaching Dharma, assembled in this place, Buddhas of ten directions all gathering in order and sitting in the eight quarters.

The *Avataṃsaka Sūtra* (trans. Thomas Cleary (1984) as *The Flower Ornament Scripture*, Vol. 1, Boston, Massachusetts, Shambhala Publications, p. 189) says:

> In each atom of the lands of the cosmos
> Rest the vast oceans of worlds;
> Clouds of Buddhas equally cover them all,
> Filling every place.
>
> In each atom are many oceans of worlds,
> Their locations each different, all beautifully pure;
> Thus does infinity enter into one,
> Yet each unit's distinct, with no overlap.
>
> Within each atom are inconceivably many Buddhas
> Appearing everywhere in accord with beings' minds,
> Reaching everywhere in all oceans of worlds:
> This technique of theirs is the same for all.
>
> In each atom the Buddhas of all times
> Appear, according to inclinations;
> While their essential nature neither comes nor goes,
> By their vow power they pervade the worlds.

The Northern Buddhist pantheon

In Buddhist cosmological theory the gods of the *Brahmāloka* are simply part of the world of beings, *sattvaloka*, that inhabit the receptacle-world, *bhājanaloka*. Strictly speaking, we should consider the world of living beings separate from cosmology, but to the early Buddhists questions of anthropology, zoology, pantheology and demonology were connected to cosmological ones. Louis de la Vallée Poussin (1911: 137) puts it thus:

> The abodes of the gods, the length of their lives, the dimensions of their bodies, and their 'non-embryogeny' are 'cosmological', while their psychology and the right they possess or do not possess to the exercise of

> virtue are 'zoological' (*sattvalaukika*). The beings, likewise, in one and the same class, inhabiting the same part of the 'receptacle-world', may differ in their method of generation; men; serpent-dragons and *garuḍas* (mythic birds) are not always born from the womb or the egg; the *cakravartin* kings resemble gods far more than men, etc. – none of this is cosmological.

One thing must be clearly understood. The gods of the *Brahmāloka* (Brahmā, Indra and other gods of the Hindu pantheon among them) play no part in Buddhist soteriology. They cannot save or bestow grace; nor are they immortal; they may live immensely long and blissful lives from the human perspective, but they are still subject to the general impermanence of conditioned things. The human realm is the only one from which liberation, *nirvāṇa*, may be gained, because only in the human condition can the First Noble Truth be fully comprehended. The gods may play a supporting role in the drama of Buddhist eschatology. For example, after he had achieved liberation under the *bodhi*-tree, the Buddha was uncertain whether to reveal the truth to other people. The god Brahmā Sahampati appeared before him and aroused the Buddha's compassion by means of argument:

> And Brahmā Sahampati adjusted his upper robe so as to cover one shoulder, and putting his right knee on the ground, raised his joined hands towards the Blessed One, and said to the Blessed One: 'Lord, may the Blessed One preach the doctrine! May the Blessed One preach the Doctrine! There are beings whose mental eyes are darkened by scarcely any dust; but if they do not hear the doctrine, they cannot attain salvation. These will understand the doctrine.'
>
> (*Vinaya* 1, 5, 6; trans. T.W. Rhys Davids and H. Oldenberg (1885) Vinaya Texts, Oxford, Sacred Books of the East, vols 13, 17, 20; repr. 1982, Delhi, Motilal Banarsidass)

Note that even before the establishment of the *saṅgha*, the *Vinaya*'s account makes Brahmā Sahampati conduct himself before the Buddha in every way like a monk. After the Buddha granted his request he bowed down before him and passed him, keeping his right shoulder towards him.

Though Buddhism has no creator-god theory in the way the monotheistic religions have, there is a place for the pan-Indian gods in the world-system, even in primitive Buddhism. Naturally, as Buddhism moved into other lands, other gods beside the Indian ones entered the scene and complicated the cosmological picture. But in addition to the accommodation of elements of folk belief within the Buddhist household, there was in the Mahāyāna a theoretical elaboration of the nature of buddhahood itself. These metaphysical speculations started with abstract enumerations of the aspects of buddhahood, but eventually the abstract forms were given iconographic representation into what are frequently called the Celestial *buddha*s and *bodhisattva*s. These figures are the iconographic representations of both the goal and the path. The goal is the state of *nirvāṇa*, represented by the fully awakened being in the state of *samādhi*, while the dynamic state of the path is represented by the highly realised compassionate being bound for enlightenment (*bodhisattva*).

L.A. Waddell (1895) gives what he calls a 'rough general descriptive list, so as to give a somewhat orderly glimpse into this chaotic crowd of gods, demons and deified saints' of what is probably the largest pantheon in the world. The following arrangement has been adapted from the one given in *Tibetan Buddhism* (1972: 327):

1. *Buddha*s – Celestial and human.
2. *Bodhisattva*s – Celestial and human, including Indian saints and apotheosised Lamas.
3. Tutelaries – mostly demoniacal.
4. Defenders of the Faith.
5. *Ḍākinī*s – female tutelary spirits.
6. Indian Brahmanical gods.
7. Country gods (*yul-lha*), and guardians, (*srung-ma*) and local gods.
8. Personal gods, household gods and familiars.

Waddell is mistaken in referring to the pantheon as a 'disorderly mob'. However, it is entirely probable that there was no uniquely Buddhist pantheon before the Vajrayāna. Following on from the notion of the transcendent Buddha developed in the Mahāyāna, the Vajrayāna came to develop a theory of celestial *buddha*s who never had an earthly existence. In works during that time various *buddha*s, other than the 'historic' ones (discussed below), are referred to;

Amitābha occurs for the first time in the *Sukāvatīvyūha Sūtra*, translated into Chinese between 147 and 186 CE. His place in the elaborate theory of five *jinas* comes later. The *Lotus Sūtra* is one of the earliest sources for the cult of Avalokiteśvara, the *bodhisattva* of compassion. In all it mentions twenty-three celestial *buddhas* and *bodhisattvas*. Other Mahāyāna *sūtras* mention more.

The earliest *bodhisattva* to attain cult status was no doubt Maitreya, the Buddha-to-come, who appears in the Pāli canon. His name is cognate with the word *mitra*, meaning 'friend', so he is the friendly or benevolent one. He is the only *bodhisattva* to be recognised by the Theravāda, making an appearance outside the Mahāyāna *sūtras*. Mañjuśrī, whose name means 'gentle glory' or 'sweet splendour', is called Kumārabhūta or 'ever young Prince Royal'. He is a kind of male Athene. He is also known as Mañjughoṣa, 'sweet voiced'. In China the Godai-Mountain, Wu-t'ai-shan, was a holy place known about in India in the seventh century CE. In his autobiography, *The Wheel of Life* (1972, London, Rider, pp. 114–55), John Blofeld describes his own pilgrimage to Wu-t'ai-shan, where he witnessed the manifestation of the *bodhisattva* in a display of meteorites. Mañjuśrī has pre-eminence in *sūtras*, such as the *Lotus Sūtra* and *The Holy Teaching of Vimalakirti*, where at the request of the Buddha and followed by eight thousand *bodhisattvas*, five hundred disciples, many hundreds of thousands of gods and goddesses, he ventures to the house of the redoubtable Vimalakirti to preach the *dharma*. When Vimalakirti gets to know who is coming, he magically transforms his house to emptiness! Mañjuśrī, as the *bodhisattva* of Wisdom, turns this into a teaching on the emptiness of all phenomena.

By the third century CE, Avalokiteśvara had become the predominant *bodhisattva*. He is the chief attendant of Buddha Amitābha in the Western Paradise, according to the *Sukhāvatī-vyūha Sūtra*. Many believe he can nullify *karma* and that he visits all suffering beings in all the realms. (Sometimes it is Kṣitigarbha who is depicted in all the *gatis* painted on the Wheel of Life. In the Far East he has the power to save beings during the period leading up to the coming of Maitreya, and in China he has become associated with rituals for transferring merit for the welfare of ancestors.) The name may mean 'the Lord who looks down' (from the mountains where he lives, like Śiva), or 'the Lord who is seen from on high' (by Amitābha who is often depicted above his head). He is traditionally associated with Potalaka in Southern India, and it was for this reason that the palace built on the Red Mountain in Lhasa was named the Potala when Avalokiteśvara incarnated as the Dalai Lamas of Tibet.[1]

In China, Avalokiteśvara was represented as Kuan Yin or 'sound regarder'. She usually appears as a woman or as an androgynous youth. This may have something to do with the Indian ideal of manly beauty as a sixteen-year-old youth, but it is perhaps not without significance that the female *bodhisattva*, Tārā, revealed herself as an emanation of the male Avalokiteśvara by being born from the tears he wept at seeing the plight of suffering beings. Tārā herself is depicted in the lotus position but with one leg unfolded ready to step down into the world to give succour.

The five *jinas*

The *maṇḍala* of the five *buddhas* (sometimes inaccurately referred to as *Dhyāni-buddhas*, but more accurately the five Meditation *buddhas*, *pañca tathāgatas*, or five *jinas*, conquerors of the *āsravas*) first appears in the *Guhyasamāja-tantra*. The three *buddhas* found in early Mahāyāna *sūtras* have two more added to their number. Some authorities give an early date to the *Guhyasamāja-tantra*, about the fourth century CE, but its contents were kept secret until the mid-seventh century. In the *maṇḍala*, the *buddhas* are positioned at the cardinal points and the centre of the cosmos. Each of them has never been anything other than a *buddha* and has never passed through the *bodhisattva* stages.

Their colouring follows solar symbolism. Akṣobhya, dark blue, suggests the deep blue of the Indian dawn sky, Ratnasambhava, yellow for the sun at noon in the south, Amitābha, red for the setting sun in the west, Amoghasiddhi, green for the Northern Lights at midnight in the north. Vairocana at the centre is white; his title is an epithet of the sun, 'resplendent'. Apart from certain features which distinguish the five *buddhas*, they are always depicted in a state of perfect meditation; all creative acts in the world are performed by one of their reflexes, the *bodhisattvas* who belong to their families. B. Bhattacharyya (1980: 129) supposes that the five *mudrās* or ritual gestures ascribed to Śākyamuni Buddha and frequently represented in Buddhist iconography, may have given rise to them, rather than the tantric tradition that they took their origin from the five *skandhas*. Whatever the case, the five *buddhas* are equipped with sets of correspondences grouped in fives. In one notable case, the ancient Buddhist triadic formula, body, speech and mind, has been incremented by two more, 'qualities' and 'action'. In Tibetan Buddhism this allows for up to five incarnations of a *bodhisattva* or holy lama to be alive at the same time, e.g., one for the 'mind', one for the 'speech' incarnation, and so on. Sometimes the position and attributes of Vairocana and Akṣobhya are interchanged.

The patterning into groups of five fits with a number of groups of five, for example, Śākyamuni with his three predecessors (see below) plus Maitreya, the Buddha-to-come, the five elements, five *skandhas*, aggregates, that constitute the psycho-physical continuum which is the human person, the five cardinal points or regions, five senses (though in Buddhism there are six – mind counts as a sense). Each *buddha* has his consort and heads a family of *bodhisattvas* and deities. In iconography the *Dhyāni buddhas* or five *jinas*, first appeared as ascetics, wearing monks' robes, with or without begging bowls. Later they have adorned bodies, holding the same postures but clothed in silks and jewels and wearing crowns. In the glorified form they hint at a representation of the *dharmakāya*, though, strictly, it is beyond representation.

Vairocana is in the centre, coloured white. A transition from Śākyamuni to Vairocana seems to take place in the early Mahāyāna *sūtras*; in the *Lotus Sūtra* the Buddha appears as the shining lord at the centre of existence, quite unlike the historical ascetic figure. Later *sūtras* refer to him as Vairocana. He is shown with his hands in the same preaching *mudrā*, or sometimes turning the Wheel of the *Dharma*. Perhaps the earliest text where Vairocana appears is the *Sarvatathāgatatattvasaṃgraha*, which teaches the unity of all the *buddhas*.

Akṣobhya in the east is coloured blue, which represents space but is also the colour associated with wrathful aspects of *bodhisattvas*. The earliest non-historical *buddha* seems to have been Akṣobhya, or 'Imperturbable', who appears in the *Vimalakirtinirdeśa*. He also appears in the *Small Perfection of Wisdom Sūtra*. He holds a diamond in his right hand and makes the earth-witnessing *mudrā* with his left, reaching down to touch the earth. The *maṇḍala* is always entered from the east, where Akṣobhya at dawn sits touching the earth in witness, in the same way that Śākyamuni did at his defeat of Māra, the Evil One. Transcendent though the five *jinas* are, they show a connection with the immanence of the historical Buddha. Hence there is an association with the elements – earth, sky, water, fire, air – and each *buddha* has a series of associated symbols, gestures, psychological states and so on. For example, Akṣobhya is seated on an elephant throne, his family is the diamond-hard *vajra*, his seed syllable is HŪṂ. He has a female counterpart, Locanā, the 'One Who Sees'. Like the other *buddhas*, he is associated with one of the five *skandhas*, in his case *vijñāna*, consciousness; his mode is mind, his sense-organ, ear. The poison which is transformed by his divine alchemy is hatred. The personality-type of this family is prone to intellectualism and must transform its over-critical conceptualising to mirror-like wisdom. Each family has this range of symbolic and psycho-physical characteristics.

Ratnasambhava in the south, is yellow, and holds the gift-bestowing posture, hands with open palms held out. His family is not large and he is never regarded as the *Ādi-buddha* (explained below).

Amitābha, whose name means 'Unlimited Light', sits in the west, coloured red and holding a lotus on his hands held in the meditation gesture, palms upwards, placed one on the other on his lap. By repeating Amitābha Buddha's name, the devotee will be reborn in his Pure Land (see below) where there are no evil destinies and everyone is assured of only one more rebirth unless they have made the *bodhisattva* vow to remain until all sentient beings enter *nirvāṇa*. He is linked with Amitayus or 'Unlimited Life', the Buddha of Long Life.

Amoghasiddhi, in the north, displays the 'Fear not!' gesture, the flat palm of the right hand raised to the shoulder and facing forward.

Later a sixth, Vajrasattva, was introduced. He embodies the five *skandhas* collectively, and is depicted holding the *vajra* and bell in each hand.

In the early tenth century, in the university of Nalanda, Buddhism came close to Hindu monism, not to say, monotheism, with the development of the notion of a primordial *buddha* behind the five celestial *buddhas*. The *Ādi-buddha* was represented in human form by Vajradhāra, coloured blue, the complexion of space, sometimes

Table 1.1 Correspondences of the five *buddha* families (adapted from Dowman K. (1984) *Sky Dancer: The Secret Life and Songs of the Lady Yeshe Tsogyel*, London, Routledge and Kegan Paul, p. 193)

Buddha	**Vairocana**	**Akṣobhya**	**Ratnasambhava**	**Amitābha**	**Amoghasiddhi**
Family	Buddha	diamond-hard sceptre	jewel	lotus	action
Position	centre	east	south	west	north
Colour	white	blue	yellow	red	green
Element	earth solidity	sky spaciousness	water fluidity	fire heat	air motion
Gesture	teaching	witness	bestowing	meditation	fearlessness
Emblem	wheel	diamond-hard sceptre	jewel	lotus	crossed sceptres
Throne	lion	elephant	horse	peacock	shangshangbird
Ḍākinī	Locanā	Dhātvīśvarī	Māmakī	Pāṇḍarā	Samayatārā
Mode	body	mind	qualities	speech	action
Skandha	rūpa (form)	vijñāna (consciousness)	vedanā (feelings)	saṃjña (perceptions)	saṃskāra (volitions)
Organ	eye	ear	nose	mouth	skin

Sense	vision	audition	smell	taste	touch
Bodhisattva	Samantabhadra	Vajrapāṇi	Ratnapāṇi	Padmapāṇi	Viśvapāṇi
Timebuddha	Krakucandra	Karnakamuni	Kāśyapa	Śākyamuni	Maitreya
Poison	sloth	anger	pride	lust	envy
Neurosis	spaced-out, dull	conceptualising	greedy, domineering	seducing	paranoid, busy
Wisdom	wisdom of all encompassing space	mirror-like wisdom	all enriching wisdom	wisdom of discriminating awareness	all accomplishing wisdom
Seed syllable	OṂ	HŪṂ	TRĀṂ	HRĪ	A
Some associated deities	Mārīcī Vajravārāhī	Heruka Yamāri Ekajaṭā Nairātmā	Jambhala Vasudhāra	Avalokiteśvara Tārā Sudhanakumāra Bhṛkuṭī Hayagrīva Kurukullā	Khadiravaṇītārā Parṇaśavarī

with a consort. In his right hand he holds the *vajra*, the diamond-hard sceptre, and in his left he holds the ritual bell, with arms crossed on his chest, or, if he is with his consort, Prajñāpāramitā, Perfection of Wisdom, his arms enfold her. Other tantrists thought one of the *jina*s was the *Ādi-buddha*; some even considered that one of the celestial *bodhisattva*s, Vajrasattva, Samantabhadra or Vajrapāṇi, was the *Ādi-buddha*.

Emptiness

It is, no doubt, due to the over-arching idea in the Buddhist *tantra*s that all the deities of the pantheon are manifestations of emptiness, *śūnyatā*, that allows Buddhism to deal with them. In so far as they are nothing but manifestations of *śūnyatā*, they are by nature non-existent. Advayavajra, a commentator who lived between 978 and 1030 CE, explains that the deities evolve through four stages: the right perception of *śūnyatā*, the utterance of the associated germ-syllable, *bīja*, visualisation of the icon, the external representation. Bhattacharyya (1980: 110) observes:

> This statement gives a direct lie to the theory that later Buddhism was nothing but gross idolatry. It shows, on the other hand, that their conception of godhead was philosophically most profound, a parallel to which is scarcely to be found in any other Indian religion.

Like all other beings in the receptacle-world, the deities of tantric Buddhism (often referred to as the Vajrayāna or adamantine vehicle), have been given a place to reside in. This is generally thought to be at the very top of the *rūpadhātu* in Akaniṣṭha heaven. However, *bodhisattva*s are never reborn here because beings never return to earth from this heaven. This, as we have already seen, is the place of *nirvāṇa* 'with remainder'. Kamalasila, however, states (Bhattacharyya 1980: 99) that beyond the Akaniṣṭha heaven there is a Maheśvara abode where the chain of consciousness of the compassionate *bodhisattva* attains omniscience; this is not the quiescent *nirvāṇa* of *arahant*s and *pratyekabuddha*s (Solitary Realisers). The oldest *tantra*, the *Guhyasamāja*, says that emptiness and compassion together make *bodhicitta*, the *bodhi*-mind of the *bodhisattva* who renounces personal *nirvāṇa* in order to work for the well-being of all beings. The deities themselves are manifested from emptiness with the three constituents: emptiness, consciousness and great bliss.

Buddha Fields and Pure Land Buddhism

The *Mahāvastu*, taking up the idea of cosmology of thousands, points out that a *buddha* is a rare being, and many of the world-systems do not have a *buddha*. In these benighted world-systems the *Buddhadharma* has never been preached. Both *buddha* Fields and Pure Lands are world-systems where a *buddha* has lived through the stages of bodhisattvahood and finally reached enlightenment. Our world is a *buddha* Field, but is not Pure Land because it contains evil destinies. In a Pure Land, the perfect *Buddhadharma* is preached by a *buddha* who may never die. Paul Williams[2] argues that the Pure Land is not a 'heavenly abode', but enlightenment itself, because impurity is just the result of impure awareness; once you recognise that all beings have the *buddha*-nature, then you must inhabit the Pure Land! Williams[3] points out that in contemporary Japanese Buddhism, the Pure Land of Amitābha cult accounts for more practitioners than any other tradition, including Zen. Pure Lands are truly wonderful places, as described in the *Sukhāvatīvyūha Sūtra*s. Those born there will attain *nirvāṇa* next birth unless, as *bodhisattva*s, out of compassion they take rebirth to help sentient beings towards enlightenment.

The Japanese commentator, Genshin, summarises the Pure Land's conditions for rapid progress to buddhahood as follows:

1. Power of Amida (Amitābha) Buddha's vows to those born in his Land.
2. Constant *buddha*-light encouraging the enlightened mind.
3. Sounds of the Land's birds, leaves, bells, etc., inducing them to reflect on the Three Jewels.
4. Constant companionship of *bodhisattva*s.
5. Long Life.
   (Kloetzli 1983: 126)

The psycho-cosmic image of the human being

In the very ancient Jain cosmology, the shape of the universe looks like the rough outline of the human form. It stretches back to an idea found in the *Ṛg-veda* that the universe was formed from the body of the Cosmic Person, the *mahāpuruṣa*, the Great Being. A similar idea is found in the ancient Norse *Eddas*, where the world is made of the dismembered parts of a giant's body. The Buddha was somehow identifiable with the *mahāpuruṣa*, so that he bore the thirty-two major bodily marks and eighty minor ones (see below). In Mahāyāna doctrine the development of the Three Bodies of the Buddha, *trikāya*, with its efflorescence into the pantheon of celestial *buddhas* undoubtedly taps into the idea of the Cosmic Being of pre-Buddhist times. The *tantras* also depend on the association between the physical body of the *yogin* and the cosmos. The spinal column is compared with Mount Meru, the axis of the universe and the whole physical organism is explained in terms of solar and lunar forces. Running through the body is the median nerve, Suṣumṇā-*nāḍī* with two *nāḍīs*, channels, coiling about it in opposite directions. The most important, Lama Govinda (1976: 87) says, are:

> The pale white-coloured Iḍā starting from the left, and the red-coloured Piṅgala from the right. Iḍā is the conductor of lunar or 'moon-like' (*candra-svarūpa*) forces which have the regenerative properties and the unity of undifferentiated subconscious life as represented by the latent creativeness of seed, eggs and semen, in which all chthonic telluric cults are centred. Piṅgala is the vehicle of solar forces (*sūrya-svarūpa*, 'sun-like') which have the properties of intellectual activity, representing the conscious, differentiated, individualised life.

Along the median there are the *cakras*, at various points, radiating centres of psychic force. The important ones are located at the perineum, navel, heart, throat and crown. The *cakra* is a solar symbol, identified with the cosmic sacrifice of the Veda. When the sun rises it does so as the universe, as the Cosmic Being (*Praśna Upaniṣad* 1.6–8). The sun moves in his orbit in a one-wheeled car (*Mahābhārata* 12.362.1). This is the wheel of the *cakravartin*, the Wheel of the *Dharma* by which the Buddha's first sermon is known (*Dharmacakrapravartana*).

The Buddha

Despite the fact that Theravāda Buddhism insists that the Buddha was a man and not a god, it does not disguise the fact that it considers Siddhartha Gautama no mere mortal, even before he became enlightened. Once a *buddha*, he attained supernormal knowledge and powers; among others are included five kinds of vision:

1. Improved human vision, so that he can see a league all round, day or night.
2. With the divine eye he can see beings coming into and passing out of existence, see their merit and see world-systems up to three thousand and beyond.
3. With his wisdom-eye he produces the unproduced path and attains omniscience of past, present and future events.
4. With his Buddha-eye he sees the degrees of purity of all beings and knows what is needed for their salvation.
5. With his all-seeing eye there remains nothing unseen by him.

Also, the conception of the Buddha as an ordinary mortal may not necessarily represent the earliest view simply because it is found in the earliest scriptures (Thomas 1975: 211).

The thirty-two marks (*lakṣaṇa*s) of the Great Being are found on the bodies of *cakravartin*s (*Dīgha Nikāya* iii 142): (1) well-set feet, (2) wheels with 1,000 spokes on the soles, (3) projecting heels, (4) long fingers, (5) soft hands and feet, (6) webbed fingers and toes, (7) prominent ankles, (8) antelope limbs, (9) hands reaching to the knees, (10) the genitals hidden by a sheath, (11) the body a golden colour, (12) soft skin, (13) one hair for each pore, (14) body hairs black, rising straight and curling right, (15) very erect of body, (16) having seven prominences, (17) the front of his body like a lion, (18) the space between the shoulders filled out, (19) height equal to his outstretched arms, (20) even shoulders, (21) keen taste, (22) a lion-jaw, (23) forty teeth, (24) even teeth, (25) not gap-toothed, (26) very white teeth, (27) a large tongue, (28) a voice like Brahmā and soft as a cuckoo's, (29) very black eyes, (30) eyelashes like an ox, (31) white hair between the eyebrows, (32) head shaped like a cap. In addition there are eighty minor marks, e.g. copper-coloured nails.

It is doubtful that any list goes back before the sculptures of Gandhāra in the first century BCE, despite the idea of special marks being an ancient one. Some of the marks are particularly interesting. For example, on the soles of his feet there are wheels with a thousand spokes and a rim and nave (solar symbol?), there is one hair to each pore on his skin and each hair rises straight and curls to the right (note that the clockwise direction is not only the way the sun apparently moves in its course, but the correct way to circumambulate a person or object of reverence), he has a white curl of hair between the brows, *uṇṇā*, and on the top of his head is a protuberance.

The twelve acts of the Buddha

Traditionally the life of the Buddha is arranged in twelve significant stages:

1. The resolve to be born.
2. The *bodhisattva* descends from *Tuṣita* heaven.
3. He enters his mother's womb.
4. The birth.
5. Accomplishments.
6. The life of pleasure.
7. The great renunciation.
8. Ascetic practices.
9. The conquest of Māra.
10. The enlightenment.
11. The teaching ministry.
12. He passes into *nirvāṇa*.

A mythic dimension is given even to events that we may consider historical, such as the birth, or the renunciation. The Buddha's mother, Māyā, gave birth in a standing position, and the infant *bodhisattva* emerged from her right side. Perhaps a standing position for giving birth was a custom of the time. More remarkable is the account that the child did not emerge through the birth canal in the usual way, but from the right side. Was this a miraculous event or was the birth by some form of caesarean section? Whatever the case, Māyā died seven days later.

The Seven Steps of the Buddha

The birth narratives say that the moment the *bodhisattva* was born he placed both feet on the ground, faced the north and took seven strides, shaded by a white parasol, and scanned the four directions.

Then with a voice like a bull he said: 'I am the top of the world, I am the oldest in the world; this is my last birth; I will not be reborn'. Mircea Eliade (1960: 110–15) examines this mythic theme for its cosmological structure and metaphysical significance. The seven steps bring the Buddha (to be) to the summit of the cosmic system, passing through seven stages corresponding to the seven planetary heavens. The significance of the cosmic North is that from there the supernal lands of the Buddha are reached. The myth of the Seven Steps expresses the new-born Buddha's transcendence of the cosmos and abolition of space and time (he becomes 'highest' and 'oldest'). Further, Eliade identifies the ascension of the Buddha through cosmic stages as analogous to a recurring myth-pattern: the universe is conceived as having seven stages with the summit located in the cosmic North, or the Pole Star, or in the Empyrean. The act of transcending takes place near a 'Centre', which may be a temple, a royal city, a sacred tree, homologised with the Cosmic Tree, or the vedic sacrificial stake (T.S. Eliot's 'axle-tree'). The cosmos was created from the summit down, so when Buddha declared, 'I am the top of the world, I am the oldest', he was returning to a transcendent state 'before the foundations of the world were laid'.

Solar myth

L.A. Waddell (1972: 346) thought of the development of the celestial *buddhas* in terms of the connection between Amitābha and Persian sun worship, but it was H. Kern who was the leading exponent of the theory that the Buddha was a solar myth. No one today would accept this as a complete explanation; it is too glib. But there is no doubt that some elements of pre-Buddhist mythology have been incorporated into historical material. Thomas (1975: 216) explains the main drift of Kern's conjecture as follows:

> In the whole marvellous legend of Buddha . . . it is all literally true, but it is the truth of myth, all the legends of Buddha being descriptions of the sun and other heavenly bodies. He did not deny that Buddha may have existed, but held that all the stories we have are mythological descriptions of natural phenomena. Buddha's meditation on the twelve fold chain of causation represents the rising of the sun at the spring equinox and the twelve months, but it is also a creation myth and more. 'The sun-god had to be represented not only as creator, but also as

physician, as Apollo, as healer and saviour. . . . Hence the four truths of the physician were also fitted in, and thus we see under the appearance of a dry scholastic formula a rational fusion of a description of the year, a combination of a myth of creation and of salvation.'

Buddha's two former teachers, who had died before him, mean two stars that disappear in the light of the sun. The Gautama who according to the Tibetan was an ancestor of Buddha, is the early dawn, or perhaps the planet Jupiter. He too fades before the rising sun. The going to Benares at midsummer to preach the first sermon, a journey of 18 hours, means that the sun was 18 hours above the horizon on the longest day. Kassap of Uruvelā, who became Buddha's disciple, is also the personified dawn, and his brightness also was lost in the glory of the sun. The six heretics are the false lights of the five planets and the moon. Rāhula is naturally an eclipse: he was born at the time when the bodhisattva disappeared. Māra is the spirit of darkness defeated and driven away by the sun-god. Buddha himself is Vishnu incarnated as Krishna.

We no longer take for granted that all myths are nature-myths, or that they are prehistoric. For example, Māra, the Tempter, whose name in Sanskrit means 'death', seems to be purely Buddhist in origin. As for the celestial manifestations of the five *jina*s, they look remarkably like solar deities despite being a development of later Buddhism.

Despite all this, the *Saṅgha* followed the lunar calendar in setting the *uposatha* days for the twice-monthly *prātimokṣa* ceremony. These monastic rules were to be recited once each half-month, on full- and half-moon days during the evening of the *uposatha* vigil.

Six previous *buddha*s have appeared in our world-system, according to the Pāli canon and Sanskrit sources, but there are also lists containing as many as twenty-four names. All agree that the first *buddha* was Dipankara before whom our historical Buddha, in his former life as the brahman Sumedha, made a vow to become a *buddha*.

Past lives of the historical Buddha

The *jātaka* is a collection in Pāli of five hundred and fifty tales of former lives of the Buddha. Each tale has a quasi-historical introduction by which the tale is yoked with some particular incident in the Buddha's life. The *jātaka*s are clearly a literary attempt to consolidate the notion of the *bodhisattva*-career; in itself this considerably alters the idea that Siddhartha Gautama was a mere man. Against the context of the Indian notion of recurring cycles of history, the career of the *bodhisattva* takes a linear progression, from the vow before Dipankara to Śākyamuni Buddha's enlightenment in the present world-age. This is one of two elements that apparently contradict the 'meaninglessness' of history. Legend also has it that Dipankara prophesied the future buddhahood of Sumedha; to this day, tantric *gurus* prophesy the buddhahood of those who take the *bodhisattva* vows before them, thereby introducing an eschatology into otherwise endless transmigrational cycles.

All Buddhists accept the phenomenon of Maitreya the Future Buddha, who, according to most views, abides in *Tuṣita* heaven as a *bodhisattva*. Early on, Buddhism may have come under the influence of Zoroastrianism. By the beginning of the Christian era the cult of a Buddhist Messiah was widespread. Kitagawa (in Sponberg and Hardacre, 1988: 19) reflect some of the complexities of the meaning of Maitreya:

> In what manner does the study of Maitreya illuminate our understanding of the nature of the Buddha and bodhisattvas? Are they saviours, 'docetic' phenomena, hypostasisations of Dharmic principles? Are we to understand that 'heavenly' bodhisattvas are personalisations of the Buddha's qualities (e.g., compassion and wisdom)? Quite apart from their 'historicity', what is their 'ontological' status? Are we to assume that they have been preordained in the cosmological scheme? Or do they come into being by means of the devotee's 'visualisation' or the adept's magical powers? . . . Assuming that Maitreya is an eschatological figure, how crucial is eschatology to Buddhist soteriology? . . . What is the relationship between the figure of Maitreya and millenarianism? Does the 'prophecy' about Maitreya have millenarian connotations? Or did millenarian movements 'discover' Maitreya as an appropriate symbol?

Transmigration and the suffering universe

Buddhism views the process of transmigration, the endless round of birth and death, with aversion. The nature of existence in the phenomenal world (*saṃsāra*) is defined in the First Noble Truth as suffering or unsatisfactory (*duḥkha*). The metaphor of an ocean that has to be crossed is not found only in Buddhism, of course. It also occurs in Judaism and Christianity. (The raft of the *dharma* on the unfathomable ocean of *saṃsāra*; Noah's ark; the barque of Peter; the Church as the one ark of salvation; even the *nave* of a church, and so on.)

The idea of transmigration, is, whatever its literal truth, a mythical, prescientific, prelogical way of thinking about the human predicament, as Keiji Nishitani (1982: 173) points out, and by questioning the factual nature of such an idea as rebirth we are not doing anything Buddhism itself has not done throughout its history; the 'meaning' of transmigration has been drawn from an existential and undogmatic interpretation of human existence that lies at the core of the myth. Reason does not negate the mythical.

The law by which one is bound to the round of transmigration is *karma*. *Karma* means action, and since actions are performed in time, it is *karma* that prolongs the suffering of the world by extending time. The Buddha, as doctor for the ills of the world, gave the Four Noble Truths (diagnosis, aetiology, prognosis and cure). One of the fruits of enlightenment is to have knowledge of all one's previous lives. In Mircea Eliade's terms (1960: 50) these remembered births are the return to *illud tempus*. He speaks of a yogic method by which the karmic residue can be 'burnt up' by retracing actions back to the Timeless, and so to regain the non-conditioned state, *nirvāṇa*.

Architecture symbolism: *stūpa*, pagoda or *chorten*

Throughout the Buddhist world, or wherever Buddhism had once been, there are to be seen distinctive monuments, known as *stūpa*s, pagodas or *chorten*s. Though the design varies from region to region, and the size ranges from something not much higher than a person to immense structures like the Great *Stūpa* of Sanchi which has a diameter of one hundred and twenty feet and a height of fifty-four feet, they all share the same symbolic structure.

Probably in origin they were pre-Buddhist monuments erected to great rulers. The Buddha stipulated that certain persons were worthy of a *stūpa* over their remains – enlightened ones, solitary enlightened ones, disciples of an enlightened one and wheel-turning (i.e., great and benevolent) Universal Monarchs (*Parinibbāna Sutta*, *Dīgha Nikāya* 16.5; trans. M. Walshe (1987) *Thus Have I Heard*, London, Wisdom Publications). In this same passage the Buddha instituted the cult of relics. This is a radical challenge to the general brahman notion of the time that human remains were polluting and certainly were not to be worshipped in any way:

> A stūpa should be erected at the cross-roads for the Tathāgata. And whoever lays wreaths or puts sweet perfumes and colours there with a devout heart, will reap benefit and happiness for a long time.

Symbolism of the *stūpa*

As viewed from the side in its later developed form, a *stūpa* may be seen to have four, or five, parts:

1. A base which may also be stepped.
2. The mound proper, which has undergone stylisation; this is called the *aṇḍa*, egg (sometimes called the *garbha*, womb) and in India it is usually a hemisphere; elsewhere it is bell-shaped, while in Tibet it looks like an upturned pot.
3. The *harmikā*, kiosk, a cube surmounting the *aṇḍa*.
4. The *htī*, spire.
5. The finial (usually in Tibet).

The *stūpa* was not a reminder of the dead hero but of one who had achieved or striven to achieve liberation from the cycles of life and death. As such it commemorated the transcendence of death. The earthly remains were powerful reminders of the Buddhist concept of *anitya*, the impermanence of all compounded things, but they had been transcended, 'gone beyond', the literal meaning of *tathāgata*.

The burial mound looks like the cosmic egg from which all things sprang in ancient Indian cosmogony. That part of the *stūpa* is also known as the womb (*garbha*), surely indicating a connection with telluric-matriarchal ideas and ancient cults of the dead where mother Earth and mother Nature were held to be the same. Lama Govinda (1976) demonstrates how both lunar and solar cults are united in the structure of the *stūpa*. The base section is said to represent earth; on it is the bubble or egg of water. These are the two elements of the moon cult. Some scholars have tried to show that Buddhism represents a solar myth. Certainly, the celestial *buddha*s of the *maṇḍala*, stationed at the compass points in the colours of the dawn, noon-day, setting sun and northern lights, are reminiscent of solar deities. But the phases of the moon are very important in Buddhism – we have already seen that the monastic calendar is a lunar one – and if the older telluric-matriarchal cult seems to have been suppressed by the patriarchal structures of the early Buddhist *saṅgha*, it was challenged, perhaps not altogether successfully, by Mahaprajapati, the Buddha's aunt, when she and her companions sought ordination as *bhkṣunī*s. The battle for women was won then but the victory has been eroded by time.

Above the *aṇḍa* is a cubic structure, *harmikā*, which actually contained the relics. Its similarity to a sacrificial altar has been observed, though the Buddhist sacrifice is only ever a self-sacrifice of the passions, never of animals. The symbolism of the vedic cosmic sacrifice is not lost, however. The *harmikā* is surmounted by the spire, *htī*, which represents and sometimes looks like a ceremonial umbrella. This is a mark of royalty, the *cakravartin*, and consequently of the enlightened being. The umbrella in its turn represents the sacred tree, the tree under which the Buddha gained enlightenment, the *bodhi* tree, below which is the place of enlightenment, the diamond seat, *vajrāsana*, the most sacred spot in the world. The spire also symbolises Mount Meru, the axis of Indian cosmology. Lama Govinda (1976: 72) identifies the two upper sections of the *stūpa* with ancient solar cults: space as opposed to the lunar terrestrial, the solar year against the lunar cycle, patriarchy superimposed over matriarchy, culture, to which Lévi-Strauss says men belong, against nature, to which women belong. Plastic, mass-creating architecture, along with the greatest works of sculpture, is supposed to be found at the beginning of each civilisation; as architecture develops the creation of space becomes primary.

Temples

The first temple complex to be built in Tibet was at bSam-yas in the eighth century CE, constructed on a cosmic plan, a *maṇḍala*. Other examples of this kind of architecture are the famous Kumbum at Gyantse built in 1440, Borobudur in Java (reckoned to have been built in the first quarter of the ninth century; covering five kilometres in all, it is basically a *stūpa* with elaborate terraces making a *maṇḍala*), and Angkor Wat in Cambodia, built at the end of the twelfth century.

Myth and ritual

Apart from representing the cosmos in the construction of temples and *stūpa*s, the two-dimensional design of the *maṇḍala* in paint or coloured sand has become a well-observed feature of tantric ritual. But the *maṇḍala* of the universe can be symbolised in further ways. One of these is by ritual gesture, *mudrā*, with the fingers of both hands held in a way to symbolise Meru and the Four Continents; the other is to use a ritual implement. The Tibetan *maṇḍala*-offering is, quite simply, the ritual offering of the Universe, with all its riches, to the Objects of Refuge, the Three Jewels, Buddha, *Dharma* and *Saṅgha*, as an act of veneration. The act is performed in three distinct modes, Outer, Inner and Secret, which represent ever deepening scholastic symbolism. The main consideration here is what is offered. It is a symbol in material and ritual terms, of the ancient Indian cosmos. The universe is 'constructed' using ritual implements: a metal base with three or four rings of metal, whose narrowing diameters allow them to fit inside each other, a top ornament and a heap of pure rice which has been stained yellow with saffron. Into the rice may be mixed jewels and precious coins. The metal of the *maṇḍala* instrument may be gold but it does not matter if it is just base metal; in the imagination it can be transmuted to the most precious of metals. Once built up, the *maṇḍala* of the cosmos is offered to all the *buddha*s and then allowed to collapse back into a heap of rice in the officiant's lap, signifying the ultimate emptiness of all created things.

Reincarnating Lamas

In Tibetan, the term *sprul-sku* (pronounced *tulku*) means the 'apparent body', *nirmaṇakāya*, the third of the three bodies of the Buddha. In this theory, Śākyamuni Buddha was the 'apparent body' or manifestation of supreme buddhahood, *dharmakāya*. Buddhahood can have no representation of itself but can manifest in a human or celestial form, the 'enjoyment body', *samboghakāya*;[4] for example, the five *jina*s. The idea that a certain teacher could let his disciples know, in advance of his death, where he would be reborn probably began with the *rNying-ma-pa* school. Their teacher, Padmasambhava, prophesied that he would return to earth to reveal scriptures that he had hidden (*gter-mas*). The returning master was not part of a series, however. The unbroken lineage of reincarnated beings who hold some office goes back to the *Kar-ma-pa* Lama Dus-gsum-mkhyen-pa who lived between 1110 and 1193. The third Dalai Lama was given the title 'Great Ocean' by Altan Khan, and conferred it retrospectively on his two predecessors. They were regarded as incarnations of the celestial *bodhisattva* Avalokiteśvara, who had already appeared in incarnate form as the King Srong-btsan-sgam-po. The Pan-chen Lama was instituted soon after the Dalai Lama, but in this case he is the incarnation of the celestial Buddha Amitābha. As an incarnate *buddha*, it may seem surprising that he does not rank above the Dalai Lama, but this is explained by the dynamic relation between the Buddha in *samādhi* and his dynamic reflex, the *bodhisattva* Avalokiteśvara.

Techniques for liberation

The contemplation of impermanence in the form of a meditation on a corpse in a cremation ground was a practice known to early Buddhists. Mircea Eliade (1960: 84), while recognising that the contemplation of skulls and bones shows the 'vanity of vanity', reveals that contemplating one's own skeleton was a technique for 'going out of time' among the *shaman*s of hunting and pastoral peoples, and Indo-Tibetan *yogin*s. He says:

> For the former, its aim is to re-discover the ultimate source of animal life and thence to participate in Being; while, for the Indo-Tibetan monks, it is to contemplate the eternal cycles of existences ruled by *karma*; and hence to dispel the Great Illusion (*māyā*) of Cosmic Life, striving to transcend it by placing oneself in the unconditioned, symbolised by *nirvāṇa*.

On the theme of shamanistic elements in Buddhism, Eliade (1960: 90) points out that, 'there is not a single one of these *siddhi* evoked by the Buddha that we do not meet with in the shamanic traditions; even the knowledge of previous lives, a specifically Indian "mystical exercise", has been reported among the shamans of North America'. *Siddhi* are paranormal powers, e.g., bilocation, flying, invisibility, that are the unavoidable corollary to advanced mystical states.

By means of the technique of 'psychic heat' (Tibetan: *gtum-mo*), the *yogin*, sitting all night on a freezing Himalayan mountainside, can cause a wet blanket to steam. Such practices of Yoga and Buddhism are identified by Eliade as 'continuations – although of course on another plane and directed to quite a different end – of the immemorial ideologies and techniques which endeavoured to change the condition of man by a change in his psychosomatic structures'.

Conclusion

When one surveys the principal distinctions between the western Judaic and the Buddhist views of history and the *mythos* associated with them, one is struck by an extraordinary parallel between them: the way that they bracket off evil. Where Hinduism allows the paradox of the evil God, the monotheistic religions make Satan the focus of evil, dynamic in opposition to God, though not equal to him in power. It is remarkable that Buddhism has personified evil as Māra the Tempter, Lord of the World. Though Buddhism has generally been able to incorporate pre-Buddhist demonology into the general pantheon inherited from the Indian cultural milieu, the establishment of Māra, as antithetical to the religious ideal, represents a distinct departure in Indian religion.

For Buddhism, evil arises from primordial ignorance, thereby giving rise to notions of a permanent self and the three poisons of existence (greed, hatred and delusion), so there would hardly seem a place for an evil agent. Nevertheless, as Trevor Ling (1962: 91) points out,

> Both Māra and Satan represent a force which proves resistant to man's search for holiness. The opposing force is conceived as being so potent and so hard to overcome by man, so universally active and so malign, that it is endowed with a will and personality.

Māra is referred to in many places throughout the Pāli canon.[5] There may be an etymological association between the name Māra and the figure *Pāpmā Mṛtyuḥ* (Death the Evil One) found in the *Upaniṣads* (Ling, 1962: 56), thereby making an appropriate connection with the First Noble Truth of Suffering. Just as suffering (*duḥkha*) is the condition of all samsaric existence, so the sphere of Māra's activity extends to every level of the cosmos except *nirvāṇa*. Māra is, in fact, everything that is not enlightened:

> Corporality is Māra: with regard to this Māra you should overcome your longing. Feeling is Māra . . . Perception is Māra . . . Mental formations are Māra . . . Consciousness is Māra . . . with regard to this Māra you should overcome your longing.
>
> (*Saṃyutta Nikāya* III, quoted in Ling 1962: 58)

Maybe not everyone will agree with Ling's view (1962: 90) that, 'Satan and Māra' are *symbols* . . . [whose principal function is] to facilitate a transition of viewpoint for those accustomed to thinking in demonic terms, rather than to embody absolute truth'. However, in Buddhism the whole of the Triple World and all it contains, including the Buddha's teachings, have only a provisional truth compared with the absolute truth of *nirvāṇa*. For Buddhists of whatever school, the absolute can be reached only through the provisional, so the pantheon of one's own school is as provisionally real as everything else.

NOTES

1. Robert Thurman (1987) 'The Buddhist Messiahs' in *The Christ and the Bodhisattva*, ed. D.S. Lopez, Jr. and S.C. Rockefeller, New York, SUNY, pp. 65–97 says:

   > . . . the bodhisattva *par excellence* [is] the bodhisattva Ārya Avalokiteśvara, one of whose incarnations is among us today, His Holiness the Dalai Lama of Tibet. Just as it is a hopeless task to try to comprehensively discuss all the bodhisattvas, so is it a hopeless task to try to talk about all the manifestations and visions and magnificent activities of this bodhisattva. In some sense he is the prime example of a divine bodhisattva, a being who already got beyond Buddhahood and as a bodhisattva, is more Buddha than all the Buddhas. He is said to be the quintessence of the universal compassion of all the Buddhas. He appears in many scriptures and has at least one hundred and eight forms iconographically. He can appear as a female, in the form of Ārya Tārā, or as a female terrific such as Bhṛkuti or Śrī Devī, and he can appear in male terrific form, as Hayagrīva. His most famous forms are the two-armed thoughtful form who utters the *Heart Sūtra*, the quintessence of the *Transcendent Wisdom* teaching of selflessness and emptiness, the four-armed pacific form that dwells in his paradise in south India, Potalaka, and the thousand-armed form of the resurrected

Avalokiteśvara. . . . His Holiness the Dalai Lama is believed by Tibetan Buddhists to have a special connection with this form [the Thousand-Armed, Thousand-Eyed, Ten-Headed Lord of Great Compassion].

2. Williams, P., (1989) *Mahāyāna Buddhism*, London, Routledge, p. 227.
3. Williams, P., *Mahāyāna Buddhism*, p. 251.
4. Tadeusz Skorupski has pointed out to me the parallel between the notions of the 'enjoyment body' and the 'glorified body' of Jesus after the resurrection.
5. For a detailed survey of the canonical coverage the reader should consult Ling's Appendix (1962: 96–163).

FURTHER READING

Bhattacharyya, B. (1980) *An Introduction to Buddhist Esoterism*, Delhi, Motilal Banarsidass.

Mircea Eliade (1960) *Myths, Mysteries and Dreams*, London, Harvill Press.

Lama Anagarika Govinda (1976) *Psycho-cosmic Symbolism of the Buddhist Stūpa*, Berkeley, Dharma Publishing.

Kloetzli, W.R. (1983) *Buddhist Cosmology: From Single World System to Pure Land: Science and Theology in the Images of Motion and Light*, Delhi, Motilal Banarsidass.

Ling, T.O. (1962) *Buddhism and the Mythology of Evil*, London, George Allen & Unwin.

Nishitani, Keiji (1982) *Religion and Nothingness*, trans. Jan Van Bragt, Berkeley, University of California Press.

Schumann, H.W. (1989) *The Historical Buddha*, trans. M.O'C. Walshe, London, Arkana.

Sponberg, Alan and Hardacre, Helen (eds) (1988) *Maitreya, the Future Buddha*, Cambridge, Cambridge University Press.

Thomas, E.J. (1975) *The Life of Buddha as Legend and History* (1st pub. 1927), London, Routledge & Kegan Paul.

de la Vallée Poussin, L. (1911) 'Cosmogony and Cosmology (Buddhist)' in James Hastings (ed.) *Encyclopaedia of Religion and Ethics*, Vol. 4, Edinburgh.

Waddell, L.A. (1972) *Tibetan Buddhism*, New York, Dover Publications. Unabridged replication of (1895) *The Buddhism of Tibet, or Lamaism*, London, W.H. Allen.

2. Christianity

Douglas Davies

From its outset Christianity has been a religion possessing sacred texts. Initially they were those of Judaism but in quick succession there emerged Epistles, which were letters written by the early Christian leaders to various new congregations of believers, followed by the Gospels, which presented outlines of the life and teaching of Jesus. Other documents, like the Acts of the Apostles, gave an account of the life of early Christians and of their experience of God and of Jesus.

The scriptures deriving from Judaism came to be called the Old Testament by Christians. As time went on some of the letters and documents of the early Christian Church were counted along with the older Jewish scriptures as part of what is now accepted as the Christian Bible. Many of these documents, such as the Gospel of John and the Epistle to the Hebrews, are not simple descriptions but are clear theological interpretations of the life of Jesus and of Christian communities. The Acts of the Apostles also has its definite theological concerns, which influence the way the activities of the Apostles and others are recounted.

So it is that, within one single book, the Bible, we find side by side material that many theologians would define as either more mythical or more historical. But, for a variety of reasons, many believers look at the Bible as a whole rather than as a collection of different material. They see it as a book inspired by God and telling the truth about God and humanity. Many such readers find it difficult to distinguish between the different kinds of literature within the Bible and, because the word 'myth' has come to assume the meaning of something that is false or untrue, such believers reject the view that the Bible has 'myths' within it at all.

Changing views

The Bible has existed for a long time. This rather obvious fact must not be ignored in trying to understand myth and history in Christianity because, as times change, so knowledge about the nature of myth and the nature of history has increased. Both myth and history have become topics of academic study, undergoing considerable analysis, and becoming more identifiable as forms of human understanding. This can influence the practice of Christian religion if believers become aware of the part myths play in their sense of their own history.

Once people know that history involves the interpretation of events, they can quickly appreciate the importance of an individual historian's outlook on the way the past is presented. In other words, history is not just about dates, happenings, and 'facts' of the past, but is very much concerned with how they are interpreted. This makes it quite obvious that, for example, Marxist, feminist, or evolutionist historians are likely to interpret the past differently. Similarly, Catholic and Protestant historians are likely to give different emphases to periods such as the Reformation. Ideology and theology are radically important influences on the way history is written.

Christianity as history

As far as Christianity is concerned there is one factor which makes this picture doubly interesting and complicated. It is that Christians believe God to have been active in or through historical events, and in this sense Christianity is often said to be a 'historical religion'. The very fact that, by what we now call the sixth century of the Christian Era, the history of the world came to be divided into two major periods, representing time Before Christ (BC) and then time after Christ (AD; Latin *Anno Domini*, meaning in the year of Our Lord), demonstrates this sense of divine activity.

This does not simply mean that Christianity has a past, though in a very simple sense this is obviously true, but that past events have had more to them than simply meets the eye. But this is where a major theoretical problem arises, because it is only to the eye of faith that certain events can be seen as the result of God's activity, and not all historians are Christian believers. As will be seen later, some theologians even speak of what they call 'salvation-history'. This is best understood by beginning with Jesus of Nazareth.

There is little doubt that there was a man called Jesus who came from Nazareth, and who was a wandering Jewish religious teacher who ended up being put to death by crucifixion. But Christianity grew and derived its very significance from the belief that this man was also divine. This belief assumed that divine activity took place amidst actual mundane events, and implies that history cannot simply involve the interpretation of human behaviour, but has to be read as possessing an additional dimension, one of divine influence and significance. This raises the critical issue of whether this sort of description of the past constitutes history or a kind of myth. Does the belief that God became 'man' in Jesus, who then died to redeem people from their sins before being resurrected and returning to heaven, constitute a myth rather than history?

Christians deal with this question in different and sometimes opposing ways because of the variety of stances adopted over ideas of faith, over the way God operates, and also over the way myth and history are defined. Much depends upon basic premises and whether someone starts from a particular doctrinal belief or from a more philosophical perspective. This chapter links the concerns of religious studies with a broad theological position, and in line with that we begin by considering human creativity as a force behind humanity's myth-making and history-writing tendencies.

Creativity and the image of God

From the Christian belief that humanity is made in God's image, this drive for meaning can be interpreted as a human reflection of divine creativity. Made in the image of god, men and women possess a creative dimension to their lives, which they bring to bear on events in the world around them. This creativity begins in childhood as the young learn about the world in which they find themselves growing up.

Reason, imagination and emotion all lie at the heart of this human creativity and are fostered by the many cultures of humanity through science, myth and history. But myth and history, like science, also exist as part of the knowledge and tradition held by certain groups, movements and societies. This total social base influences myth and history, and needs to be considered in its own right.

Social framework

The words science, religion and history all point to the fact that western society has divided information into distinct categories which are taught as separate bodies of knowledge. Although there are advantages in doing this, there is also the danger of thinking about the world and human existence in a fragmented way, and of assuming that other cultures, or people of former ages, also classified life in a similar way when they often did not do so.

This is a very important point for interpreting Christianity, because over its two thousand years' existence Christianity has become established in many different cultures, with their own attitudes to the world of nature and to the realm of faith. For this reason it is important to understand something about the culture of a people when talking about myth and history. This is where the academic discipline of social anthropology is useful within religious studies because it concerns itself with the pattern of human cultures and social life.

Traditional, modern and postmodern societies

Although it involves an over-simplification, societies may be divided into three types according to their approach to knowledge. These are traditional, modern and postmodern societies. It is probably best to think of these terms as describing trends or broad attitudes rather than as describing an entire society. Indeed, many question the very idea of a 'postmodern' trend, and there is considerable debate over the whole issue of defining 'modernity' and 'postmodernity'.[1] But the issues are so important that they are worth sketching even though accepted definitions do not exist. With this caution in mind, we outline some distinctive features of these different social attitudes to knowledge, time, and life's significance to give a framework for understanding myth and history.

TRADITIONAL SOCIETIES

A traditional society is one where knowledge is handed down from generation to generation as a precious commodity. In the history of humankind traditional societies have included very many tribal groups of hunters and gatherers, of pastoralists and agriculturally based peoples, who often were preliterate. Knowledge in the form of songs, stories of the past and religious beliefs, along with basic practical knowledge of nature and crafts, was passed from parent to child over many generations. Great respect was shown to such traditional wisdom, and care was taken to instruct particular people capable of perpetuating it.

Many of the so-called primitive peoples studied by anthropologists over the last hundred years have been of this type. In Europe, too, many rural communities have operated in this way until fairly recently.

MODERN SOCIETY

Over the last hundred years many deeply significant changes have come about in what is called the developed world of industrial and modern agricultural societies. Urbanisation and the great development of industry involved science and engineering to a great extent. A key feature was discovery.

Discovery involves new things. New ideas came from science and new techniques from engineering. Old ideas and ancient traditions were no longer prized simply because they were old. Old things were abandoned as new discoveries offered possibilities of development that quite transformed human life. Perhaps electricity and the steam engine were two fundamentally important discoveries, but many drugs and medical techniques also changed the pattern of human life.

Modern society emerged as the desire for discovery replaced respect for traditional knowledge. Modernity itself shifted respect to newly discovered ideas and to principles that now held sway over life. The theory of evolution was one such principle of modernity, and was applied to aspects of social life just as it was to animal life. In its own way Marxism also offered a modern theory of social existence. As we shall see, modern society, especially since the middle of the nineteenth century, has had a considerable impact upon religious life and in particular upon religious belief.

POSTMODERN SOCIETY

It is only since perhaps the 1970s that the idea of postmodernity has been discussed by intellectuals. In simplest terms, postmodernity refers to life that has no simple theory to unite people in their motives for living and for interpreting the world. A deep awareness of the way social customs influence people leads the postmodernist into a sense of the fragmented nature of each individual. There is no overarching focus to guide thought in any collective way. Meaning becomes a shattered concept, and each thinker has to make do with the fragments that lie to hand. Language itself becomes the very tool to tear to bits theories of life that have guided many.

The three forms and Christianity

The three forms of social outlook have dramatically different consequences for religious belief, and especially for the Christian faith. It is important to spell out some of these even though the terms traditionalism, modernism, and postmodernism involve a simplification of social situations.

People in traditionalist societies speak in the plural and say 'we have always believed' that such and such is true. They accept a belief because it has been handed down to them. They learn the stories of old times and pass them on to their children because they are important in maintaining their identity as a tribe, group or nation. Old things are good and must be preserved through their customs.

Modernist societies speak in the singular and say 'I believe' that such and such is true. Individuals are important as they commit themselves to a theory of life whether it is Christianity, Marxism, liberalism, evolutionism or whatever.

Postmodernists doubt the existence of a definite individual, deny the truthfulness of any one theory of existence to which individuals might commit themselves, and certainly deny the worth of simple acceptance of schemes of life-interpretation passed down from the ancient past.

As far as the Bible and religious teachings are concerned, traditionalists accept the past because the source of religious inspiration was located in the life of Christ, his apostles, the written scriptures, and the early decisions of the church. Modernists qualify traditional teaching in the light of discoveries about evolution and the development of the Bible. They develop theories about the sources and forces lying behind scriptures and doctrines, and seek to interpret these for their own day. Postmodernists deny the wisdom of seeking interpretations of texts to find out what their original meaning might have been. They deny the right of great institutions to pronounce on truth or on theories of truth which others should accept. Instead, the postmodernist prefers to play with ideas which are seen as flitting aspects of questions rather than arrive at concrete answers to problems. Postmodernists toy with the surface of things, while the modernists reckon to seek the depth beneath the surface, and traditionalists assert the ancient wisdom in the depth and in the transmission of its truth to future generations.

Traditional churches, modernity and postmodernity

In the light of what has already been said, one issue becomes dramatically obvious. It is that most mainstream Christian churches have strong traditional dimensions to them even when they exist in largely modern, and increasingly postmodern, societies. As traditional bodies, they perpetuate beliefs and values from the past and seek to hand them on to future generations. Many aspects of church life foster this attitude, including the existence of bishops, celibate priests, and many forms of ritual which have an authority of their own. So, too, when it comes to doctrine, the very idea of discovery seems to contradict that of divine revelation.

But, at the same time as they emphasise their obligation to the past, churches often strongly assert the need to be part and parcel of modern society and to speak in ways that are relevant to the present day. In saying this they may not fully appreciate the contradiction that exists between tradition and modernity, between perpetuating the past and discovering new things, as far as basic attitudes are concerned.

Cultures and Christianity: types and time

Sometimes this paradox is not obvious because Christianity has long ago penetrated societies that are traditional. In many such cases, as in Catholic South America, a Christian-influenced mythology has replaced, or merged in a significant way with, pre-existing myths, just as Christian ideology has come into close relations with the thought-forms of modern societies.

TRADITIONAL CONTEXT AND TIME

Two interesting features are to be found in the traditionalist perspective on life-experience and events that take place in society. First, traditionalists see some period in the past as a golden age, or as a period when the supernatural world was very close to the world of humanity. Often God was nearer then than now. In many tribal religions this is a major area in which myth operates to describe the original time of creation when gods, humanity, animals, plants, and the rest of nature had distinctive relations to each other. Invariably this scene of idyllic relations is brought rudely to an end by some sort of wickedness on the part of human beings. The creation myths in the early chapters of Genesis are typical of this depiction of a primal time when God walked in the Garden in the cool of the day and spoke to Adam and Eve, and when there was a serpent that tempted the unfortunate pair (Gen. 1–4). In a slightly similar way the Acts of the Apostles speaks of the nearness of God through the Holy Spirit, expressed through the flames of fire that danced on the Apostles' heads on the day of Pentecost when the Christian movement was propelled into a new intensity of life (Acts 2).

Secondly, ordinary life in the present world operates according to a cyclical programme. This repetitive scheme of things was often associated with the cycle of the year, grounded in the economic life of a society. In agricultural societies there were times for seed-sowing and harvest, just as in pastoralist and nomadic societies there were times for moving flocks to different pastures.

The paradox of Christianity in this kind of society is that in theological terms, it cannot simply accept time as a constantly repetitive cycle of events because of the Christian belief that God started with creation and is now working towards a future goal which will overthrow the present ordinariness of life. This was part of a problem that Augustine devoted himself to in the fourth century in his book, *The City of God* (XII, 13–15). In developing his own philosophy of history, he argued that God had actually created time which passed in a flowing way rather than as a repetitive cycle.

This is symbolised to a certain extent in those ritual moments when the doctrinal-mythical domain penetrates the cyclical and repetitive life of everyday existence. These moments can be viewed as 'outside' time, expressing a kind of 'ritual time', when the normal routine of life is put aside to enter into ritual activity where mythical material is rehearsed. These moments can be backward- or forward-looking, as in Mass or Eucharist. During the service people are reminded of the events of the passion of Christ and of the Last Supper and, in some sense, come to share in those past events through the ritual events of today. But the Eucharist also looks forward to the coming Kingdom of God.

Early Christian traditions developed an annual calendar to govern worship, prayer and theological thinking. It focused on events in the life of Christ from his birth to his resurrection and the sending of the Holy Spirit. But this calendar was directly related to pre-existing Jewish festivals such as Passover. The particularly important factor in this Jewish background is that key festivals, such as Passover, were held to acknowledge divine acts in the history of Israel. Even though their timing was linked to phases of the moon, as Easter still is in Christian churches, this was not because of any power of nature but because of a way of timing events. Over the centuries many other days were incorporated into what is now called the Liturgical Calendar, and these celebrated the lives of various saints or theologically important events.

Such ritual knowledge is a fundamentally important aspect of human experience, and it probably exerts a great influence on how people think about their religion. It is likely that people come to a sense of their religion as being true because of experiences they have in life, often in connection with worship, prayer or other religious activity. We explore this dimension shortly in connection with the Eucharist.

MODERNISTS

Using the term in a general cultural sense, modernists see their own day as radically important as a period of discovery and advance. Tradition hands things on, discovery finds new things. But the 'things' that are found tend to be theories, broad-scale ways of interpreting reality. So, for example, both evolutionism and Freudianism were nineteenth-century discoveries of 'theories' which explained many aspects of life.

The word 'modernist' also has a specifically theological meaning, used to describe a group of Roman Catholic scholars of the late nineteenth and early twentieth centuries, including A. Loisy (1857–1940), G. Tyrrell (1861–1909), and the Anglican, F.B. Jevons (1858–1936). All these saw deep significance in the symbolic meaning of doctrine rather than in its literal truth.

In the mid- and late nineteenth century other western Christian thinkers also developed the idea of 'salvation history' (a translation of the German *heilsgeschichte*) to interpret the way God deals with humanity. In many respects salvation history resembles evolutionism and Freudianism as a theory explaining human destiny. Like Marxism, it suggests that history is not simply a series of random events but involves the outworking of underlying principles.

Some Christians combined grand theories with basic Christian doctrine so that their explanations of the meaning of life could make its appeal at both levels. So, for example, both F.B. Jevons and his close contemporary, Teilhard de Chardin, combined evolutionary thinking with a belief in a progressive revelation of Christian truth.

The general scheme that salvation history followed argued that it was God's initial action which created the world, after which divine activity was focused on humankind through the people of Israel, their prophets and spiritual leaders, until, in a new way, God entered human life through the person of Jesus of Nazareth. His life, death and resurrection herald a new and distinctive phase within the history of salvation and lead on to a future kingdom of God in which the divine purpose is fulfilled.

Many religious movements, such as the Jehovah's Witnesses and Seventh Day Adventists, have become narrowly interested in *dispensations*, or particular phases of divine activity, during which God is believed to be engaged in particular tasks working towards the salvation of people. Very often such groups use biblical texts, especially from books such as Daniel and Revelation, to provide blue-prints for the pattern of history which they believe God has revealed to them.

Theologians of more mainstream traditions, such as Karl Barth and Paul Tillich, have also set about interpreting God's work in connection with humanity through various time series. Barth stressed the nature of faith in perceiving the events of Jesus's life as a work of God, events which ordinary historians would read in a secular way. Tillich showed how time can be divided into categories depending upon its quality or significance. *Chronos* refers to 'clock-time', or the constant passing of equally significant moments, while *kairos* refers to periods of deep significance for Christian people (1964, Vol. 3: 395). This distinction between *chronos* and *kairos* shows how important the perception of events is in interpreting historical events.

Another fundamentally important contribution comes in Oscar Cullman's book, *Christ and Time* (1962). This was first published in 1946 and is an important analysis of Christian ideas of time and history. For him, the coming of Christ provides the central focus (which he calls 'the middle' of time) for a Christian understanding of history – a history which he calls 'redemptive history'. Basic to this perspective is the fact that Christianity inherited the idea of 'linear' time from Judaism. Time has a beginning in the creation of the world and presses on in a linear way towards a goal set by God. The coming of Christ is the profoundest of all events, punching its way into the midst of time and providing a significance for all other periods both before and after it. Both preaching and, as we see below, the Eucharist are moments when the significance of Christ's intervention into time becomes apparent and deeply significant for many Christians.

POSTMODERNITY

Postmodernists announce the death and end of history. They believe there is no validity in grand theories of history grounded in underlying principles or laws. Inevitably, postmodernists assume that there can be no overriding theories of existence, including religious theories. This means that it is impossible to interpret the past in ways that imply an inherent reason for events and occurrences. Individualism and personal idiosyncrasy are the best that can be anticipated and even the idea of an individual is radically questioned.

The idea of an eternal truth can have no place in a postmodern outlook, whether that truth is experienced through a cyclical view of nature or in a sense of linear time working towards a goal. This makes postmodernity an uncomfortable context for Christianity, with its commitment to aspects of historical tradition and to a divinely influenced future.

We have already said that Christian churches exist in a paradoxical situation as far as these three approaches to knowledge are concerned. In what follows we see some of the ways in which Christianity has responded to this problem.

Birth of tradition

In Christianity's Jewish background, the view was held that God acted in particular events set within history. The message of the prophets about a coming reign of God set a stamp on the idea that times would change and that there was a purposeful flow to history.

Christianity emerged within this pattern of thought, and was specifically rooted in a group of disciples of the historical person Jesus of Nazareth. Early generations of Christians believed that Jesus had overcome death through the resurrection, and many seemed to hope that quite soon a supernatural event would take place with the risen Christ's Second Coming to inaugurate the Kingdom of God (1 Cor. 7:29–31). As time went on, the Second Coming did not take place, but believers did not simply give up their faith; they went on to develop it in complex ways. Of central importance was the increasing commitment to the belief that Jesus was both human and divine.

In this doctrine of the Incarnation the belief is expressed that God participated in real human life and human nature through the individual, Jesus of Nazareth. This was believed to have taken place in a quite literal sense. Someone whose very nature was divine in a way that no other human had ever been divine, had walked the streets of Jerusalem. God had, in a quite new sense, 'entered' history and changed the way time was viewed. Central to this scheme was the ancient history of the Jews which was part and parcel of early Christian self-reflection. The Christian Bible came rapidly into existence as sacred scripture over the early centuries of Christianity. It was divided into Old Testament and New Testament, the clearest example of a cutting up of time into periods of differing significance. In the first, God dealt with the Jews through prophets, priests and kings, and in the second with all humankind through a 'Son'.

Church and Bible

Throughout the subsequent history of Christianity, this sense of a historic foundation for belief has been significant in two major ways; one focuses on the church, and the other on the Bible. In the

Catholic and Orthodox traditions great stress is placed on the belief that the church continues the ministry of Jesus. The Roman Catholic Church sees itself as having the successor of Saint Peter as its head, and regards the Pope as a guardian of true doctrine. Great emphasis is placed on the line of succession, or Apostolic Succession as it is called, from Peter the Apostle to the present Pope. Bishops are also a central feature of this line of authority, and they ordain priests as part of the total ministry of the church. God is believed to guide the decisions of the church, not least in the way it understands and interprets the Bible. The Early Church Fathers are also relied upon as sources of theological material, so that the past remains an important centre of gravity of belief.

In a similar way, the Greek Orthodox Church sees itself as a guardian of tradition, and places great emphasis on the ritual of the Holy Communion, or the Liturgy, as it is called. In many ways Orthodox tradition consists in maintaining the faith through maintaining the Liturgy and the bishops and priests.

The Protestant churches, stemming from the Reformation (including the Anglican and Lutheran Churches), stress the importance of the Bible as an authoritative basis for faith, precisely because it deals with periods when God is believed to have communicated with humanity through prophets, the historical Jesus and the Apostles. These accounts of early Christians are as important to Catholic as to Protestant strands of Christianity and demonstrate the importance of history to Christian theology and religion.

Church rites and time

Ritual activity also gives believers an experience of the historical aspects of religion. The Christian Eucharist is a fine example of this, working as it does to link the present day with the earliest days of Christian history. It takes the Last Supper, which Jesus held with his disciples, as the model for today's Eucharist. The Eucharist is a kind of memorial. Christian traditions differ in quite subtle ways in the interpretation they give to this memorial. In Roman Catholicism and in the Catholic tradition within Anglicanism, a link is made between the Last Supper, Christ's death on the cross, interpreted as a sacrifice, and the present day rite of the Mass. The emphasis on what is called the Eucharistic Sacrifice is associated with another doctrine, that of the 'real presence' of Christ in the bread and wine used in the ritual. In this way there is a kind of 'collapsing' of time into one moment of devotion and worship. Historical events of the past are integrated with a theological interpretation of those events and with the individual's own inner experience of God in the present day.

There is yet another dimension to this spiritual tradition of Catholic thought which is related to the Eucharist. For not only do believers share in what happened in the past, they also share in what, in a sense, also happens now 'in heaven'. The sacrificial offering of Christ in his death has an eternal significance to it, and each Mass or Eucharist enters into that eternal mystery of Christ's sacrificial death. Past, present and eternity are related through the Mass.

In more Protestant traditions time and worship are viewed in quite different theological terms. The historical death of Christ is emphasised by saying that he died once in a completed sacrifice (which does not have that eternal dimension to it) in which later worshippers may share. Protestant Communion services stress a memorial, a looking back in thanks for the forgiveness of sins, rather than a looking into an eternally present sacrifice. There are many theological arguments involved in this difference, including a radically different doctrine of the priesthood and ministry.

Churches make history

Despite these variations in doctrine, one vitally important point emerges from the variously named Christian ritual of the Eucharist, Mass, Holy Communion or Lord's Supper. It is that a present-day rite is believed to be integrally linked with deeply significant past events. In a very significant way Churches sustain and develop a sense of history, so that Christian ritual not only grows out of past events but also generates history.

This raises a theoretically interesting question. Does the idea of tradition arise in the past and then get passed on to today's generations, or does the present-day life of churches generate the interest and energy which gives life to past events? In terms of common sense, the answer is obvious. Tradition starts in the past and comes on to the future. But from another perspective it is perfectly possible to say that it is the present-day activity of religious groups which gives the past any significance at all. In practical terms there is an interplay between these two perspectives.

For Christianity, as a living religion, this is a very important point. Christian tradition is not, for example, like the 'tradition' of ancient Egyptian religion. It is possible to study ancient Egyptian religion and many other 'dead' traditions which no longer have active groups of believers. But those traditions do not have the power and significance found in religions which still have adherents. It is contemporary Christians who make Christian tradition live. There are many institutions which help sustain the past and which place a tremendous emphasis upon it, so much so that the centre of gravity of the religion seems to lie in history rather than in the present. Some people might see the Pope and the hierarchy of the Roman Catholic Church in this way, possessing a weight of tradition coming from earlier centuries.

Other Christians see God at work today in such a way that the centre of gravity of Christianity lies in their own group in the here and now. This is especially important in newly emerging religious groups, as in the case of many sects. They will, almost always, see the Bible as important in recording the times of Jesus but they tend to jump over the intervening centuries as periods of reduced Christian commitment until they come to the present day, when God's power through the Holy Spirit restores the fullness of faith to humanity.

In these ways Christian churches 'make history'. They draw significance from historical events at the same time as they give significance to them. And as with the Eucharist, so with other rites. Baptism, for example, and the washing of feet, are used in Catholic traditions and also in other groups such as the Seventh Day Adventist Church. Biblical accounts of these rites feed into present use and often validate what is done today.

Is history dead?

It is in this sense that dynamic religious groups are likely to stand in firm opposition to the postmodern idea that history is dead. To speak of the death of history may sound odd but, as already mentioned, some contemporary scholars argue that history has come to an end in the sense that postmodern people can no longer believe that history is influenced by laws, trends or processes. The collapse of Communist regimes in many European countries in the 1990s offers one example of this. But, one major objection to the idea of the death of history comes from Christian religious practice.

From what has already been said, it is obvious that active Christian groups and congregations do see themselves as an expression of God's activity in the world. In this sense the idea of the 'Kingdom of God' stands in sharp contradiction to a postmodern world-view. This opposition is not simply philosophical, but is grounded in the practical life-experience of believers who think of themselves as part of a long series of divinely influenced events. Their commitment can be either widely or narrowly conceived. Some churches see their own history as the truest and surest expression of God's activities, and, to be certain of salvation, people should be members of that particular group. Here the Catholic Church has traditionally argued that individuals need to receive the sacraments of that church before they attain salvation, while many Protestant groups have argued that the individual needs a personal experience of God's forgiveness. Some other Christian churches think more in terms of a broad movement of God's activity in the development of many Christian churches. But for all these groups history is not dead but dynamic and alive.

Facts of history and myth

The importance of faith in interpreting history as a divine process cannot be overemphasised, because what may appear to one person as a divine history, to another can seem to be a simple mythological account of events.

Two well-known phrases summarise the difference between history and myth. One is, '1066 and all that', and the other is, 'once upon a time'. The first reminds us that history is grounded in past events, in dates when things happened. But history is about more than simple dates; it concerns the significance and interpretation of events and periods in the life of human societies. The second signals the fact that the account that follows the introductory phrase is a story, and does not refer to events that have actually taken place.

In one sense, 'facts' are very rare in the realm of human behaviour. They seldom come 'pure'. Each culture deeply influences the way its members look at things. This is true of simple objects and is even more significant when it comes to ideas, values and beliefs. This is exactly the case with history and with myth. It is often said that it is the victors who write the history of a society, and recent times have witnessed the writing and rewriting of history in the decline of the Communist world of the USSR. So, though for many people history means a list of dates which are seen as basic facts about events that once took place, in practice, history also involves complex debates about the relative significance of different interpretations of events.

In the Bible this is the case, as scholars argue over the way different authors present the story of the life of Jesus. Do they do it as historical fact or more as a story that reflects a mythical concern over issues of God, and truth, of life and death? A good biblical example of the shaping of historical accounts concerns the event when Jesus made a whip and drove out the traders from the temple at Jerusalem. In the gospels of Matthew (21:12), Mark (11:15) and Luke (19:45), this takes place towards the end of Jesus's earthly ministry, as events move to the climax of his passion and death, while in John's gospel it is placed very early on, at the outset of the public life of Jesus (2:14ff.). For a variety of reasons it is likely that, historically speaking, the event that lies behind these accounts took place once, and towards the end rather than at the beginning of Jesus's ministry. But the theological significance John wishes to develop, that Jesus is more significant than the temple in the life of believers, makes him bring the event forward in the account.

This kind of emphasis is not far removed from stories that are told to make a point without the events contained in the story ever having taken place. In fact many people think of myth as interesting stories about persons and places which exist in imagination but not in real life.

Literal, poetic and mythical ways of thinking

'Truth' is the most important theological issue at stake in the relationship between myth and history, but it is not easy to define truth, as another biblical example will show. The early chapters of the Book of Genesis focus on the creation of the world and of the human race. Some Christians see these chapters as myths. They do not for a minute think that there was an actual garden in which a real-life Adam and Eve walked in the cool of the day and heard God speaking to them. Even so they think that the stories do present truth because they speak of God's responsibility for creation and of human responsibility towards God. The truth of the story does not lie in whether the events actually occurred, but in the ideas expressed through the events of the story.

But there are other Christians who do believe that there was a real garden possessing the real first parents for humankind. For these believers, the truth of the story lies in the events actually having taken place. The first kind of interpretation accepts that some biblical material is mythical in form and resembles the myths of many other cultures, while the second line of interpretation says that the biblical material must be accepted in a literal rather than in any allegorical or metaphorical way.

This is a fundamentally important point for Christianity, because it adds a further dimension to the question of truth, and truth is a key concept in the Christian religion.

TRUTH AND MYTHICAL THOUGHT

The literal-minded Christian believes that God has inspired the Bible in a way that makes the printed book authoritative as a source of religious truth. All human attempts at interpretation must be secondary to the Bible itself. But almost all modern scholars accept that the Bible must be approached through other forms of interpretation before its significance becomes apparent. This assumes that reason and scholarship and a knowledge of the development of ideas and social life play a tremendously significant part in understanding the Bible. The problem is that literal-minded Christians often accuse others of not accepting the plain meaning of the Bible, just as the more liberal thinkers see the literalists as naive fundamentalists. In other words, the very word 'myth' has come to be a kind of short-hand term expressing quite different attitudes towards knowledge, literature and faith.

In terms of religious studies, scholars like Mircea Eliade have paid particular attention to what they call mythopoeic thought (1960). This refers to the human ability to create and use mythical stories as a way of expressing particular ideas about life. For Eliade, mythical forms of thinking are associated with the idea of the sacred, which reflects a constant capacity of human consciousness rather than a phase in the evolution of consciousness. From the work of historians and anthropologists of religion, the importance of myth in the kind of traditional societies often studied by social anthropologists is well established. What is less easy is to grasp the significance of myth-like aspects of stories, accounts of events, and of more clearly historical occurrences.

Especially since the nineteenth century, science has come to play an increasingly important part in influencing the idea of truthfulness and certain knowledge in the population of modern societies. The experimental method is specially important in this process, so that the phrases, 'prove it', or, 'can it be proved?', throw light on how some people at least think about particular ideas.

Sigmund Freud's psychoanalysis is one example of an interlinking of what appear to be both scientific and mythical ideas. He reckoned to have discovered the existence of the unconscious mind, with its power to influence ordinary life. Taking the Oedipus myth as the model for what happened in humanity's earliest history, he argued that early men grouped together to kill their father to gain access to the forbidden women. Overcome by guilt, they initiated the incest taboo in human culture. The great majority of psychologists do not accept that there is any truth in Freud's interpretation, yet it has profoundly influenced western society.

Freud interpreted Christianity as an extension of Judaism and as an outworking of the Oedipus complex. The death of Christ becomes another kind of killing of the primal father, with the holy communion as a meal related to the reduction of the sons' guilt after murder. In *Totem and Taboo* Freud spelled this out, with history being a process of human encounter with guilt.[2] In *The Future of an Illusion* Freud depicted religion as an illusion preventing individuals from encountering the harsh realities of existence.[3] Knowing that parents ultimately fail, people put their trust in a heavenly father, thus failing to mature and stand alone. This theory of history and culture is fundamentally mythical and has influenced many, despite its complete lack of any scientific base.

Anthropology and myth

Some social anthropologists have been among the most influential group in the study of myth because, unlike Freud, they lived among peoples who used myth in a normal and regular way as part of their ritual life and as a way of explaining aspects of their own social custom.

The French anthropologist, Claude Lévi-Strauss, argued that myths were a way of trying to overcome problems posed in a society through a series of binary oppositions. These were statements giving opposite views of a cultural problem through stories which explored various options for its resolution. Lévi-Strauss tended to avoid using biblical material, but the English anthropologist, Edmund Leach, specifically took up myths from the Old Testament to study by this method of 'structuralism' (1969). The Old Testament scholar John Rogerson has analysed this work, along with many others, and presented a reliable analysis of many approaches to myth in the Old Testament (1974).

Doctrine and myth

One key issue in this often hostile debate lies in the fact that Christianity asserts as doctrinal fact things which are regularly regarded as myths when found in non-Christian religions. Obvious examples lie in the creation stories, the Virgin Birth of Jesus, the miracles associated with the life of Jesus, as well as the idea of the Incarnation itself. There is probably no doctrine more central to Christianity than the belief expressed in the doctrine of the Incarnation, that God actually became human in the person of Jesus of Nazareth. The Creeds of the Christian churches have this teaching at their heart, as does all Christian worship.

At one level, it is an incredible statement and begs to be interpreted along with other human myths about the gods coming to visit humanity. But the Christian faithful, along with the great majority of Christian leaders, are adamant in their view that God actually became human in Jesus at one point in time. A story which has the marks of myth about it is said to be true in the sense that the events it describes actually took place within human experience. In other words, it is said to belong to history and not to mythology. Many of the writings of the popular theologian, C.S. Lewis, flow around this idea that the wonder of Christianity lies in the fact that what seems almost totally impossible actually happened.

The doctrine of the Incarnation came to assume an increasingly important place in the history of western culture, notably from the establishment of the Holy Roman Empire by Constantine in the fourth century. It became focused in the Mass or Eucharist, and from that ritual base exerted a strong influence on church architecture, music and art. With the subsequent establishment of theology as a major subject in European universities from the middle ages, Christian doctrine became established as a statement of fact about reality.

Power and truth

This is a particularly important point that is often ignored in theological studies. It concerns power in society. Each society explains its significance in terms of some theory of origin or principle of life, and these religious, political and ideological explanations become normative and authoritative for its members. Christianity has been one such explanatory principle, and Christian ideas or doctrines, such as that of the Incarnation, came to be unquestioned and even unquestionable. Although the rise of modern thought from the Enlightenment, and especially since the nineteenth century, has altered this state of affairs, it still remains true that Christian doctrine is often treated differently from the beliefs of other world religions and from the 'myths' of preliterate societies. For complex social, historical and philosophical reasons centred on cultural ideals of status, influence and power, it is difficult to equate a Professor of Theology with a local myth-teller and wise-person of a preliterate society, yet for many practical purposes they serve a similar purpose.

In this sense, European history itself gave an authority to Christian doctrine which allowed it to function as a factual and empirical truth. For there is a sense in which the accepted truthfulness of an idea or belief is associated with the assent given to it by those who hold and control power in a society. This was the case, for example, in the USSR until the 1990s, with the Marxist interpretation of history as a struggle between social classes in an evolutionary development of society. With the decline of the Soviet Union, the history of Russia and aligned countries is being rewritten, and Christian groups are free once more to express their own theory of history in relation to the Kingdom of God.

The history of many countries in other parts of the world was also deeply influenced by Christian ideas of history as a result of European colonisation and missionary work; this was especially true, for example, in South America and South Africa. The South African theory of apartheid involved a Christian doctrine of racial groups and of the duty and prerogative of white people in relation to black races. This, too, has undergone serious change as other Christians have argued against the Dutch Reformed background to white South Africans' religious views of history.

Story and truth

As times change, the status of belief alters. In Christianity, for example, the centrality of the Mass led to an entire theology explaining its nature. In the thirteenth century this was explained by transubstantiation, the doctrine which argued that the inner, actual and real nature of the bread became the body of Christ even though its outer and apparent nature remained that of bread. And so, too, with the wine. For Catholics this was a vitally important doctrine which helped feed their faith and form the ritual of the Mass. For many Protestants it is simply not accepted as a true explanation of how Christ is present for the faithful at the Eucharist. To non-Catholics, and especially to non-Christians, the transubstantiation doctrine can easily be viewed as a myth, explaining how divine power comes to inhabit material objects.

Following on from the life and death of Jesus, his earthly representatives, the official priests, whose ordination makes them stand in a historical succession to Saint Peter as Christ's prime Apostle, perform the ceremony and say the prayer of consecration through which God miraculously transforms the inner nature of the bread and wine so that the very body and blood of Christ can be eaten and drunk by believers today. Is this a myth or is it a doctrine? Is it a myth that functions as a doctrine, or a doctrine that functions as a myth? Or are the words 'doctrine' and 'myth' largely interchangeable and avoided only because of the cultural status of Christian religion compared with preliterate religions or religions long dead?

Myth and spiritual development

Christian doctrine has to battle with the relationship between history and fact, myth and doctrine, just as many individual Christians, past and present, have to do for themselves. This is particularly important in an individual's religious and intellectual development in relation to a maturing idea of God.

To think of God as a pleasant and generous old man living among the clouds is obviously an immature and vastly childish image. Yet many Christians probably do think of heaven as a place and of God as an identifiable 'person'. The work of theologians such as Paul Tillich, who have spoken of God in a less literal and more existential way as 'the ground of being', has not been particularly welcomed by people at large. This was made very obvious in the 1960s when the then Bishop of Woolwich, John Robinson, wrote several books, including the famous *Honest to God* (SCM Press, 1963), in which he simply reflected the existential theology of Tillich and denied the simple images of a supernatural heaven etc., much to the dismay of many ordinary Christians.[4] Many felt that he was taking away the truthfulness of the faith they had held throughout their life.

Since the 1970s a similar concern has been expressed by the Cambridge theologian, Don Cupitt, whose many books basically argued that all religious ideas were constructed by human imagination and influenced by social contexts, so that Christian doctrine was not basically different from preliterate mythology. For Cupitt, along with a significant minority of Christians, this view must be accepted as part of a maturing of thought and faith, while for many others it involves an abandonment of the Christian claim to exclusiveness through an actual divine revelation.

Part of the issue of history and myth concerns the way individuals evaluate their religion, because the distinction between history and myth is, at one popular level, simply the distinction between fact and fancy. For some, it would be impossible to believe and live as Christians if they felt that there never was an actual historical pair called Adam and Eve. For others, it is perfectly possible to continue in faith even if, for example, Jesus had not actually been raised from the dead but that a memory of him had somehow inspired his disciples with hope for the future and love among themselves.

Many Christians who give serious thought to doctrine find these issues of tremendous importance as their life proceeds. Many people are brought up as Christians, or are converted to Christianity as children or teenagers, and tend to have a relatively simple view of God, Jesus and the Bible. For them the factual and historical nature of Christian religion is important because it has formed part of the belief which is intrinsic to their sense of identity. As time goes on, and especially if they engage in academic study of religion, some of these perspectives no longer hold. They come to see parallels between stories of supernatural persons and miraculous events in other religions, and wonder whether Christianity works in the same way. There is no easy answer to this question, because a simple, rationalistic perspective gives a clear negative answer even to the existence of God, let alone to more particular religious ideas. One problem lies in the fact that the idea of history has been accorded high intellectual status, while that of myth has been given a low status because of its association with 'primitive' peoples. This was especially true in the nineteenth century, but it also continued into the first half of the twentieth century.

Biblical myth and de-mythologising

Scholars have discussed the idea of myth in relation to the Bible from the later part of the eighteenth century until today. Originally the greatest weight was placed on the Old Testament (Rogerson 1974), but the New Testament has also received considerable attention (Bultmann 1960[5]), not least in connection with the doctrine of the Incarnation which has been derived from it.[6]

The German New Testament scholar and theologian, Rudolph Bultmann, broached this question in 1941 with his study of *The New Testament and Mythology*. He provoked one of the most famous recent debates in theology with his argument that the New Testament emerged from a world where mythological forms of thought and expression were commonplace. We, in the modern western world, educated by science, philosophy, and not least by a growing awareness of history, no longer found the mythological perspective persuasive. On the contrary, myth spoke more of error and immature thought than of educated insight. Accordingly, he proposed a scheme of demythologising which sought to translate the meaning of biblical myths into a message which could be understood by contemporary believers. Mythology must be translated into existentialist philosophical terms appropriate to the modern world. Bultmann was worried that modern people would pay no attention to the Bible because of its obviously mythical and therefore (according to popular thought) untrue content; they would throw out the baby with the bath-water. In a characteristically Lutheran way, Bultmann saw the crux of Christian belief lying in the decision that individuals had to make within their own lives in relation to God's grace. They should not be hindered in doing this by outmoded biblical images, expressions and stories. He retained as central, Justification by Faith as the key-note doctrine which made Christian faith authentic. In fact Bultmann saw his own task as resembling that of Luther:

> De-mythologizing is a task parallel to that performed by Paul and Luther in their doctrine of justification by faith alone. . . . De-mythologizing is the radical application of the doctrine of justification to the sphere of knowledge and thought. Like the doctrine of justification, de-mythologization destroys every longing for security.
>
> (1960: 84)

The last sentence is particularly important because Bultmann's prime concern is with the life of faith and not with an attempt at destroying faith by rationalising it away. He defines faith as 'the abandonment of man's own security and the readiness to find security only in the unseen beyond, in God', and argues that 'faith itself demands to be freed from any world-view produced by man's thought, whether mythological or scientific. For all human world-views objectivize the world and ignore or eliminate the significance of encounters in our personal existence' (1960: 40, 83).

History as myth?

But history was also central to Bultmann's discussion. This became very apparent, for example, in a discussion on myths and demythologising between him and the German philosopher and psychiatrist, Karl Jaspers, especially in their small but significant book *Myth and Christianity* (1958), subtitled *An Inquiry into the Possibility of Religion without Myth*. Bultmann wants to keep a stress on the historical revelation of God to humankind in Jesus despite a strong avoidance of the language of miracle, but Jaspers criticises him for retaining the idea of God speaking to humanity at particular historical moments, for to claim that God does such things is to speak in a mythical way; that, at least, is what Jaspers thinks.

Jaspers was not opposed to mythological thought. On the contrary, he resembled another influential figure, the psychologist

Carl Jung, and considered myth to be a basic element of religious reflection upon life. For Jaspers, myths composed 'a language of images, ideas, figures, and events . . . which point to the supernatural. When translated into mere ideas their actual meanings are lost.' More than this, he saw that myths are important, not as 'objects of historical study, but as presences, as legitimate modes of existential insight' (1958: 85).

Jaspers included the idea of a divine revelation in history as also belonging to the mythical world of understanding. This is an important point, for it is the issue which divides thinkers. On the one hand, there are those who see Christianity as a fundamentally historical religion because at one place and at one time God was revealed through the actual man Jesus; on the other hand, there are those who see that belief itself as a mythical statement about reality. It is, after all, a matter of faith as to whether the historical Jesus was anything other than a Jewish teacher who won disciples and influenced the subsequent history of the world.

In practical terms, this division is likely to continue for as long as some Christian theologians identify myth as a category of thought alien to theology and to the human nature of Christians. These will continue to stress the literal truth of Christian doctrine focused on the wonder of the Incarnation. For others, and here the study of religions exerts a strong influence, myths are categorised as a perfectly normal mode of thought in the lives of people of all levels of society and in every culture. Religious life for such people may well include a commitment to accept the mythical formulation of belief, knowing full well that it is not a literal statement of truth but a way of formulating their inner experience. For some contemporary Christians, especially some who have been born into a more traditional and literalist form of religion, this outlook can be a freeing possibility, enabling them to develop in their experience of God.

Myth and history continue to exist as directly related categories. Where history is prized as the medium of religious revelation, myth will be ignored or devalued. Those who see history as a radically problematic medium for gaining religious certainty will value myth highly. But other important consequences follow these trends, not least the significance given to non-Christian religions. A spirit of exclusivity rules if history is deemed the canvas on which God is revealed through events in the life of Israel, through Jesus of

Nazareth, through early church councils and their creeds and doctrines, and then either through the great tradition of Thomas Aquinas and ongoing Catholic tradition, or else through the Reformation of Martin Luther and others. Catholics argue that their history gives more of the total revealed truth than the history of the Protestants. The Protestants see the Reformation as a major turning point in religious knowledge and freedom. The Eastern Orthodox see their constantly ongoing liturgical tradition as continuing the Christian truth through history and not losing out as the other two Christian streams have done. Smaller Christian groups then add their own version of historical revelation to show how their doctrine is closer to God's truth than the doctrine of the other churches.

But through all this there is the doctrinal certainty that God is revealed in Christian history in a way that is not the case for non-Christian religions. Their gods, scriptures and worship are seen to be strongly mythical and to lack the stamp of religious truth, which is none other than a direct contact from God in history. Any idea that the supernatural world may have interacted with this world through actual personages, such as the *avatāra*s of Viṣṇu in Hinduism, tends to be quickly relegated to the realm of myth and thereby to a lower order of knowledge. In other words, Christianity's sense of being a historical religion is part of its own identity as a superior form of religious knowledge when compared with 'mythological' religions. This is why many theologians would deny that Christian doctrine was mythological in any real way.

Narrative, myth and theology

The constant importance of myth and history within Christian theological thinking can be seen in Narrative theology. This theological approach emerged in the second half of the twentieth century as a way of allowing groups of ordinary Christians to develop their own theological understanding of their life and local circumstances. It has been an important aspect of Christian thought in disadvantaged social groups in South America and South Africa. Instead of approaching the Bible through a detailed analysis of the text, they see it as an extensive set of stories about God's dealings with many earlier believers. Because no great scholarly skill, in knowing many languages and how to interpret the Bible, is required, ordinary believers can practise this kind of theology. They are encouraged to see their own life circumstances as another story of God's relationship with people.

The idea of a narrative lies behind this approach, which is why it is often called Narrative theology or the theology of Story. As people see their own local history as a narrative of events, often focused on elements of injustice, they find it easy to see the Bible as one large set of narratives concerning God's people and their search for justice and salvation (Stroup 1981).

This approach shows the clear importance of history as the framework within which Christians see themselves as related to God. But it also involves a kind of myth-making activity, a sort of mythologising of events which otherwise might be seen as economic, political, or ordinary social history. This approach resembles the nineteenth-century idea of salvation-history but with a focus not on past events but on today's deliverance.

NOTES

1. See Harvey, D. (1989) *The Condition of Postmodernity*, Oxford, Blackwell, and Turner, B.S. (ed.) (1990) *Theories of Modernity and Postmodernity*, London, Sage.
2. Freud, S. (1960) *Totem and Taboo*, London, Routledge and Kegan Paul.
3. Freud, S. (1973) *The Future of an Illusion*, London, Hogarth Press.
4. See Towler, R. (1984) *The Need for Certainty*, London, Routledge.
5. Bultmann, R. (1960) *Jesus Christ and Mythology*, London, SCM Press, pp. 40, 83.
6. See Hick, J. (ed.) (1977), *The Myth of God Incarnate*, London, SCM Press.

FURTHER READING

Bultmann, R. and Jaspers, K. (1958) *Myth and Christianity*, New York, Noonday Press.

Cullman, O. (1962) *Christ and Time*, London, SCM Press.

Eliade, M. (1960) *Myths, Dreams and Mysteries*, London, Fontana.

Leach, E. (1969) *Genesis as Myth and Other Essays*, London, Cape.

Lévi-Strauss, C. (1964) *Structural Anthropology*, Vol. 1, London, Allen Lane.

Rogerson, J. (1974) *Myth in Old Testament Interpretation*, Berlin, Walter de Gruyter.
Stroup, G.W. (1981) *The Promise of Narrative Theology*, London, SCM Press.
Tillich, P. (1964) *Systematic Theology*, London, Nesbitt.

3. Hinduism

Jacqueline Suthren Hirst

It is often said that Hinduism is not interested in history, that it is ahistorical. Historians, both European and Indian, have followed Rawlinson in suggesting that, before the coming of the British, the pre-Muslim history of India did not exist.[1] On the other hand, Hinduism has rarely been accused of lacking myths. Retellings, anthologies and analyses of Hindu myths abound. It might be expected, then, that this chapter would be largely concerned with myth, giving perhaps passing consideration to histories of India. However, the matter is not that simple.

'Myth' and 'history' are, of course, western terms, both of which are used in many ways with different nuances of meaning. Put very crudely, the distinction is sometimes assumed to be this: where myths deal with God or the gods and 'events' which may not literally have happened, history deals with past facts and so reports what actually did happen. The impression may be given that myths are, at least in some senses, 'false', whereas historical accounts are 'true'. This is implied by Walker when he says of the brahmanical court chronicles, 'Mythology is the framework of their fanciful outpourings, replete as they are with eulogies of patrons and heroes, and theological and moral didacticism'.[2] Not exactly a sympathetic view!

Yet the kind of crude opposition implied here will not do. The interests of myth and history converge in so far as both are concerned with human existential questions about meaning, values, a sense of identity, causation, continuity and change. Without denying their differences, this chapter will explore some of these common concerns as they are expressed in Hindu traditions, whose variety at any one period and across the centuries is well known. It will also try to show how different senses of history have affected Hindus' self-understanding. First, though, we shall look at two key terms and types of textual source for myth and history in Hinduism.

Itihāsa-purāṇa

'*Itihāsa*' is used in some modern Indian languages as the word for 'history'. '*Purāṇa*' is frequently rendered as 'myth'. So it looks as though here are neat Hindu equivalents for 'history' and 'myth'. However, because the words often occur in a compound (*itihāsapurāṇa*) meaning 'history and myth', it has been suggested that Hinduism makes no great distinction between the two, backing up the view that it is fundamentally ahistorical.

To the question of ahistoricality, we shall return. For the moment we shall look more carefully at the usages of '*itihāsa*' and '*purāṇa*' in some key textual traditions.[3] Both words appear together in the *Śatapaṭha Brāhmaṇa* and the *Bṛhadāraṇyaka* and *Chāndogya Upaniṣads*, for types of oral wisdom. They seem to refer to entertaining stories which were recited during the Horse Sacrifice to keep the sacrificer alert!

Śaṃkara, the most famous exponent of classical Advaita Vedānta (seventh or eighth century CE), gives examples for each within the Veda. For *itihāsa* he refers to the story of Urvaśī and Purūravas, found, among other places, in the *Śatapaṭha Brāhmaṇa* (11.4.4.1). This is the famous story of a nymph and a king who marry, which later inspired a play by the great poet Kalidasa. Because the king, Purūruvas, fails to keep one of the conditions of their marriage, Urvaśī disappears. The heartbroken Purūruvas is finally granted a boon by the *gandharva*s (celestial musicians) through which he becomes the initiator of a crucial fire ritual. In calling this story *itihāsa*, Śaṃkara is probably referring to its aetiological function, explaining how the particular sacrifice came to be. '*Itihāsa*' literally means 'thus it was'.

For *purāṇa*, Śaṃkara quotes *Taittirīya Upaniṣad* (2.7): 'This universe was in the beginning Non-being'. The passage goes on to describe how Being emerged from Non-being to form itself into *ātman* (the self), with bliss as the quintessence of its being. It is, then, an origination story or 'creation myth'. *Purāṇa* literally means 'ancient'.

Others suggest different interpretations. Yaska (a grammarian of the fifth century BCE) discusses many vedic etymologies in his *Nirukta*. In one example, he is trying to ascertain the identity of the Aśvins, twin celestial gods (12.1). He points out that some people identify them with sun and moon or with day and night, but that the *aitihāsikas* (specialists in *itihāsa*) say they are two famous kings. The *aitihāsikas* look for a historical basis for the Aśvins, whereas others look for a mythological basis in parts of the cosmos. What is important is that there is awareness of story of various kinds, whose interpretation is open to discussion.

In devotional Hinduism, the terms refer to particular texts which may well be based on the earlier *itihāsas* and *purāṇas*, at least in part. *Itihāsa* comes to denote the Epic *Mahābhārata* and, often, the *Rāmāyaṇa* as well, though strictly the latter is a *kāvya* (poem). The *Mahābhārata* has as its centre the legendary history of the war between two sets of cousins, one side, the Pāṇḍavas, aided and abetted by (Lord) Kṛṣṇa. In many ways, it acts as a key source of historical consciousness for (Hindu) Indians as we shall discuss further below.

The *Rāmāyaṇa* tells the story of Rāma, his birth, marriage and banishment into the forest, accompanied by his wife, Sītā, and his loyal half-brother, Lakṣmaṇa. Sītā's kidnapping by Rāvaṇa, the ten-headed demon king of Lanka, gives rise to a great search and battle in which Rāvaṇa is defeated. At this, Rāma reclaims Sītā, puts her through a fire ordeal which proves her purity, and returns with her victorious to be enthroned in Ayodhyā. Sītā subsequently goes into exile once more, suspected of unfaithfulness. She dies, swallowed up by the earth which finally attests her innocence. The *Rāmāyaṇa*, especially in its various vernacular versions, may well be the best-known story in India, particularly since its serialisation on Indian television in 1987–88. In both past and present, its narration has been bound up with issues of social and political identity, some of whose implications will be discussed towards the end of this chapter.

The *Purāṇas* are the sources from which many of the well-known stories of the gods and goddesses are drawn. Traditionally, there are said to be eighteen major *Purāṇas* and eighteen minor, though in fact there are many more. According to Vaiṣṇava tradition, six of the major *Purāṇas* belong to each of the Vaiṣṇava, Śaiva and Śākta devotional schools. This is certainly an oversimplification, but it does indicate the (sometimes competitive) devotional milieux of these texts.

The following story is from the *Kūrma Purāṇa* (quotations from Dimmitt and van Buitenen 1983: 205–6). It will give a flavour of the kind of stories to be found in the puranic literature. For collections of other puranic stories, Dimmitt and van Buitenen (1983) and O'Flaherty (1975) make excellent introductions (in the following, square brackets indicate author's summary).

> [Long ago, when the cosmos was in a period of dissolution, Śiva appeared to awaken Lord Viṣṇu and Lord Brahmā. Both claiming to be the creator of the worlds, they argued about who was greater.] While the argument was going on like this there appeared by the illusion of the supreme god a matchless *liṅga* whose self was Śiva. . . . It was bright as the fire of Doomsday, wreathed with garlands of flame, free from growth and decay, without beginning, middle or end.
>
> [Brahmā and Viṣṇu agreed to explore the limits of this fiery pillar but could find no end though they searched for a hundred years. Chanting *Oṃ*, they praised Śiva, who manifested himself as the great Yogin, with trident, tiger-skin and snake for sacred thread. Then the great god spoke:] 'I am pleased with you both, O best of the gods. Now see that I am the greatest god and fear no more! Ages ago the two of you eternal ones were produced from my limbs. Brahmā, Grandfather of the worlds, lies in my right side. Viṣṇu, the protector, dwells in my left. And Hara [a form of Śiva] is born in my heart. . . . I will give to you both whatever you desire.'

Prostrating themselves, Brahmā and Viṣṇu claim their boon. It is constant devotion to Śiva. The myth thus makes a clear statement about the identity of the Supreme Lord and also provides an explanation of the significance of the *liṅga*, the aniconic form in which Śiva is generally worshipped. While many other myths (and indeed sculptures) stress the *liṅga*'s phallic form, the symbolism of the ungraspable nature of Ultimate Reality is often preferred by Hindus in the West who feel the balance of male and female in *liṅga* and *yoni* can be misunderstood by outsiders.

Traditionally, a *Purāṇa* is said to cover five topics: the origination of the world cycle, its dissolution, genealogies, world ages and the successive deeds of the descendants of the dynasties mentioned. Klostermaier notes that scholars are increasingly prepared to accept the historical value of some of these dynasty lists (1989: 91). Besides these topics, not all of which feature in every *Purāṇa*, is a wealth of other material covering religious observances, image worship, pilgrimage, astrology, the aims of life, the nature of *Brahman* and so on. Iconography, ritual and a sense of time and tradition are thus underpinned by the puranic stories. To see how these stories of *itihāsa* and *purāṇa* are viewed, we shall turn to the ways they are told.

Telling the stories

In the villages of India, besides perpetual informal family retellings, it is the *paurāṇika*, the storyteller, who keeps these stories alive. R.K. Narayan describes such a figure, living in conformity with the *śāstra*s and knowing by heart the 24,000 verses of the *Rāmāyaṇa*, the 100,000 of the *Mahābhārata* and the 18,000 of the *Bhāgavata Purāṇa*. For him, he says:

> The characters in the epics are prototypes and moulds in which humanity is cast, and remain valid for all time. Every story has implicit in it a philosophical or moral significance. . . . To the storyteller and his audience the tales are so many chronicles of personalities who inhabited this world at some remote time, and whose lives are worth understanding, and hence form part of human history rather than fiction.
>
> (Narayan 1987: 5)

In her delightful book, *Storytellers, Saints and Scoundrels* (1989), Kirin Narayan shows the reverse process employed by the holy man whose stories she recorded. Swamiji's audience is drawn into his stories, as his listeners hear themselves featured among the characters in his tales, individual human histories becoming part of fiction in order to be perceived more truly as they are. Story is about self-perception and identity. Its sources need not be limited to the Epics and *Purāṇa*s, but may include traditional *kathā* (narrative) collections, like the *Hitopadeśa* fables, regional stories in local languages and tales told to accompany and explain particular practices like a fast for a certain goddess.

Storytelling is not simply a rural phenomenon. Jackson and Killingley describe a South Indian storyteller, many of whose recitations are for town dwellers, helping them to keep in touch with their religious traditions (1988: 114–16). Hearing a *Purāṇa* acts as an efficacious substitute for the highest and most complicated rituals. It is said to yield many benefits, including purity and the removal of the contamination of the Kali age. Puranic recitations provide the easy path of *bhakti* (devotion) for busy urban people, and bring refreshment and inspiration into their lives.

Increasingly, such narrations are gaining popularity in the West. Storytellers from India undertake tours which draw thousands of Hindus, some choosing to spend their annual holiday in this way. The tellers may narrate in Sanskrit or Hindi with commentary in Gujarati and English, say, and draw in the younger generation with competitions and jokes as well as more serious teaching. The *Rāmāyaṇa* and *Bhāgavata Purāṇa* are particularly popular texts. Based on his oral retellings, Morari Bapu's *Mangal Ramayan* is the English translation of his Gujarati commentary on the sixteenth-century Hindi version of the *Rāmāyaṇa*, the *Rāmcaritmānas* of Tulsidās.[4] He emphasises that this is not just a story or a recitation, but the wish-fulfilling tree, the bodily incarnation of God Almighty. To hear it helps to build up inner purity and moral conduct which lead to nearness to Lord Rām. To bring out its significance, Morari Bapu has a fund of stories, some emphasised as true anecdotes – life really is like this. With others, it is the 'hidden message' which is 'very appealing'. However, this should not be taken to imply that the events of the Epic may or may not have occurred. The link with actual geography (and hence with a current pilgrimage location) is stressed in the following:

> It is not only a belief but a substantiated fact that the Lord himself had his permanent abode in Chitrakoot [Rāma's first home in exile] . . . Chitrakoot was and is, thus, a permanent abode of Lord Ram.
>
> (p. 7)

It was in Chitrakoot, explains Morari Bapu, that Rāma established *Rāmrājya* (reign of all for the benefit of all), where he denied himself all luxury in food, transport and shelter till he could provide amply for all his subjects. In such a place, chanting of his name is particularly efficacious. Yet Morari Bapu also speaks of the 'Chitrakoot of our hearts' where God can dwell. For this reason, the return of Rāma and Sītā to Ayodhyā is for him the climax of the whole story. There the ideal of selfless service flourishes as, joyfully, the couple are enthroned together, just as they can be in our hearts today. Morari Bapu believes that Tulsidās wisely ignores the end of

Valmīki's saga where Sītā goes off into exile, accused again of unfaithfulness, because 'it is not useful to humanity at large'. Events in themselves are not enough for him; nor is their narration in esteemed versions from the past. It is their continuing uplifting significance which makes them retellable.

'So indeed it was'

In 1989, Peter Brook launched his massive nine-hour English stage version of the *Mahābhārata*, based on Jean-Claude Carrière's French retelling. It subsequently became a televised film. With an international cast, Brook made it clear that his intention was to show the epic's story as the story of the world, of all humans, of universal concern. This is 'how things are'.

Many Hindus preferred the Hindi version, shown in ninety-one episodes on British television, with interpolations from other texts like the *Bhāgavata Purāṇa*. As one friend of mine put it, 'Krishna really looked like he does in the Hindi version. He just didn't look like God in the other one'. He also did not look Indian, played as he was by Bruce Myers, an Englishman. My friend is not naive. She would be quick to agree that God is beyond all human ideas. Yet her vision of Kṛṣṇa is shaped by the *Bhagavadgītā*'s description of his four-armed form, holding conch and discus, and represented iconographically with the equivalent of a halo around his head. The Hindi version which reproduced this rang more true for her, though she agreed with Brook that the epic story deals with the fabric of all human experience.

The *Mahābhārata*, 'the Great [Epic] of India', sees itself as *itihāsa*. It portrays itself fundamentally as Vyāsa's account of the victory of the Pāṇḍavas over their cousins, the Kauravas. This is retold on two subsequent ritual occasions, augmented by a mass of material on *dharma* and other topics. It even says, 'Whatever is written here, may also be found elsewhere; but what is not found here, cannot be found anywhere else either' (quoted in Klostermaier 1989: 78).

The *Mahābhārata*, then, infuses awareness of past events in its hearers but goes well beyond this in a claim to comprehensiveness which works at several different levels. Madhva, the great thirteenth-century Dvaita Vedānta teacher, believed the *Mahābhārata* conveys three different layers of meaning: *āstikādi*, 'in so far as it is a relation of the facts and events with which Śrī Kṛṣṇa and the Pāṇḍavas are connected'; *manvādi*, 'by which we find lessons on virtue, divine love . . . sacred duty and righteous practices, on character and training, on Brahmā and the other gods'; and *auparicara*, 'by which every sentence, word or syllable' names or glorifies 'the Almighty Ruler of the universe' (see Klostermaier 1989: 78).

Modern commentators have found allegorical as well as political significance in the war, as the struggle between *dharma* and *adharma*, or between the higher and lower natures of the self. Gandhi's interpretation of the *Bhagavadgītā*, part of Book 6 of the *Mahābhārata*, works with the latter view. It would, then, be incorrect to say that the *Mahābhārata* has been understood simply as history. On the other hand, to deny that it is in some sense 'historical' ignores one of its most vital dimensions. In his foreword to a book entitled *Mahābhārata: Myth and Reality: Differing Views*, Niharranjan Ray writes:

> And the people of traditional India have been believing that the *Mahābhārata*, despite its being a store house of legends and stories, is an *itihāsa* or history according to their conception, since it records at its core the story of the Kuru-Pāṇḍavas, the Pañcālas and a host of other contemporary *jana*s [tribes], as faithfully as the live story of a fraternal feud leading to a devastating war could be, but all put in a literary form by an imaginatively effective poet. They have been singing and reciting it through the ages and allowing the characters, events and situations presented in it, affect their lives very deeply and widely . . . the *Bhāratayuddha-kathā* [Vyāsa's poem] has been, through the centuries, woven into the very texture of India's life and culture, and is thus an important and inalienable part of the lives of countless millions of people of this land, and hence an essential fact of Indian history, and this, even from the point of view of the modern concept of history.
>
> (Gupta and Ramachandran 1976: vii)

Ray suggests that the original historical events have been mythicised and that this myth has then become part of history. This latter point cannot be stressed too strongly. However, because of this, attempts to confirm the *Mahābhārata*'s historicity by straightforward archaeological means seem, to Ray, futile. Nonetheless, this does not render all historical exploration useless. Even more importantly, he stresses that there is no need to choose between myth and reality.

> In actuality [myth] is a 'true story' of the life of any society, the essence extracted out of the very process of human life of a given time and space. . . . [Myths] incorporate deep-rooted traditions and provide 'living' entities in the sense that they supply models of human behaviour, and by doing so, give meaning and value to the flowing current of life in a given social situation. . . . A myth is a socio-psychological phenomenon, and hence a reality which historians can hardly afford to ignore.
>
> (Gupta and Ramachandran 1976: xiv)

Ray, then, makes two points. First, there is a historical core to the *Mahābhārata*, though this is not recoverable in any easy way. Secondly, the *Mahābhārata* has become inextricably bound up with Indian (Hindu) self-consciousness and therefore has become part of Indian history. The collection of articles following Ray's balanced introduction stems from a controversy which raged in the front pages of the Indian press during 1975 over the date of the Bhārata war. Romila Thapar, a prominent Indian historian, relates the storm to cultural nationalism at a time of social and political change. She suggests that the contenders are caught in their own battle, one side trying to dismiss the epic as valueless because not historically authentic, the other seeking to verify its authenticity with what are thought to be the most up-to-date scientific methods. The limits of these she sharply delineates. However, elsewhere she rejects a view of history which limits it to a modern western form and seeks to explore what she calls 'embedded history' and 'externalised history' in an Indian context. The *Mahābhārata* she finds to carry the seeds of a more conscious (hence externalised) and less embedded approach than earlier myths and eulogies. In her view, 'it is a later age reflecting on an earlier one' as a state system replaced the pastoral-agricultural world of the epic's heroes.[5]

Is Hinduism ahistorical?

Thapar's work brings us back to the question of the supposed ahistoricality of Hinduism. As indicated above, many Orientalist writers clearly thought it was ahistorical, condemning such a stance as sorely inadequate. They based their views on observations of the following sorts. Hindu texts show a decided lack of interest in recording dates of any sort. Accordingly, it is difficult to date even such major events as the entry of the Aryans into India (supposing that there was such an entry). Texts, too, are notoriously difficult to date, partly because of the lack of records and partly because they are often oral composites (see above on the three 'tellings' of the *Mahābhārata*). Dates that are given are often based on the accounts of foreigners, Chinese pilgrims, for example, or on Indian Buddhist material. The *Rājataraṃgiṇī*, a Kashmiri work dated to 1160 CE, 'represents the only Sanskrit chronicle which can lay claim to being regarded as history'.[6] Texts of a 'properly' historical kind are to be found only after the Muslim conquests in the thirteenth century CE.

This lack of historical writing is linked with the often-mentioned Hindu cyclical view of time which is contrasted with western linear views of history as moving from a beginning to an end. If events repeat themselves from cycle to cycle, the argument goes, they are not really significant in themselves nor open to historical explanation in terms of socio-economic conditions, for example. Another argument points to the denial of change in the transmission of texts and their interpretations. Thus a sub-commentator claims merely to reproduce the views of the earlier major commentator who in turn was simply elaborating on the meaning of the text itself, say *Upaniṣad* or *Bhagavadgītā*. Yet the various works show clear evidence of differences which might be linked with changing social conditions, so this again shows a lack of historical awareness.

It is possible to challenge the deductions drawn from the above points in a number of ways. For example, the assertion that a writer is simply being faithful to the original texts whose authority is beyond question, is commonplace across religious traditions before the modern period. The contrast between linear and cyclical views of time may be overdrawn, as we shall consider in more detail below. Hindu texts may well contain embedded historical records, for example, in the puranic genealogies. Historical consciousness in terms of a present shaped by a past tradition is wholly characteristic of, for example, the *Mahābhārata*, past and present! Moreover, it can be shown that a sense of cumulative progress, of freedom and contingency of human action, is present in the myths and concepts of Hindu classical traditions (Lipner 1994: Chapter 11).

Histories of (Hindu) India which have been written by or under the influence of modern western writers also have their own advantages and drawbacks. K.M. Panikkar, in his *Survey of Indian History*, published in 1947, urges: 'Today when we talk of the Mauryas, the Guptas, the Chālukyas and the Pallavas, let it be remembered that these great ages of Indian history were recovered to us by the devoted labours of European scholars'. Thapar acknowledges such work in providing a chronological framework 'around which fresh interpretations can be constructed which will place the ideas and institutions of Indian civilization in their correct perspective' (Thapar 1966: 22). Yet she indicates how the concerns of nineteenth-century western scholars (mis)shaped Indian history, concentrating as they did on dynastic histories, brahmanical (idealised) texts and comparisons with Greek achievements. If such history claims to report 'events as they really happened' in contrast with the testimony of despised eulogy and myth, it deceives itself.

One response, then, to the contention that Hinduism is ahistorical is to challenge the basis on which that claim is made and the notions of history that are associated with it. Another response, typified by Pratima Bowes, is to accept the basic data, especially the lack of interest in chronology and the cyclic view of time, but to reject the deductions that may be drawn from these points. She strongly denies that the Hindu intellectual tradition 'took history to be meaningless or even life itself to be so' (Bowes 1977: 15). She rather takes the *yuga* theory of the four ages to be a sign of profound interest in progress and decline in human affairs and one which does not adopt the simplistic view of progress found in much western history. Granting that the Hindu view of the four ages takes a mythological approach and may involve a 'relative devaluation of history' (Bowes 1977: 17), she feels that in compensation it gives a greater breadth and resilience to a civilisation which can accept decline as part of a larger pattern.

A third response is given by Madeleine Biardeau, who also points out the many difficulties faced by historians using modern historical methods to construct early histories of India. She shows how the theory of the Aryan invasion and suppression of Dravidian peoples has great appeal because of its supposed explanatory properties. Thus the *varṇa* system of four 'social groups' (see below) is understood as the product of the dominance of pure Aryans (twice-born) over impure vanquished Dravidians, now *śūdra*s (later, untouchables as well). The many features of devotional Hinduism which seem strikingly different from those of the sacrificial vedic religious system are explained as Dravidian resurgences. Perhaps, Biardeau allows, such an incursion did take place.

> But what if this seemingly historical structuring only existed in our minds; and perhaps even implicitly took its model from our most recent history? Between the assertion that ethnically and culturally different peoples must have learnt over the centuries to coexist, and the assertion that their cohabitation explains the present-day socio-religious structure of Hindu India, there is a gulf which cannot be crossed without examination.
>
> (Biardeau 1989: 6)

In writing her book on *Hinduism: The Anthropology of a Civilization*, Biardeau therefore eschews 'the historical overview' and 'linear continuity that is visibly lacking' (Biardeau 1989: 14). Rather, she seeks to find the 'complex, stable system of values, beliefs and practices that still underlines [*sic*] the surface variations [of different forms of Hinduism, including those affected by the impact of the West] and which alone makes them comprehensible' (Biardeau 1989: 15).

For some, Biardeau's proposal will liberate Hinduism from a western historical straitjacket. For others, it will seem like another western denigration of India, denying it the 'proper history' of the West. For still others, it will undercut their very claims about self-identity. Dalit consciousness, for example, is based on a view which sees themselves as the 'oppressed', the original people subordinated as untouchables by the Aryan invaders, from whom they wish to distinguish themselves sharply. In the South, such views are reinforced by readings of the *Rāmāyaṇa* such as that of the Tamil writer, E.V. Ramasami. He heard its story as 'a thinly disguised historical account of how North Indians, led by Rāma, subjugated South Indians, ruled by Rāvaṇa'.[7] Writing in a political context before and after Indian Independence in 1947, in which anti-Northern, anti-brahmanical feeling ran high, he received enthusiastic support from his Tamil audience. His book, *Characters in the Rāmāyaṇa*, is now translated into English and Hindi, and hence has wider impact. Against such interpretations, Biardeau points out that Rāvaṇa is himself an *ārya*, a Brahman, though one who has overreached himself. Followers of Ramasami would simply point out how ensnared she has become in a brahmanical view of history.

What is certain is that the question of (a)historicality and the relation between myth and history in Hinduism is not simple, nor of merely academic interest. It is highly complex, affects people's sense of identity and has political and social ramifications too. We shall explore some of these below. First, though, we shall return to a few key concerns shared by history and myth – origins, time, causation, continuity and change – and see how these are approached in various Hindu traditions.

Stories of beginnings

In her book, *The Origins of Evil in Hindu Mythology*, Wendy O'Flaherty notes that many of these myths use a pseudo-historical framework to tell how evil arises. So, for example, in this story from the *Vāyu Purāṇa* (1.8.77–88), corruption comes simply through the power of time (*kāla*).

> In the beginning, people lived in perfect happiness, without class distinctions or property; all their needs were supplied by magic wish-fulfilling trees. Then because of the great power of time and the changes it wrought upon them, they were overcome by passions and greed . . . the wishing-trees disappeared; the people suffered from heat and cold, built houses, and wore clothes.
>
> (Quoted in O'Flaherty 1980: 24)

However, as O'Flaherty rightly emphasises, though the myths are often set 'in the beginning', 'implicit in them is a concern for the way things *are*' (O'Flaherty 1980: 9). They help explore and explain the kind of cosmos in which we live and hence may contain recommendations for human behaviour now.

One famous origin myth is found in the *Puruṣasūkta* in the *Ṛg-veda* (10.90.1–16). It tells of the Cosmic Person, who is dismembered in a sacrifice by the gods. From parts of his body spring the four social groups of human society and elements and regions of the cosmos. 'His mouth was the brahmin (*brāhmaṇa*s), his arms were made into the nobles (*kṣatriya*s), his two thighs were the populace (*vaiśya*s), and from his feet the servants (*śūdra*s) were born' (O'Flaherty 1975: 28). Thus the *varṇa* system is legitimated as being part of the very structure of the universe. By implication, human beings should uphold that system to maintain cosmic order. But because there is a legitimating myth, that is not to say there has been no further discussion about what constitutes a person's *varṇa*. From the *Upaniṣads* on, it was stressed, in a number of important texts, that a Brahman was not simply a Brahman by birth, but by behaviour befitting a Brahman. When, in the 1990s, European members of the Hare Krishna movement claim Brahman status, they are tapping into the latter emphasis in this ancient tradition as developed within the Caitanya movement and made explicit by the two teachers who preceded their leader, Prabhupāda (A.C. Bhaktivedanta Swami). In their rejection of the (multiple *jāti*) caste system, they follow the trend of many nineteenth- and twentieth-century reform movements. Retaining the four *varṇa*s as suitable for people of different intellectual abilities, they stress the vedic grounding of the *varṇāśrama* system of four social groups and stages of life. The underlying myth continues to provide an ideal for society, variously interpreted (or rejected) in modern Hindu contexts.

Such myths are not limited to the Sanskrit tradition. David Shulman gives an interesting analysis of some Tamil stories about the legendary figure Agastya, author of the first Tamil grammar. The Agastya legend, he says, 'is in essence an origin myth explaining the beginnings of Tamil culture' (Shulman 1980: 6). Since Agastya is a vedic seer who is said quite explicitly to have come from the North, the legend shows that the Tamil tradition looks to the North as the source of its inspiration and prestige.

There was once a dispute, runs one story, between Agastya and Vyāsa over who was the greater. Agastya worshipped Śiva, who told him to worship in two places for a year, one famous as a Sanskrit place of study, and then return to Śivagiri to be instructed in Tamil by Śiva's son, Murukan. When Agastya returned to the sages, they, with Vyāsa, greeted him, saying, 'You have enabled all to taste the divine drink of Tamil'.

Shulman comments, 'Agastya is thus a symbol of Tamil learning, not as independent from or opposed to Sanskrit, but rather in harmony and conjunction with it' (Shulman 1980: 8). Here is a somewhat different picture of the relation of Tamil and Sanskrit from that which Ramasami, for example, espoused.

Many stories of beginnings are on a much smaller scale. They relate not to society or a whole culture, but to local places of worship or pilgrimage. Thus many temples have their own *sthalapurāṇa* or story of founding, sometimes in Sanskrit, sometimes in the vernacular. Shulman gives Tamil examples. Such stories of founding are not confined to the past. Maureen Michaelson records the story of a Lohāna man from Uganda, who settled with his family in Leicester.[8] One night, in Uganda, he dreamed that Jalarām, a nineteenth-century Gujarāti saint revered for his devoted service to others, would appear to him. The following night, after a lightning storm, an image of Jalarām appeared on the white kitchen tiles. Many people came to take *darśan* (seeing the manifestation and realising the presence of the divine). When the family were driven out of Uganda, they brought the tiles to England. Their house remains a centre for a Jalarām *satsaṅg* (group singing devotional songs). Parents also take their children there for their first outing, so it has become a small place of pilgrimage. In explaining its origin, a historian would have to acknowledge that for this family and the other devotees, the explanation lies in a perception of Jalarām's self-manifestation.

The three previous stories have been about the origins of society, culture and devotional practice. Many other myths deal with the origination of all things: from the Cosmic Egg, from the desire of a lonely creator or, more metaphysically, from Non-being or Being or the disruption of the cosmic equilibrium. Śaṃkara, the great Advaitin teacher, was not inclined to mistake origination myths as accounts of the way things came to be. For him, the various Upanisadic origination myths are usually classified as *ākhyāyikā*, stories, a form of secondary passage or *arthavāda*. For Śaṃkara, the stories of *arthavāda*, though they may be veridical, are there to direct people's thoughts to the true Self, identical with *Brahman*, Ultimate Reality, goal of realisation and hence liberation. So a story which speaks of fire, water and food arising from Being (*sat*) (*Chāndogya Upaniṣad* 6.2) directs the mind to the source of everything, *Brahman*, and hence to the desire to realise one's identity with that Ultimate Reality. As Śaṃkara comments on the origination myth in the *Aitareya Upaniṣad*:

> There is no worthwhile result from knowing the story of origination (*sṛṣṭyākhyāyikā*). But the result from knowing the proper nature of the one Self is immortality, well-known from all the Upaniṣads.
>
> (*Aitareya Upaniṣad Bhāṣya* 2.1)

Within Hindu traditions, then, stories of beginnings are interpreted in a range of different ways: as literal accounts of the way certain things came to be; as stories conveying crucial values shaping actions now; as pointers to the deepest truth about the way things are. In many ways, historians have played similar tunes, albeit in different keys.

Concepts of time

At this point, we shall turn back to examine the view that the Hindu understanding of time is cyclical. Roger Hooker suggests that the observation of the recurring seasons is one key factor in Hindu concepts of time, which is balanced by the sense of linearity found in each individual's movement from birth to death. Certainly the pattern of the mythological and ritual year is strongly affected, for example, by the monsoon. Thus Viṣṇu is said to sleep for four months from the eleventh of the bright half of Āshāḍha to the eleventh of the bright half of Kārttika, roughly mid-July to mid-November, spanning the rains. This is the time of rife disease, when Viṣṇu is absent, yet also the marriage season in some parts of India, for other activities are suspended. The great autumn festival of *Navrātrī* takes place once the rainy season has ended. C.J. Fuller has shown how royal celebrations of *Navrātrī* at once identified the ruler with, and subordinated him to, the Goddess who slew the buffalo demon and so allowed order to be restored under proper kingship.[9] He suggests that the king was also identified with Rāma, as still clearly happens in Vāranāsi (Benares). Thus the festival legitimates rightful rule, through myth and ritual, and marks the commencement of the battle season, once the rains are over. Myth, time and history are interwoven in a complex repeated pattern.

In mythology, it is said that one human year is just a day to the gods. Their year comprises three hundred and sixty human years. In this way, suggest Dimmitt and van Buitenen, observations of days, lunar months and solar years are 'given divine and universal significance' (1983: 20). Besides this pattern of time based on observation is another scheme, that of the four *yuga*s (explained below). A third scheme involves the *manvantara*s – fourteen ages of the earth, each having an original ruler called a *Manu*. Dimmitt and van Buitenen suggest that there may have been a connection with actual human rulers, the *Manu* acting as the legitimating source of kingship. Here seems to be another example of human history being underpinned by a mythological view of time.

Whereas the *manvantara* scheme fits uneasily with the other two schemes, the relation between observed years and the *yugas* is quite straightforward. Jackson and Killingley (1988: 137) give a chart (adapted in Table 3.1) to show how twelve thousand years of the gods make up a cycle of four ages or *yugas*.

Table 3.1

Name of *yuga*	Years of the gods	Human years
Kṛta or *Satya*	4,800	1,728,000
Tretā	3,600	1,296,000
Dvāpara	2,400	864,000
Kali	1,200	432,000
Total:	12,000	4,320,000

The ages are named after the four throws of the dice in ancient Indian games. The *Kṛta* Age is perfect. It is represented by a cow standing on four legs. Each subsequent age gets shorter and worse. Humans live shorter lives, there is less food and morality declines. By the *Kali* Age, in which we now live, the cow is left wobbling precariously on only one leg. The *Kaliyuga* opened with the war of the *Mahābhārata*, traditionally dated to 3102 BCE. In this sense, our current period of world history is shaped by the aftermath of these events. It will end when Kalkin, Viṣṇu's tenth *avatāra*, comes to begin a new *Kṛtayuga* or perfect age. Then the cycle of the four *yugas* will start all over again. After one thousand cycles, a *kalpa*, or cosmic day, the world will end through fire and/or flood and undergo a cosmic night of similar time. Then it will be manifested again, a cosmic day. And so on, *ad infinitum*.

With this immense time perspective, it is not surprising that a modern Advaitin can write:

> Advaita Vedānta and the Hindu tradition in general, unlike almost all other traditions, had long been familiar with vast time periods and scales; for this reason, the modern cosmological estimate of the age of the universe – the time since the Big-bang to the present – as approximately eighteen billion years is neither shocking nor blasphemous to Advaita Vedānta.[10]

The impression is sometimes given that a biblical view of history with a beginning and an end just needed a little stretching to make it into a modern scientific view of time. Authors like the above claim, rather, that the view of time found in Hindu mythology accords more readily with a modern scientific worldview.

We saw earlier that Bowes argues that the Hindu view of *yuga*s also gives a more realistic attitude to the rise and fall of civilisations within the historical process. Some, though, have been inclined to draw on the *yuga* pattern to idealise as a perfect age the time before Muslim and British domination. Other commentators have felt that the idea of the *Kaliyuga* has led to a rather fatalistic acceptance of events, since decline is programmed into the times, so to speak. Only when Kalkin appears will things improve. Yet others have found the idea more flexible, galvanising people into political action. Orators in the Panjab in the 1920s spoke in a traditional manner of the evils of the *Kaliyuga*, time of food shortages and falsehood. But then they urged that the perfect age would be restored, once the British were overthrown. That their hope was not borne out has not discouraged others from urging political action to improve the state of the age.

The concept of cyclical world ages or *yuga*s is developed in texts like the Epics and *Purāṇa*s. It is not found in the *Upaniṣad*s or other vedic texts. In consequence, ideas like the *mahāpralaya* or destruction of the world at the end of a cycle are not found in the Pūrvamīmāṃsā school. Moreover, sophisticated metaphysical discussions about the nature of time take place in other classical schools without overt reference to this mythological background. These discussions are concerned with such matters as the origin of time, its relation to *Brahman*, the nature of continuity between past, present and future, the role of memory in perception and error, and the way in which the results of actions are experienced by an individual in future embodiments.

For most of these writers, the *yuga* framework is an implicit part of their 'mental furniture'. However, this does not usually mean that their thought is dominated by a cyclic view of time where the events of this age become insignificant because they are in some sense repeated. Rather, such writers emphasise the importance of one's present human birth, for their concern is ultimately soteriological. Liberation of the self from *saṃsāra*, the entrammelling world of rebirth, is most easily or only achievable from a human birth, however that liberation is conceived. In future cycles, there is no duplication of events happening in this *yuga*, and hence no evasion of the present moment.

In the *Bhagavadgītā* (8.19), it is said that all beings come into existence again and again, and are then dissolved into the Unmanifested at the coming of the (cosmic) night. Śaṃkara explains that this verse has at least two purposes. One is to remind people that they will not escape from the consequences of their actions, for they will be reborn again and again in different births. Another is to create detachment from this interminable process of *saṃsāra*. So, again, such teachings serve primarily to foster the desire for liberation. It is often alleged that this in itself devalues the significance of the world and hence of history. If it does, it is not for the reason that the cyclic view of time is seen as repetitive, but that it is unrelieved. Moreover, since the very structures of this world provide the clues for realising the Ultimate Reality within, their importance should not be too lightly dismissed, even for the Advaitin.

From a rather different angle, the idea that cycles of time necessarily diminish the importance of the historical present can be challenged by looking at the modern Brahmā Kumārī movement. In the late 1930s, its founder, Dada Lekhraj, predicted the end of the world from natural catastrophe, civil strife and (apparently) nuclear holocaust. In visions, he saw that these catastrophes would be succeeded by a paradise on earth, whose tiny population would enjoy complete equality in a wholly balanced environment. This remnant would consist of those who heeded the warnings to purify themselves in the face of others' disbelief. Lawrence Babb shows how Lekhraj actually works within the traditional Hindu context which sees the world periodically ending in calamities, but invests this with special urgency by speeding up the cycle. Thus, the Brahmā Kumārī world time of four *yuga*s lasts only five thousand years, by contrast with the 4,320,000 of the puranic accounts. The 'endlessly repeating cycles of world creation, degeneration, and destruction',[11] which the Brahmā Kumārīs accept, apparently do not detract from the urgency of adopting a *sāttvic* (pure) life-style, practising a form of *rāja yoga* and belonging to a movement which has attracted considerable opprobrium for its ideal of female celibacy.

In this section we have tried to show from a variety of perspectives that to contrast a Hindu repetitive cyclical view of time with a western linear one is too stark. There is not just one Hindu (nor indeed one western) scheme of time. Even the *yuga* scheme varies in significance in different contexts. It can stress the vastness of time scales in the cosmos, as much as their repetitive nature. Within this *Kaliyuga*, the focus can be sharply on an individual life or on the legitimation of a ruler in an immediate historical situation. Myth, with its purview of millions of years, becomes rooted in ritual on an annual or even weekly basis, say, a fast for Santoshī Mā, the recently popular North Indian goddess of contentment, whose story is released on video. Speeded up, the cycle pressurises decisions about life-style and equality for members of the Brahmā Kumārī movement. Considered in its awful infinity, it directs the modern Rāmakrishna Mission Advaitin both beyond it to liberation and within it to social service. Finally, as Roger Hooker observes: 'While some contemporary Hindu thinkers appeal to the past in a nostalgic way, others are trying to give positive significance to time and change, and therefore to history' (1989: 74).

Continuity, change and causation

Much has been written on continuity and change in Hinduism, especially on the place of the Veda in this process.[12] Rather than engage in this large question, we shall look at one way in which Hindu traditions have themselves consciously envisaged continuity and the possibilities for change that this has allowed. We shall then briefly consider two forms of causation, one mainly developed in myth and hagiography, the other in philosophical analysis, to see how these compare with historians' accounts of causation.

> Now the line of teachers. The son of Pautimāṣī (received this teaching) from the son of Kātyāyanī; the son of Kātyāyanī from the son of Gautamī . . . Yājñavalkya from Uddālaka . . . Prajāpati from Brahmā (or Brahman). Brahmā (or Brahman) is the self-existent. Adoration to Brahmā.
>
> (*Bṛhadāraṇyaka Upaniṣad* 6.5.1–4)

So ends the great *Upaniṣad*, with its line of teachers going back to the creator god, or perhaps even to the Ultimate Reality, *Brahman*, for the Sanskrit could be read either way. The pupil who receives teaching today does so conscious of the unbroken *paraṃparā*, the succession of teachers who from time immemorial have seen the truth and passed it on unchanged through their teaching tradition (*saṃpradāya*). The concept of *saṃpradāya* is fundamental to many Hindus' sense of religious identity as well as to the legitimacy of a *guru*'s teaching. So the complex arguments about whether the International Society for Krishna Consciousness (the Hare Krishna movement) is a Hindu movement, often centre on teaching tradition. Those who wish to legitimate it trace Prabhupāda's lineage back through the Goswāmis to Caitanya (and thence to Viṣṇu). Opponents point out that the succession of teachers was interrupted until the nineteenth century, hence ISKCON's claims are not well-founded.

A sense of identity with one's forerunners from the past is heightened in those traditions where membership is through personal initiation by a *guru* only. So, for example, children of Pushti Mārg members in Britain can only become members themselves when a Mahārāj or deputed *guru* comes from India to perform such ceremonies. 'Pushti Mārg' means 'Path of Grace', and was founded by the vedantin teacher, Vallabha (fifteenth century CE), who, of course, traced his teaching back to the *Upaniṣad*s themselves.

There is a danger, found in all religions, that a tradition can fossilise if successive teachers see their task as one of mere repetition or simplification. At its best, though, the many different *saṃpradāya*s within Hinduism have produced profound thinkers of great calibre who responded to the challenges of their times and whose influence continues to the present day. It is not surprising that such thinkers have inspired their followers to write of their lives. Hagiographies abound, often reflecting the concerns of a much later age and premises which modern historians might not share. Thus Mādhava's *Śaṃkara Digvijaya* records how the gods approached Śiva at a time when religious practice had degenerated, partly under Buddhism's sway, and begged him to re-establish the vedic religion.

> When the Devas had completed their submission, the great God Siva said: 'Taking a human body . . . I shall establish the Dharma, conquering all the leaders of the perverse paths. I shall produce a commentary on the Brahma Sutras, setting forth the true teaching of the Vedas. I shall do this, taking the form of a great Sannyasin, Sankara by name. . . . All of you . . . should also take birth on earth like Myself and assist Me in My mission'.[13]

It is perhaps as unwise to dismiss such stories as of no historical significance as it is to accept them as literal account. The translator is circumspect in granting their mythological content, yet he maintains:

> They are living traditions that transmit a little of their original impact to the generations that have come later, whereas pure historical productions are only like dead specimens . . . preserved in the corridors of Time's museum.[14]

It is not a question of seeking historical evidence in the hagiographies for Śaṃkara's own time. Rather, we should note their engagement with questions which still occupy historians and sociologists: what is it that makes an original thinker – charisma, the needs of the times, the readiness of people to recognise a new 'solution'? If the intervention of the gods seems to create too radical a disjunction from preceding human teaching, consciousness of the *saṃpradāya* may be seen as a counterbalance to this view.

Perhaps the most well-known Hindu approach to causation is through the notion of *karman* (literally, action, and originally, ritual action). Although it takes various forms, the common idea is that all actions have results, some of which are immediate, but others long-term, perhaps not maturing until many lives hence. The results of actions then create the conditions for a person's rebirths in a linear development. They do not 'determine' the future, but create the conditions in terms of which human beings live and make choices which in turn affect the future both contingently and remotely. John Brockington notes that, 'the concept has at times had a similar function in Hinduism to the idea of history in Western thought, though with the important qualification that it operates at the individual rather than societal level'.[15] It is also different in that while the historian hopes to use evidence to understand both immediate and more long-term causes, such evidence is unavailable to ordinary mortals at a personal level since the trauma of birth effaces all memory of previous lives. Popularly, a person may well say, 'I must have done something terrible to be undergoing this now', but the particular cause is unlocatable. Nonetheless, the karmic principle that all events are due to past and complex causes is one shared by historians, whose interests if not methods overlap with the myths and traditional teachings yet again.

History, myth and nationalism

Finally, we shall turn to a modern phenomenon to explore some of the political ramifications of our topic. The factors influencing the growth of Indian nationalism in the late nineteenth and early twentieth centuries are extremely complicated, but concern us in at least two ways. The first is the reaction to Orientalist portrayals of Indian history which led writers like the Bengali Bankim Chandra Chatterjee to search their own heritage to repudiate assertions about Indian lack of military prowess, for example. The second related factor is the inspiration which was provided by both *Mahābhārata* and *Rāmāyaṇa* at this time. With his historical novels, political satire and poem, *Bande Mātaram*, which became the anthem of the Swadeshi (nationalist) movement, Bankim was undoubtedly a key figure, but his ideas and influence have been variously interpreted. He tried to use historical methods to show that the *Mahābhārata* represented life in the period between the vedic and Buddhist ages. The *dharmarājya* (rule of righteousness) established by its war, he saw not as a fact of remote history but as a goal to be realised in contemporary India. Importantly, he seems to have envisaged this *dharmarājya* in an open sense which saw love of one's country as the highest of all smaller loves, provided that it did not militate against the selfless, God-directed love of humanity. Other writers, like Bipin Chandra Pal, developed ideas of a specifically Indian form of democracy which would recognise the divine equality of every human being, whether Hindu, Muslim, Buddhist or Christian. More recently, Pandit Nehru's pride in the history of India, embracing the achievements of the Buddhist emperor Asoka and Muslim ruler Akbar, as well as Harappa and the sacred geography of Hindu India, reflects the inclusive attitudes of those who drew up the constitution of India as a secular state.

In the 1980s and 1990s, this secularism has come under strong pressure for a web of reasons, many associated with weakness in the ruling Congress Party. Once more, an Epic, the *Rāmāyaṇa*, colours the debate. In December 1992, the Babri mosque in Ayodhya was destroyed by militant Hindus, the culmination of a long dispute which had been simmering for decades. Ayodhya is the traditional birthplace of Lord Rām, the mosque having been built over the site of a Hindu temple, a claim for which historical evidence is mustered. During the election campaign of 1989, the Vishwa Hindu Parishad

(VHP), a highly organised religious group linked with the political opposition party, the BJP (Bharatiya Janata Party), encouraged Hindus from all over India to carry consecrated bricks to Ayodhya to rebuild the Rāmjanmabhoomi (site of Rām's birth). Rajiv Gandhi, Prime Minister, had earlier supported the laying of a foundation stone, then stopped further work. His assassination on 21 May 1991 perhaps reflected his failure to understand the growing communalism among many Hindus who feel that secularism has favoured Muslims.

Some observers feel that the Hindi *Rāmāyaṇa*, screened on Indian television in 1987–88, contributed to sentiment worked on by the VHP in its overt anti-Muslim stance, which intends to target other mosques built over Hindu temples in future elections. Some more extreme VHP propaganda even suggests that the Taj Mahal was originally a Hindu building. What is notable is the way that history is being made the issue: first, the historicity of Rām; secondly, rights over land and sacred places going back some five hundred years. Earlier western attitudes, which denigrated myth and looked down on aspects of the Hindu past and its lack of records, have surely seeped down, transmuted in reaction in this popular consciousness.

The BJP is supported by many educated middle-class Hindus disillusioned with the Congress Party. Its appeal should not be underestimated. Yet a potter quoted in *India Today* in December 1990 was pragmatic about historical issues: 'We don't know about the past, we don't know if Ram was born in Ayodhya or not or if there was a temple before the masjid [mosque] was built. We know only one thing: because of this controversy our livelihood is in jeopardy' (December 31 1990: 46).

At Dassehra celebrations in Delhi, following the screening of Ramanand Sagar's *Rāmāyaṇa*, Mark Tully watched two Sikhs and three Hindus circling an effigy of Rāvaṇa together and setting its fireworks alight. For him it was a sign of hope that the Epic serialisation could unite communities as well as divide them (1992: 152). Whichever it does, it will be as a consequence of the sense of identity imbued from the past by the present.

Conclusion

The subject of myth and history in Hinduism is vast. It is only in passing that we have been able to indicate some of the many functions of myth in Hindu traditions: as common cultural reference points, as stories relived through festivals and pilgrimage, as sanctions for rituals, iconography and order in society, as the basis for devotion, meditation and purification, as testimony to those deities experienced in one's own life, as pointers to the Ultimate Reality beyond all human description and conceptualisation. We have not been able to discuss the many different approaches used to analyse Hindu myth, for example, the Jungian stance of Heinrich Zimmer in *Myths and Symbols in Indian Art and Civilisation*, the structuralist method of Wendy O'Flaherty in *Śiva: the Erotic Ascetic*, or the narrative analyses in the collection edited by Paula Richman, *Many Rāmāyaṇas*. Nor again have we been able to consider the 'silence' of women in Indian history and the ways in which Hindu women are seeking to reclaim both history and myth today. (For this last point, see the Hinduism chapter in *Women in Religion* in this series.) What we have tried to examine is the relation between myth and history in different Hindu contexts, to challenge the view that these are mutually opposed categories.

'"Indian history"', says Gonda, is 'an expression by which I mean the process of development of the *humanitas indica*'.[16] If Indian history is this development of what makes India India, the embodying values of Indian civilisation, the constitution of a people's sense of identity, then the contribution of Hindu myths and legendary history is a highly significant factor. In particular, the ways in which myths together with rituals are constitutive of social order profoundly affect those within and outside the caste system.

Yet this is a complex issue. For Indian history is by no means synonymous with Hindu traditions, as Nehru tried to show in his letters to his daughter. To predicate modern Indian belonging on acceptance of the great leaders of Indian history, like Lord Rām and Lord Kṛṣṇa (*sic*), as a BJP MP did in a recent speech in Britain, would seem highly problematic for Muslims and Christians, who would reject their divinity, if not their historicity. On the other hand, to dismiss the importance of these Epic figures in Indian historical consciousness would be foolish. *Rāmrājya*, the rule of Rāma, need not be interpreted in an exclusivist sense, and indeed has not been by many great Hindu thinkers. Nor is the *Rāmāyaṇa* bound to only one telling: it has Jain and Buddhist versions as well as modern political narrations, as we saw above. Thapar sees cultural strength in these various recensions, which reflect different social aspirations and ideological concerns.

Since these stories were first told, they have always affected Hindus' understanding of past and present. They were, after all, seen as *itihāsa*, accounts of how things were. We have also seen how some scholars are increasingly recognising the historical value of both *itihāsa* and *purāṇa*, for genealogical material and for more or less 'embedded' historical evidence. Yet we have heard the warnings of eminent Indian historians against historicist approaches to such texts, which try to press them into the service of a modern form of history alien to their nature, and read them in a literalistic way.

Story is central to Hindu traditions. It is not then surprising that there is a plethora of terms for different types of story, and sophisticated interpretations of story in both classical and modern traditions. 'What is not here is not anywhere'. May the stories be heard and retold.

NOTES

1. Rawlinson quoted in 'Historiography' in Walker, B. (1968) *The Hindu World*, Vol. 1. London, George Allen & Unwin, p. 455.
2. Walker, B. (1968) *The Hindu World*, Vol. 1. London, George Allen & Unwin, p. 456.
3. For more detail on different texts and schools of interpretation, see the volume *Sacred Writings* in this series.
4. *Mangal Ramayan* as narrated by Ever Revered Sant Sri Morari Bapu, Bombay, Prachin Sanskriti Mandir, 1987.
5. Thapar, R. (1986) 'Society and Historical Consciousness: the Itihāsa-Purāṇa Tradition' in S. Bhattacharya and R. Thapar (eds) *Situating Indian History, for Sarvepalli Gopal*, Delhi, Oxford University Press.
6. Walker, B. (1968) *The Hindu World*, Vol. 1. London, George Allen & Unwin, p. 453.
7. Richman, P. (1991) 'E.V. Ramasami's Reading of the *Rāmāyaṇa*' in P. Richman (ed.) *Many Rāmāyaṇas: The Diversity of a Narrative Tradition in South Asia*, Berkeley, University of California Press, p. 178.
8. Michaelson, M. (1987) 'Domestic Hinduism in a Gujarati trading caste' in R. Burghart (ed.) *Hinduism in Great Britain: The Perpetuation of Religion in an Alien Cultural Milieu*, London, Tavistock Publications, p. 45.

9. Fuller, C.J. (1992) *The Camphor Flame: Popular Hinduism and Society in India*, Princeton, New Jersey, Princeton University Press.
10. Puligandla, R. (1988) 'Modern Physics and Advaita Vedānta' in S.S. Rama Rao Pappu (ed.) *Perspectives on Vedānta: Essays in Honor of Professor P.T. Raju*, Leiden, E.J. Brill, p. 189.
11. Babb, L.A. (1986) *Redemptive Encounters: Three Modern Styles in the Hindu Tradition*, Berkeley, University of California Press, p. 112.
12. Gonda, J. (1965) *Change and Continuity in Indian Religion*, The Hague, Mouton & Co; Smith, B.K. (1989) *Reflections on Resemblance, Ritual and Religion*, Oxford, Oxford University Press.
13. Madhava-Vidyaranya, *Sankara-Dig-Vijaya: The Traditional Life of Sri Sankaracharya*, trans. Swami Tapasyananda, Madras, Sri Ramakrishna Math, 2nd edn, 1980, p. 5.
14. Ibid., p. vii.
15. Brockington, J. (1992) *Hinduism and Christianity*, Basingstoke, Macmillan, p. 118.
16. Gonda, J. (1965) *Change and Continuity in Indian Religion*, The Hague, Mouton & Co, p. 7.

FURTHER READING

Biardeau, M. (1989) *Hinduism: The Anthropology of a Civilization*, trans. Richard Nice, Delhi, Oxford University Press.

Bowes, P. (1977) *Hindu Intellectual Tradition*, New Delhi, Allied Publishers.

Dimmitt, C. and van Buitenen, J.A.B. (eds and trans.) (1983) *Classical Hindu Mythology: A Reader in the Sanskrit Purāṇas*, Calcutta, Rupa & Co., by arrangements with Temple University Press.

Gupta, S.P. and Ramachandran, K.S. (eds) (1976) *Mahābhārata: Myth and Reality: Differing Views*, Delhi, Agam Prakashan.

Hooker, R.H. (1989) *Themes in Hinduism and Christianity: A Comparative Study*, Frankfurt am Main, Verlag Peter Lang.

Jackson, R. and Killingley, D. (1988) *Approaches to Hinduism*, London, John Murray.

Klostermaier, K.K. (1989) *A Survey of Hinduism*, Albany, State University of New York Press.

Lipner, J.J. (1994) *Hindus: Their Religious Beliefs and Practices*, London, Routledge.

Narayan, K. (1989) *Storytellers, Saints and Scoundrels: Folk Narrative in Hindu Religious Teaching*, Philadelphia, University of Pennsylvania Press.

Narayan, R.K. (1987 reprint) *Gods, Demons and Others*, Delhi, Vision Books.

O'Flaherty, W.D. (trans.) (1975) *Hindu Myths: A Sourcebook Translated From the Sanskrit*, Harmondsworth, Penguin.

O'Flaherty, W.D. (1980) *The Origins of Evil in Hindu Mythology* (paperback edn), Berkeley, University of California Press.

Shulman, D.D. (1980) *Tamil Temple Myths: Sacrifice and Divine Marriage in the South Indian Śaiva Tradition*, Princeton, N.J., Princeton University Press.

Thapar, R. (1966) *A History of India*, Vol. 1, Harmondsworth, Penguin.

Tully, M. (1992) *No Full Stops in India* (paperback edn), Harmondsworth, Penguin.

4. Islam

Martin Forward

Myth and history, as practised in the West, are Enlightenment constructs. The modern study of history rests on three major assumptions. First, history is the story of humanity's life on earth, as recorded in written materials that have survived through the process of time. Secondly, history is about meaning. As opposed to narrators or chroniclers, who simply record the past, historians try to understand and interpret it, to unlock what it says about the human story. Thirdly, if historians are to comprehend the past, they need to recognise its 'otherness'. L.P. Hartley, in his novel *The Go-Between*, famously wrote: 'The past is a foreign country: they did things differently there'. If this is true of an individual's own past, as Hartley believed, how much more true it is of the long, passing years of human history.

Myth is a means of conveying momentousness through story or dogma, where historical research is not the only, or even necessarily the best, tool to uncover truth. However, it is closely related to history. There is little history that does not have a mythic dimension, and *vice versa*.

Myth and history are in a particularly interesting symbiosis when they are related to religion. History challenges myths about their accuracy. Myths can also challenge history. Ever since the Enlightenment, the study of history has tended to assume a closed universe, and has thus discounted the influence on the human story of the supranatural or supernatural. In particular, God has been excluded from the study of humankind. Therefore, historians may be tempted to describe religious matters such as prophecy and revelation simply in terms of what individuals or groups have said and believed about them. Myth encourages historians to examine the question of truth: for example, it is one thing to say that many people have believed that Muhammad is the Prophet of God, as historians do; it is another to assume and describe the truth of that statement, as myths do.

Islam has had a particularly tense and ambivalent relationship with western Europe. What, then, is its attitude to myth and history? Islam certainly believes that history is the story of humankind on earth. It is a religion which centres on God's role for the human species. It regards human beings as the vicegerents (in Arabic, *khalīfah*) of God on earth. It also believes that history is about meaning. The human quest is to receive and obey God's will. This is achieved by recognising that the Qur'ān ('recitation') is the last scripture. It was revealed to Muhammad, the seal of the prophets, through the agency of the angel Gabriel (*Jibrā'īl*), in piecemeal fashion from 610 CE until shortly before Muhammad's death in 632.[1] Upon the basis of the Qur'ān, Muslims have constructed the *Sharī'ah*, the holy law of Islam, binding upon all Muslims, and governing all aspects of life. When Muslims follow this law, they can be certain that they are obeying God, since they believe that it is the divine 'highway', revealed by God and leading people to him. Many western historians regard this as the stuff of myth: we have already noted the Enlightenment conviction that historians can describe the origin and content of faith-systems, but not the questions of truth and meaning that they offer.

In one respect, Islam recognises the 'otherness' of the past. It sees a sharp distinction between the world before Muhammad's ministry, and since. The former is *jāhiliyya*, a state of ignorance. But, in another sense, Islam is built upon the past, or rather, a particular part of the past, the time of the Prophet, as a controlling model for all believers since. Through the *ḥadīth*, the 'tales' or 'traditions' told of Muhammad by his closest followers, Muslims uncover a life whose details are to be followed by them. So, the Prophet's life furnishes information about how to pray, sleep, wash, visit the bathroom, greet people, treat animals, and deal with a whole range of human activities. Here, then, is another difference from contemporary western convictions about the mystery of the past.

Islam is a monotheistic religion. The Qur'ān condemns Jews and Christians for giving only lip-service to the belief that God is one (9:30). *Tawḥīd*, the unity of God, is a fundamental Islamic doctrine, so that Muslims look for a unity of the sciences, of humankind and of all aspects of life on earth, to reflect the sovereign unity of God. Islam's unforgivable sin is *shirk*, 'association' or polytheism. The one God guides humankind. Indeed, the Qur'ān is *hudan li'l-nāṣ*, 'guidance for humankind'. It describes how God has spoken through previous prophets, and through *āyāt*, 'signs' of nature as well as revelation. Islam does not believe that this is a closed universe, devoid of God's presence and activity. In Islam's view, it is not so much the duty of historians to scan human activity for the signs of God, still less to explain it without reference to him; rather, they should assume the divine presence in the story of humans on earth.

Thus, great Muslim historians have never shirked mentioning God. One of the greatest of all, Ibn Khaldun (1332–1406), a sociologist as well as a historian, prefaced his famous *Muqaddimah* or 'Introduction' (to history and historiography) with praise to God, Muhammad and his *ṣaḥābah* (earliest followers or 'companions'). And at the end, he wrote, 'Knowledge comes only from God, the Mighty One, the Wise One' (Ibn Khaldun 1967: 459). This might be discounted as pious phraseology, but ought not to be. There is no reason to doubt Ibn Khaldun's piety, or the conviction of Muslim historians, then and in other times, that God is the beginning and the end of the human enterprise.

Thus, of the three assumptions of the modern western study of history that this chapter describes, Islam accepts that it is the story of people, and that it is a search for meaning. But, unlike many western historians, it has located that meaning in the One God, and regards his exclusion from the human quest as aberrant, indeed, as grotesque and shocking. Furthermore, it has assumed the fundamental solidarity of humankind across the ages, not the overwhelming mystery and strangeness of the past.

What of myth?

Orthodox Sunni Muslims[2] are deeply suspicious of myth as a description of stories which yield religious meaning. For them, the Qur'ān is a 'clear sign' (e.g., 15:1), and the stories that it tells, being revealed by God, are clearly true, and clear in their meaning. Many Muslims fall into the category of those believers who treat their religious stories and beliefs as historically true (that is, they happened at a point in time exactly as they document), but immune from historical investigation. Revelation has spoken and renders history irrelevant. Thus, there are considerable differences of opinion between Muslims and contemporary western scholars about the appropriateness of myth and history as interlocked subjects relevant to and illuminating the study of religion.

There is another, historical, reason why Muslims are reluctant to accept the tools of modern, western scholarship; it arises from Islam's fraught relationship with western Europe. Scholars have been used as part of a whole system of intellectual, colonial and economic domination of Islam by the West. Edward Said, born a Christian of Palestinian origin, and now working in the United States of America, has been an influential critic. In a number of books, he denounces 'orientalists', western scholars of the east, especially of the world of Islam, who see the world through their own fantasies, rather than in its own light.[3] He notes the prurience that drove the West's interest in the Orient, particularly Islam, with its emphases upon the harem, the submissiveness and voluptuousness of women and the insatiability of men. In his view, most western books about Islam display attitudes of dominance, confrontation, imperial conquest and cultural aversion.

Some of these western scholars of Islam have been secularists. Maxime Rodinson, for example, is a French Jewish Marxist and atheist who, while accepting the integrity of the Prophet, locates the origin of the Qur'ān in the mind of Muhammad: 'he was able for a short period to produce, from his unconscious, phrases of disturbing poetic quality'.[4] Others have been overtly religious. Scholars like Hamilton Gibb, Arthur Arberry, and Kenneth Cragg may appreciate Islam, but are profoundly influenced by their Christian convictions which lead them to challenge and even undermine what they purport to admire. One common recent response by Muslims has been to dismiss all such scholars as orientalists, as though that absolved them from the responsibility of responding to their challenges and, indeed, affirmations. However, Akbar Ahmed, a Pakistani Muslim who teaches at Cambridge University, argues that Said overstates his case. Not all orientalists are driven by a hatred of Islam. Some have formed close friendships with Muslim saints and scholars. They have done worthy work, such as translating seminal Arabic texts into English, and asking searching questions that Muslims need to answer. However, he agrees that, 'In time, the ideas and views of the orientalists have tended to ossify. Their vitality snapped, they have become mimetic, a storehouse of oriental stereotypes and exotica' (Ahmed, 1992: 179–83).

The rest of this chapter will describe Muslim self-understandings, but also try to suggest that Muslim and western understandings of history and myth need not be hermetically sealed against each other, and can be mutually enriching. It will use the word 'myth' neutrally, to indicate religious stories and beliefs which historical research may have much to say about, but which convey more meanings than historical ones. It will examine a source which many Muslims have condemned as wholly mythical and unrepresentative of Islam, *The Book of the Thousand and One Nights*. Then it will explore the early years of Islam, especially the collection of the Ḥadīth, and the Qur'ān, hugely controversial areas for any discussion of myth and history. Then it will look at contemporary issues, to see what light, if any, the categories of myth and history can cast upon them.

The thousand nights and one night

The stories of Aladdin and Sinbad and other tales from *The Book of the Thousand and One Nights* have become part of the western heritage of storytelling. They conjure up pictures of fabulous wealth, genies and giants, supernatural powers, and an inscrutable oriental deity. Precisely for this reason, many Muslims condemn them as of no value in understanding Islam: they have fed too many 'orientalist' fantasies. Yet these tales existed long before westerners read them. They are virtually unalloyed myth; the historical setting given to them is deliberately imprecise. They arise out of a mainly illiterate society and, for our purpose, their value lies in what they reflect about the influences of Islam on the societies in which they were told.

Some (including the great British 'orientalist', E.W. Lane, who wrote an early – and rather dull – translation in 1839–41), have claimed that the yarns were written by one or, at most, two people. This has not gained widespread currency. The tales seem to come from many lands – India, Persia, Greece, Syria and Egypt – and also from different epochs. Some are very ancient indeed; others may date from as late as the fifteenth century. An index list of Arabic works, the *Kitāb al-Fihrist*, dating from 987, reveals that the framework of the book, the story of Shahrazad (Scheherazade), was Persian in origin, and taken over by the Arabs who recounted and embellished the tales and added others. Some modern scholars suggest an ancient Indian source for the framework. The book was known in Egypt in the twelfth century in a form which must have been similar to the present text.

The tales have become thoroughly islamicised. They immortalise the great city of Baghdad, home of the ʻAbbāsid caliphs, and particularly the caliph Harun al-Rashid (766–809), of whom many tales abound. In its final form, the book's preface offers praises to God, and invokes blessings upon Muhammad, his family and companions. The stories are full of references to Allāh. Indeed, the fact that their number is one more than a round figure may correspond to the fact that there are ninety-nine names of God in Muslim theology: only God encompasses totality and wholeness. What light, then, do the tales cast upon medieval Muslim society?

The framework-story of Shahrazad tells the tale of King Shahryar, a ruler of Sasan, in the isles of India and China, and his brother, Shahzaman, lord of Samarkand. Both were cuckolded by black men. In vengeance against the infidelity of women, Shahryar ordered his *wazīr* (chief minister) to bring him a virgin every night, whom he would ravish and then cause to be slain. After three years, one of the *wazīr*'s daughters volunteered to be the king's victim. She kept him fascinated by her sexual charms (she bore him three sons) and her prowess as a teller of tales. After one thousand and one nights, the king revoked his plan to kill her, and his brother married her sister.

This framework-story reveals a cruel, racist, sexist and élitist view of the world. We shall pick up women's issues as a contemporary theme later in this chapter, so it is worth emphasising the implications of the story of Shahryar and Shahrazad for this theme. Women are the victims of men's belief that they are libidinous unless severely guarded. Their value is as objects of desire, passive and submissive. Shahrazad survives by working within this world-view, not by challenging it: at the end of each night, the book gives the formula, 'At this point Shahrazad saw the approach of morning and discreetly fell silent'. The story is probably pre-Islamic in origin, but, as with other religions, misogyny flourished in Islam in spite of core religious teaching, and could be seen as acceptable to the central tenets of faith, so that such a story could be easily assimilated.

The stories are captivating. Rather than analysing one or two of them, this chapter urges its readers to buy and peruse a copy of the tales! They offer two suggestive points about myth. The first is that scholars of a religion do not always locate where its power lies for most people. The *'ulamā'* (religious scholars) and other learned Muslims of Sunni Islam (the milieu in which these stories flourished) have emphasised the importance of obedience to God's law. Stories offer different possibilities of hearing and responding to the power of religion in a society. Many of the stories reinforce stereotypes; the amenable woman is one such stereotype. Another is that of a remote, elusive and omnipotent deity, which has been a strong emphasis in orthodox Islam, but is by no means the unquestionably true reading of the Qur'ān and the earliest sources: indeed, the escapades and pranks of the tales' protagonists assume a large measure of human freedom within God's sovereign control of the world. So some stories reflect certain Islamic values, but add to them or give them an unorthodox twist. Others, instead, question the widespread acceptance of some theoretically core beliefs and practices.

This is the second point: the tales enable certain beliefs and practices frowned upon by the orthodox scholars to be entertained, explored and even celebrated. For example, Islam has always condemned homosexuality. The Qur'ān inveighs against it (7:80–4). The tales are well aware of this teaching, but are also aware of the fact of same-sex relations between men (not, significantly, between women). Some descriptions of this theme are amusingly as well as erotically portrayed, as, for instance, the story of the youth and his master (Mardrus and Mathers 1964, Vol. 2, p. 368f.).

Where a myth points out the power of a practice traditionally denounced by a religion, what is to be done? In this case, does it reveal that Islam can condemn and repress homosexuality, but not uproot it? Or does it suggest that the traditional teaching needs to be reappraised in the light of growing knowledge about human potentialities? The vast majority of Muslims would not accept the second possibility, where that knowledge is seen to conflict with God's teaching, and the Prophet's practices. So to these areas, we must now turn.

The early years of Islam: myth and history

When Muhammad died, revelation died with him. He was succeeded as temporal leader (*khalīfah*) of the Muslim community by his friend, contemporary and father-in-law, Abu Bakr (*c.* 573–634), but nobody could follow him as a prophet: God had already called him the seal of the prophets (33:40). Revelation had guided the nascent community's actions. What was to happen now that it was taken from them? One answer was that the Prophet himself had already, in his lifetime, become a model for believers. The Qur'ān says: 'You certainly have in God's Prophet a beautiful model for anyone whose hope is in God and the Last Day and who often praises God' (33:21). So *ḥadīth* became a secondary level of revelation. Where the Qur'ān failed to address a problem, a saying or action of the Prophet could guide the community.

The collection of *ḥadīth* took several generations. The word comes from a verb meaning 'recount'. Each *ḥadīth* was the testimony of the *ṣaḥābah*, or of the first generation (*al-tābi'ūn*, 'the followers') or the second generation (*tābi'ūn al-tābi'ūn*, 'the followers of the followers') thereafter. The collector had to record faithfully each *ḥadīth*, and to establish its *isnād*, the 'chain' of people from its source, that source being one of the Prophet's close companions. Each companion quoted had to be close to Muhammad, the possessor of a good character and a good memory. People involved in the transmission of *ḥadīth* became the subject of biographies. This is important, because it provides a way of furnishing believers with information which enables them to decide whether they are worthy of credence or not.

Muslims subject each *ḥadīth* and *isnād* to a wide variety of classifications. A basic one is to classify a *ḥadīth* as *ṣaḥīḥ* ('sound'), *ḥasan* ('fair') or *ḍa'īf* ('weak'), depending on the reliability of the *isnād*. Some western historians of Islam have criticised the Muslim science of *ḥadīth* criticism, on the grounds that it concentrates on the *isnād*, the chain of transmitters, rather than the *matn*, 'text' or substance of each *ḥadīth*, but though their comments have been too summarily dismissed by many Muslims, who have not usually responded to the substance of their criticisms, these scholars have overstated their critique. The biographies do provide information which enables people to make reasonable judgements about the reliability of transmitters.

One of the most quoted transmitters is Abu Hurayra (died *c.* 678). al-Bukhari (810–870), in his famous *Ṣaḥīḥ* (so-called because his is a particularly highly regarded collection of *ḥadīth*), listed eight hundred experts who regarded him as their source. He is said to have remembered 5,300 *ḥadīth*. However, some of the closest followers of the Prophet were sceptical about his facility. 'Umar (*c.* 591–644), the second *khalīfah*, is supposed to have said of Abu Hurayra: 'We have many things to say, but we are afraid to say them, and that man there has no restraint'. One source even has 'Umar say that 'the worst liar among the *muhaddithun* [narrators of *ḥadīth*] is Abu Hurayra'. Even al-Bukhari wrote that 'people said that Abu Hurayra recounts too many *ḥadīth*'. 'Ā'isha (*c.* 614–678), the Prophet's third wife, also criticised him:

> They told 'Ā'isha that Abu Hurayra was asserting that the Messenger of God said: 'Three things bring bad luck: house, woman and horse'. 'Ā'isha responded: 'Abu Hurayra learned his lessons very badly. He came into our house when the Prophet was in the middle of a sentence. He only heard the end of it. What the Prophet said was: "May Allah refute the Jews; they say three things bring bad luck: house, woman, and horse."'[5]

This discussion about Abu Hurayra raises serious questions about the authenticity of the Ḥadīth. Muslims have recognised that many were fabricated, to gain factional, sectarian or even personal advantage. al-Bukhari's achievement was to reduce about 600,000 *ḥadīth* to 7,257, if the repetitions, about 4,000, are eliminated. He had a high reputation for collecting a large number of variant accounts of the same *ḥadīth*, to include repetitions so as to give all the nuances, and for an instinctive distrust of witnesses and transmitters. He was also a godly person, priding himself on the fact that he would never enter any *ḥadīth* without having carried out the ritual purification and prayer twice.

Nevertheless, there are grounds for questioning the veracity even of some of the *ḥadīth* recorded by al-Bukhari. Some Muslims have attacked them for perpetuating outlooks which distort or overemphasise certain qur'anic teaching. For example, he wrote down *ḥadīth* which encourage misogyny, which overemphasise *qadar* (divine 'will' as opposed to human responsibility), and embellish stories about the events surrounding the Last Day.[6]

It is clear that there is much more serious critical Muslim appraisal of the *ḥadīth* material than many western scholars have known or, at any rate, admitted. Muslims do not treat all or even most *ḥadīth* as historically accurate, giving material upon which believers can construct their daily acts of obedience to the divine will. It is not just modernists who have found aspects of the *ḥadīth* distasteful. Ahmad b. Hanbal (780–855), the founder of the Hanbali School of Islamic Law (the most conservative of the four schools), is recorded by Ibn Taymiyya (1263–1328), a Hanbali jurist, as having said: 'Three things have no basis [in Arabic, *isnād*]: *tafsir* [qur'anic commentary], *malāḥim* [eschatological stories] and *maghāzī* [stories of the battles]'. Moreover, the great historian, Ibn Khaldun, attacked the methodology which some of the historians of early Islam employed:

> Historians, Qur'ān commentators and leading transmitters have committed frequent errors in the stories and events they reported. They accepted them in the plain transmitted form, without regard for its value. They did not check them with the principles underlying such historical situations, nor did they compare them with similar material. Also, they did not probe with the yardstick of philosophy, with the help of knowledge of the nature of things, or with the help of speculation and historical insight. Therefore, they strayed from the truth and found themselves lost in the desert of baseless assumptions and errors.
>
> (Ibn Khaldun 1967:11)

More controversial is the fact that it is arguable that some of the most unreliable *ḥadīth* are about the Prophet himself, when they portray him as incomparable in all respects. One companion narrated that, 'Allāh's messenger was the handsomest of all the people, and had the best appearance. He was neither very tall nor short'. Another testified that, 'I have never touched silk or Dibaj [i.e., thick silk] softer than the palm of the Prophet nor have I smelt a perfume nicer than the sweat of the Prophet'. Yet another revealed that, 'The Prophet was shier than a veiled virgin girl' (Khan, Vol. 4, nos 749, 761, 762).

Moreover, a number of *ḥadīth* are recorded about a demand by the pagans to the Prophet to show them a miracle, so he showed them the splitting of the moon (Khan, Vol. 4, nos 830–2) – even though the Qur'ān denies that Muhammad had any miracle to offer, save the miracle of the Qur'ān itself (e.g., 20:133). Indeed, another *ḥadīth*, narrated by Abu Hurayra, is a statement of the Prophet:

> Every Prophet was given miracles because of which people believed, but what I have been given, is Divine Inspiration which Allāh has revealed to

> me. So I hope that my followers will outnumber the followers of the other Prophets on the Day of Resurrection.
>
> (Khan, Vol. 6, no. 504)

This could suggest that Muhammad had no miracle to offer, other than the Qur'ān. Many Muslim modernists solve the problem by not mentioning such *ḥadīth*, and by stressing his reasonableness. So, for instance, Ameer Ali (1849–1928), an Indian high court judge and privy councillor, in his highly influential book, *The Spirit of Islam*, which has rarely been out of print since its first edition in 1890 (which was based on a previous work of 1871), wrote:

> Disclaiming every power of wonder-working, the Prophet of Islam ever rests the truth of his divine commission entirely upon his Teachings. He never resorts to the miraculous to assert his influence or to enforce his warnings. He invariably appeals to the familiar phenomena of nature as signs of the divine presence. He unswervingly addresses himself to the inner consciousness of man, to his reason, and not to his weakness or his credulity.
>
> (Ali 1922: 32f.)

Most of the adulatory descriptions of Muhammad in al-Bukhari's collection, in other compilations, and throughout Muslim history, read more as myth than as history. It is a tendency of many religions to grant to their heroes superlative, indeed miraculous, qualities. Certainly, Muhammad has the quality of a mythic, supra-historical figure for Muslims, past and present. He is the 'the Beloved' of God and the faithful. Every time his name is mentioned or written down, a Muslim adds 'Peace be upon him' (PBUH), or 'May God bless him and grant him salvation'. When a film about him came out in 1977, it evoked a storm of protest from some Muslims, who believe that so holy a life cannot be adequately represented in a physical medium, even though no shots were taken of the actor who read Muhammad's lines. In the wake of the controversy surrounding the publication of Salman Rushdie's book, *The Satanic Verses* (London, Viking, 1988), the anger of many Muslims was directed at its perceived distortion, demeaning and trivialisation of the Prophet. Pakistan introduced a law which made blasphemy against the Prophet a capital offence.

It is not just the Prophet whose virtues some Muslims have extolled. Shi'ah Muslims have heaped adulation upon 'Ali b. Abi Talib (*c.* 598–661), the Prophet's cousin and son-in-law, who, they believe, should have succeeded Muhammad as political and religious leader of Islam. Even so dedicated a modernist as Ameer Ali, himself a Shi'ah Muslim, reserved paeans of praise for 'Ali:

> On Osman's ['Uthman b. Affan, *d.* 656, the third *khalīfah*] tragical death, Ali was elected to the vacant Caliphate by the consensus of the people. The rebellions which followed are a matter of history. . . . The dagger of an assassin destroyed the hope of Islam. 'With him', says Major Osborn, 'perished the truest-hearted and best Moslem of whom Mohammedan history has preserved the remembrance.' Seven centuries before, this wonderful man would have been apotheosised; thirteen centuries later his genius and talents, his virtues and his valour, would have extorted the admiration of the civilised world. As a ruler, he came before his time. He was almost unfitted by his uncompromising love of truth, his gentleness, and his merciful nature, to cope with the Ommeyades' [the Ummayad dynasty was the first major one in Islamic history – 651–750] treachery and falsehood.
>
> (Ali 1922: 283)

Ameer Ali is here revealing the Shi'ah myth of its origins, and its crucial failure to establish an Alid dynasty. History asks serious questions about this myth, not least in raising the subject of 'Ali's competence to rule. He was passed over as *khalīfah* twice and, when he became the community's leader, many, including 'Ā'isha, would not accept him. His weakness helped cause the first major split in Islam, when the Kharijites (*khawārij*, 'those who seceded') condemned him for agreeing to arbitration after the battle of Siffin in 657, instead of seeking the judgement of God. They were later joined by other former supporters from Kufa, a city in Iraq, where 'Ali was assassinated in 661.

Later Shi'ah mythology made elaborate claims for the descendants of Muhammad through 'Ali and Fatima. These underpin a conviction that the succession of Muhammad should have been to members of his family and was spiritual as well as political, beliefs which Sunni Muslims have never accepted. History certainly casts doubts on the myth of the family's political and spiritual acuteness, at least as illustrated by 'Ali.

Sunni Muslims call the first four caliphs 'rightly-guided'. The period until 'Ali's death is regarded by them as a golden age, when Islam spread across North Africa and into the Persian and Byzantine empires. History casts doubts on aspects of this myth. If it was an age of gold, why were three of the caliphs killed? The glamorising and myth-icising of this period runs the risk of failing to ask what lessons it has, warts and all, for the contemporary world.

Muslim myths about the early years of Islam challenge the third characteristic assumption of contemporary western understandings of history, its 'otherness'. The *ḥadīth* survive into the modern world in the belief that Muhammad's sayings and customary practices continue to influence each succeeding generation of believers, in the actual ways that its members model their lives on his. This conviction has caused problems to contemporary Muslims. Times of prayer, and, still more challengingly, the length of hours required to fast, in a British summer, vary greatly from the time these practices were instituted in Arabia, where dawn to dusk varies little from one part of the year to another. There have been moves towards modernisation and not only in avowedly secular Turkey. For example, in Tunisia, there was an unsuccessful government attempt to interpret fasting, not in a literal sense, but as an inner discipline.

Islam is, in one sense, an attempt to live out a way of life appropriate to seventh-century Arabia in vastly different circumstances. Muslims would say the way of life is of timeless value. Western historians would say this begs questions about attitudes and assumptions which cannot cross the barrier of more than 1,300 years. Is there scope here for fruitful debate, or is it best to recognise that cultic practices of one religion are not best understood or interpreted by historians and other scholars from different traditions?

The Qur'ān

The Qur'ān, in relation to the connection between myth and history, raises two momentous questions. The first concerns the question of the Prophet's status: what is his involvement in the revelation? The second is, what is the nature of the qur'anic language about revelation?

The vast majority of Muslims have believed that the Qur'ān is the actual word of God:

> Orthodox opinion has, from the earliest times, rigidly maintained that the illiterate prophet faithfully conveyed to his amanuensis the heavenly words that came to him, through Gabriel, taking scrupulous care not to confuse the inspired utterances with his own ordinary speech. The oral revelations preserved in the Koran are in fact, it is held, portions of a celestial speech whose original is inscribed on a guarded tablet in Heaven (K:85:22). The contra-natural descent of parts of this supernatural language marks a pivotal event in mortal history (K:97) completing Allah's gracious self-disclosure to men. The Koran in the original Arabic, safeguarded in Muslim memory and devotion, is therefore the literal and immutable word of Allah, infallibly dictated to his messenger and constituting the final and conclusive expression of the divine will in relationship to mankind.
>
> (Akhtar 1990: 40)

This is an admirable summary of the classic Muslim position on revelation, though other Muslim scholars have seen difficulties with it, especially where history probes the assertions of myth. For example, in the somewhat complicated process of collecting the qur'anic text (which early Muslim sources describe[7]), what are the implications of the length of this process, and the resultant variant texts, for the conviction that all the revealed words, neither more nor less, form the Qur'ān as we now have it?

However, the particular question under review here is the Prophet's involvement in the revelation. Akhtar writes that, 'There cannot of course, for the committed Muslim, be two opinions about the authorship of the Islamic scripture'. In his view, either God or the Prophet must be the author of the Qur'ān, and he avers, 'I shall assume that these two possibilities are mutually exclusive: the Koran is not some amalgam of the divine and the human' (Akhtar 1990: 41).

A small number of Muslims have thought otherwise. Ameer Ali boldly wrote, specifically about the idea of a future life in Islam, that:

> A careful study of the Koran makes it evident that the mind of Mohammed went through the same process of development which marked the religious consciousness of Jesus. . . .
>
> The various chapters of the Koran which contain the ornate descriptions of paradise, whether figurative or literal, were delivered wholly or in part at Mecca. Probably in the infancy of his religious

> consciousness, Mohammed himself believed in some or other of the traditions which floated around him. But with a wider awakening of the soul, a deeper communion with the Creator of the Universe, thoughts, which bore a material aspect at first, became spiritualised. The mind of the Teacher progressed not only with the march of time and the development of his religious consciousness, but also with the progress of his disciples in apprehending spiritual conceptions.
>
> (Ali 1922: 220f.)

Ameer Ali was not a careful or learned scholar of Islam, though his works have been widely read, and some are still available.[8] It may be that he was propounding a view of the sole authorship by Muhammad of the Qur'ān but, if so, it is extraordinary that he did not seem to realise the singularity and unorthodox nature of his conviction. It is more likely that he was trying, rather clumsily and simplistically, and with too much reliance on nineteenth-century European notions of the progressive development of humankind, to restate orthodox views in ways that his audience could appreciate and affirm. However, he failed, crucially, to describe *how* God speaks his word through the Prophet.

A recent and more revealing attempt to find some space for Muhammad in the revelation given by God to him and then through him, is that of Fazlur Rahman (1919–87), who wrote:

> The Qur'ān itself certainly maintained the 'otherness', the 'objectivity' and the verbal character of the revelation, but had equally certainly rejected its externality *vis-à-vis* the Prophet. It declares, 'The Trusted Spirit has brought it down upon your heart that you may be a warner' (XXVI, 194), and again, 'Say: He who is an enemy of Gabriel (let him be), for it is he who has brought it down upon your heart' (2, 97). But orthodoxy (indeed, all medieval thought) lacked the necessary intellectual tools to combine in its formulation of the dogma the otherness and verbal character of the Revelation on the one hand, and its intimate connection with the work and the religious personality of the Prophet on the other, i.e. it lacked the intellectual capacity to say both that the Qur'ān is entirely the Word of God and, in an ordinary sense, also entirely the word of Muhammad. The Qur'ān obviously holds both, for if it insists that it has come to the 'heart' of the Prophet, how can it be external to him?[9]

Fazlur Rahman's book was controversially received by Muslims, though by no means all have rejected his scholarship. Although his argument is more learned, assured and compelling than Ameer Ali's, like him, he falls short of spelling out, with sufficient clarity and detail, *how* the revelation can be wholly God's, yet in some sense, Muhammad's. He is, however, more compelling an advocate than Ameer Ali for a more flexible and modernist interpretation of Islam, because he offers precise qur'anic material to underpin a more interesting development of the concept of revelation. In a later work,[10] he develops these ideas further, arguing that Muslim scholars must re-evaluate their methodology and hermeneutics. The implication of his book's title is that Islam and modernity are not mutually antagonistic. Yet if history and myth, as this chapter has described them, are characteristics of modernity, he ultimately fails to answer the questions they raise. He falls short of subjecting Islam on the one hand and myth and history on the other, to fruitful mutual interrogation.

So Shabbir Akhtar's assertion represents the concept of revelation as it is held by nearly all Muslims. In another book, he emphasises Muhammad's central importance for Muslims:

> Muhammad is unique in the respect and honour afforded him by his followers. Though not regarded as divine, Muhammad is held in the highest possible esteem. No pictorial representations are allowed; mention of his name warrants, among the pious, the invocation of the divine blessing upon him, his family and his companions. His wives are seen as mothers of the faithful. Every detail of his biography has been preserved and countless millions seek to imitate him daily in every aspect of their lives. . . . Muhammad is dead. But he is dead only in the least significant sense. For he is ideologically alive – and well.
>
> (Akhtar, S. (1989) *Be Careful with Muhammad*, London, Bellew, p. 2f.)

Where the traditional form of the myth, as expounded by Akhtar, could be said to fall short of complete credibility is precisely in making Muhammad a cipher (Akhtar says that he received revelation 'like a robot') with regard to the primary revelation of the Qur'ān, yet wholly crucial to the secondary revelation of the *ḥadīth*. Muslims have argued that the myth is coherent: the Qur'ān upholds both, on the one hand, the traditional view of its divine origin and the Prophet's passive receptivity of it (17:105f.) and, on the other, his role as a model for believers (33:21). However, the point at issue is not its coherence but, rather, its relevance and flexibility. It makes perfect sense of certain qur'anic verses. But does it make sense of the contemporary world in which Muslims live? And is it the only way in which the qur'anic material can be interpreted?

The question of how qur'anic material is to be read was widely and controversially discussed in the early Islamic centuries. One otherwise diverse group, the Mu'tazila, held two views which were later regarded as unorthodox: the createdness of the Qur'ān; and an allegorical attitude to the physical attributes of God mentioned in the Qur'ān. Their convictions are known through their opponents (*Mu'tazila* means 'seceders'), and so must be treated with extreme caution. But they seem to have held to the createdness of the Qur'ān because the belief in an uncreated Qur'ān compromises the central Islamic tenet of *tawḥīd*, 'the unity of God'. In the end, they and their views were rejected, and those of their former member, al-Ash'ari (873/4–935/6) prevailed. Perhaps in reaction to his Mu'tazila past, he came to believe that the anthropomorphic expressions about God in the Qur'ān, such as references to his face, must be accepted, but without stating how (*bilā kayfā*).

Sunni orthodoxy has held these views ever since. There are, however, at least two problems. First, logically, as the Mu'tazila contended, the doctrine of the uncreated Qur'ān sits ill with an uncompromising monotheism. Secondly, *bilā kayfā* is a device which, accepting a literal reading of the text, attempts to solve the problems that then arise, only to create more.[11] Specifically, what does it *mean* to talk of God's face as being his face, without knowing how? It renders parts of God's revelation literally 'meaningless' – beyond the power of humans to understand – when the Qur'ān calls itself 'the book that makes things clear' (43:2).

Contemporary issues

One of the chief questions that modernity raises for all religions is the fact of religious and ideological pluralism. This creates a problem for Muslims, because a central belief of Islam is *tawḥīd*, the 'unity' of God and therefore of all things he creates. In particular, many Muslim scholars, from the early days of Islam, have emphasised the need for a united *ummah*, 'community' or 'nation' of Islam, to be an obedient sign of God's one-ness in a forgetful and fragmented world. In practice, and ironically, this emphasis has sometimes caused division rather than unity. For example, the demand for a separate Muslim state in the South Asian subcontinent when the British quit India in 1947 led to the creation of Pakistan, but at the cost of leaving millions of Muslims in secular or Hindu India. Furthermore, since Bangladesh seceded from Pakistan in 1972, there have been more Muslims in India than in Pakistan. That secession questioned the 'myth' that a single Islamic *ummah*, stretching from North Africa to Indonesia, is more powerful for all Muslims than regional, linguistic and other loyalties.

That particular 'myth' is a potent one in Islam. The Prophet's ministry broke tribal loyalties in Arabia in favour of commitment to Islam. Within a few years of his death, Islam had destroyed the Persian empire, and encroached into the territory of Byzantium, the eastern Roman empire. Thus, Islam embraced a variety of racial groups, and provided the means of holding them together. Islam's early years of success meant that it has always aspired to be a community which has temporal as well as spiritual power. When it has ruled, it has often done so magnanimously, granting to smaller, usually monotheistic groups, the status of *dhimmī* (*dhimma* means 'an agreement of protection'), allowed to practise their own faith, provided certain taxes were paid.

The conviction of a united community, exercising temporal power, forms a potent myth. Even Ameer Ali, a Shi'ah, strove in the early years of the twentieth century, and especially during and after World War I, when Turkey was an enemy of Britain, for the retention of the caliphate as a focus of world-wide Muslim unity. At that time, the Sultan of Turkey claimed to be caliph (*khalīfah*) of Islam. When the Turkish government of Mustafa Kemal Ataturk (1881–1938) abolished the caliphate in 1924, Ameer Ali expressed his anger at an action he believed could only be taken by all Muslims.

The myth of Islam as a united, politically powerful force lives on. For example, during the Gulf war of 1991, many Muslims justified the actions of Saddam Hussein on the grounds that nation states like Kuwait and Saudi Arabia are modern concepts, not worth defending, particularly when led by arguably corrupt rulers. Zaki Badawi, the Principal of the Muslim College in London, has argued that there is no theory in Islam of being a minority (Badawi, Z. (1981) *Islam in Britain*, London, Ta Ta Publishers, p. 27). Many Muslims are proud to be Muslim and Egyptian, or Saudi, or British, or whatever. But when Muslims, inspired by this myth, act as majorities when they are, in fact, minorities, this sometimes causes a backlash from the community at large. For example, the concept of a Muslim parliament in Britain challenges the long-standing British myth that the Westminster parliament represents everyone in the land by the principle of universal adult suffrage.

The myth of a united and powerful single Muslim nation is challenged by history. For example, the Ottoman Sultans claimed that the caliphate was passed to the Ottoman Sultan Selim by the last 'Abbāsid caliph in 1517. However, there had not really been a universal caliphate since the fall of Baghdad in 1258, and, even before then, it had for many years been a shadowy, theoretical power. The caliph provided the myth of a united and politically powerful *ummah*, when the reality was, for many centuries, a variety of Muslim leaders holding power over particular areas. Even earlier, the unity of all Muslims had come under threat. When the Prophet died, many tribes broke away from loyalty to Islam, and had to be brought back by military force. The early successions to the caliphate showed a tension between dynastic family claims, and those of 'the best man for the job'. When 'Ali was killed in 661, the succession of Mu'awiyah (*d.* 680) was the triumph of dynasticism. It caused anger and schisms throughout the Muslim world.

A second aspect of the contemporary world's religious and ideological diversity is theological rather than political. Muslims regard Islam as the last and final religion. We have noted the space that it creates for other monotheistic religions. Some Muslim modernists have extended the range to include other faiths: in lectures, Zaki Badawi has included Hinduism and Buddhism as among the divinely revealed religions; and Ameer Ali included, Jesus, Moses, Zoroaster, the Buddha, and even Plato as predecessors of Muhammad, whose mission he was called upon to fulfil (Ali 1922: 111).

The Qur'ān points out that every community has had a warner (13:7), although it condemns many people for failing to heed them, and some communities, notably Jews and Christians, for failing to live up to the demands of monotheistic belief (9:30). Jews, Christians, and Sabaeans, as well as Muslims, indeed, all who believe in God and in the Last Day, and do good deeds, will have nothing to fear (2:62; 5:69). Yet, it also says that the true religion with God is Islam (3:19), and that anyone who accepts another religion will be among the losers (3:85). Western and some Muslim historians would argue that there are contextual reasons for these apparently contradictory statements. Let us take the example of the Jews. There were many Jews in Madinah, who would not accept that the Prophet had a ministry from God, and worked against him. Eventually, two Jewish tribes in Madinah, the al-Nadir and Qaynuqā', were expelled by the Prophet. Another, the Qurayza, was accused by him of treachery after the siege and battle of al-Khandaq in 627. The men were executed, and the women and children enslaved. The Qur'ān pronounced that the Jews were strongest in enmity towards the Muslims (5:85), and that they will listen to any lie (5:44).

Nevertheless, in later centuries, Jews were often honourably treated in Muslim lands when their co-religionists were suffering persecution in Christian countries.

> The relationship of Jews to Islam was complex, at times positive, at times negative. During the tenth century, Jews living under the 'Abbasids in the east were experiencing a major breakdown, while Jews in Andalusia were embarking on a golden age. In the twelfth century, Maimonides fled from a hostile Islam in Andalusia, tarried briefly in hostile Islamic North Africa, only to be welcome in Islamic Egypt, where he became physician to the vizier of Saladin. Islam created climates favourable to Jewish creativity and climates altogether inimical to Jews. The record is clear: the differences setting Islam apart from Judaism did not always generate hostility.[12]

Since the creation of Israel in 1948, and the dispossession of their land by Muslim (and Christian) Palestinians, many Muslims the world over have emphasised the stories in their tradition which illustrate Jewish perfidiousness. The author of this chapter was once roundly denounced in a remote, rural part of Pakistan for admitting that he had visited Israel, even though none of his interrogators had ever met a Jew. There are Islamic resources for a different relationship, which would stress the fact that Jews are *ahl al-kitāb* ('People of the book'). In the modern world, the choice people make from their store of history and myth colours their attitudes in ways that have important consequences.

One final example of contemporary issues is the status of women. The fact that there is a book in this series on *Women in Religion* illustrates how important this item has become. The section on Islam in that book discusses it in detail. In relationship to history and myth, it is important to note that from the beginning of Islam, men have attempted to suppress women by creating a myth of their inferiority on the basis of a partial reading of historical evidence, just as men have in other religions. They have quoted *ḥadīth* such as: 'Those who entrust their affairs to a woman will never know prosperity'. Yet women are discovering that aspects of the tradition defy such dismissive posturing, and some men aid them in their endeavours to change the status of women in Islam today. For example, the Muslim College in London, which, among other tasks, trains *imāms* for work in an English-speaking environment, has women students. Its Principal, Zaki Badawi, argues that in Britain mosques which mirror the South Asian cultural practice of excluding women should open their doors to women to meet and pray together, because this is what was practised in early Muslim history. Fatima Mernissi puts it this way:

> The image of 'his' [a Muslim man's] woman will change when he feels the pressing need to root his future in a liberating memory. Perhaps the woman should do this through daily pressure for equality, thereby bringing him into a fabulous present.[13]

Mernissi's acute judgement could be extended more widely. In the end, history and myth must work to create a liberating memory of all our religious traditions, appropriate for the extraordinarily diverse world in which we live.

NOTES

1. Muslims date their calendar from the year 622 of the Common Era (or Christian Era) when, after persecution in his hometown of Makkah, Muhammad emigrated to Madinah. They follow the lunar year, different from the Gregorian, western system based on the sun's rotation. I have used the Common Era dating. Muslims often give both dates in their works.
2. Muslims who follow the *sunnah*, or customary practice, of the Prophet Muhammad, his specific actions and sayings. The word means 'trodden path'. Sunni Muslims are far more numerous than the second largest Muslim group, the Shi'ah, or 'party' of the Prophet's son-in-law, 'Ali, who they believe should have succeeded him as temporal and spiritual head of the Muslim community.

3. Of special interest are: Said, E. (1978) *Orientalism*, London, Routledge and Kegan Paul, and Said, E. (1981) *Covering Islam: How the Media and the Experts Determine How We See the Rest of the World*, London, Routledge and Kegan Paul.
4. Rodinson, M. (1973 edn) *Mohammed*, London, Pelican, p. 313.
5. Mernissi, F. (1991) *Women and Islam: An Historical and Theological Enquiry*, Oxford, Blackwell, p. 76. I am indebted to chapters 2, 3 and 4 of this book for information used in this section of the chapter.
6. On misogyny, see the chapter on Islam in *Women in Religion*, and on *qadar* and the Last Day the chapter on Islam in the book *Human Nature and Destiny*, both in this series.
7. For a short account of the collection of the Qur'ān, see the chapter on Islam in the book of this series entitled *Sacred Writings*.
8. Most of his major works are available in pirate editions in Pakistan.
9. Rahman, F. (1979, 2nd edn) *Islam*, Chicago, Chicago University Press, p. 31.
10. Rahman, F. (1982) *Islam and Modernity: Transformation of an Intellectual Tradition*, Chicago, Chicago University Press, 1982.
11. Another such device is *kasb*, 'acquisition', which attempts to resolve the dilemma of human freedom and divine will by asserting that God creates all actions, which humans then 'acquire'. This is further described in the chapter on Islam in the book of this series entitled *Human Nature and Destiny*.
12. Epilogue by Ellis Rivken, in Ahmad, B. (1979) *Muhammad and the Jews: A Re-Examination*, New Delhi, Vikas, p. 126.
13. Mernissi, F. (1991) *Women and Islam: An Historical and Theological Enquiry*, Oxford, Blackwell, p. 195.

FURTHER READING

Ahmed, A.S. (1992) *Postmodernism and Islam: Predicament and Promise*, London, Routledge.

Akhtar, S. (1990) *A Faith for all Seasons: Islam and Western Modernity*, London, Bellew.

Ali, S.A. (1922 edn) *The Spirit of Islam*, London, Chatto & Windus.

Ibn Khaldun (trans. Rosenthal, F.) (1967) *The Muqaddimah: An Introduction to History*, London, Routledge and Kegan Paul.

Khan, M.M. (1987 rev. edn) *Ṣaḥīḥ al-Bukhārī*, vols 1–9, Delhi, Kitab Bhavan.

Mardrus, J.C. and Mathers, P. (1964 edn) *The Book of The Thousand and One Nights*, vols 1–4, London, Routledge and Kegan Paul.

5. Judaism

Sybil Sheridan

History is central to Jewish belief. The religion revolves around the worship of a god that is intimately connected with the history of the world and in particular the history of one people. God is the God of History, continually involved, intervening in events, supporting human beings and ensuring the divine purpose is carried out. The Jewish God is identified as the God of Abraham, Isaac and Jacob, as the Lord who brought the children of Israel out of Egypt – specific historic points in the drama of one nation. The uniqueness, described in the Bible, is not only that God is creator of the universe, but also creator of time.

> It was the glory of Greece to have discovered the idea of cosmos, the world of space; it was the achievement of Israel to have experienced history, the world of time. Judaism claims that time is exceedingly relevant. Elusive it may be, it is pregnant with the seeds of eternity. Significant to God and decisive for the destiny of man are the things that happen in time, in history. Biblical history is the triumph of time over space. Israel did not grow into being through a series of accidents. Nature itself did not evolve out of a process, by necessity; it was called into being by an event, an act of God. History is the supreme witness for God.[1]

As God is involved in time, so are the people who follow him. Jewish destiny is seen as a gradual unfolding of God's purpose in the world from the first act of creation to the end of time with the coming of the Messiah. The destiny is marked by the celebration of specific historical events: the Exodus, the destruction of the two Temples, etc., and looks forward to specific future events, the coming of the Messiah, the ingathering of the exiles.

Those celebrations that are clearly of agricultural origin have historical events superimposed upon them. The harvest festival, *Shavuot*, becomes the time when the Torah was given; *Sukkot* marks the wanderings in the wilderness.

In this process, much that is mythological becomes part of history. The agricultural origins of many celebrations predate Israel's settlement in the land of Canaan, and they contain elements of the cults that the Hebrew religion replaced. Other aspects have been demythologised to suit the theological needs of the Israelites. Some of the alterations are so great that the original myth becomes barely recognisable. On the other hand, important historical events appear to have been turned into myth. History, in Judaism, does not mean an enumeration of facts – accuracy is most certainly not its strongest point – rather it is a theological interpretation of events designed to involve the believer and effect a specific response.

Contemporary Jews are to regard themselves, not only as the inheritors of such historical traditions, but also as participants. Thus all Jews at the *seder* table are to think of the Exodus as if they too were in Egypt at that time, and all are understood to have stood at the foot of Mount Sinai and been witness to the theophany that there took place. In this way, history becomes myth. It is not so much the event itself, but its meaning that is central to the belief, and the reinforcement of that meaning through a large variety of symbols and celebrations. This is particularly clear in mainstream Orthodox Judaism which, though holding history at the core of its beliefs, does not approach it historically, but thematically. Exile and return, sin and repentance, are ideas demonstrated again and again in the narratives of the Bible. From creation to the end of time, the same pattern of events unfolds. The patriarchs, Moses and other heroes have their place in this history, but they also act as pious examples that ordinary people can follow, and most of Jewish literature addresses these figures in such a vein. In this they belong in every age, offering a timeless quality and an immediate appeal.

Other movements within Judaism take a radically different line. Reform Judaism originated in Germany in the early decades of the nineteenth century and was greatly influenced by Christian biblical scholarship of the time. It therefore takes the Bible less literally as the Truth, and rather views it as expressions of truth as conceived in particular ages under particular circumstances. Non-Orthodox Judaism relies very heavily therefore on a historical approach to the religion, careful to separate the different strands of belief as they developed. Only through this approach can one make a distinction between myth and history in Judaism, for to Orthodoxy, myth is history and history myth.

The beginnings of time

THE FIRST CREATION STORY: GENESIS 1–2:4A

> In the beginning God created the heavens and the earth. The earth was without form and void, and the darkness was upon the face of the deep; and the Spirit of God was moving over the face of the waters.
>
> (Gen. 1:1–2)

The first creation story recounted in the Bible appears to have used elements found in the Babylonian creation epics. *Enuma Elish*[2] recounts how the primordial Apsu, Mummu and Tiamat are defeated by the gods they engendered. The heavens and earth are formed from the split body of Tiamat, and the triumphant god, Marduk, then holds a celebration and builds a city for his supporters.

There are clear similarities to be found in the primordial origins of the universe as a watery waste, and in the order of creation described, but, unlike *Enuma Elish*, Genesis records no indication of a battle for supremacy. God alone is. He creates out of emptiness. There are no other gods – even the use of the plural, thought to indicate the presence of a heavenly court, is in no way specific and such lesser beings have no part to play in the creative process. While, for Genesis, creation is the central theme of the narrative, in *Enuma Elish* creation seems almost incidental to the main story, that of the great battle.

Other creation narratives in the Bible record more of the primeval battle. For example, in Psalm 74:13–14:

> Thou didst divide the sea by thy might;
> thou didst break the head of the dragons on the waters.
> Thou didst crush the heads of Leviathan,
> thou didst give him as food for the creatures of the wilderness.

Here the enemy is not Tiamat, but Leviathan, which recalls the Ugaritic battle between the god Baal and Yam (the sea) in which the serpent Lotan figures. Yam is also mentioned in Job 26:1–13, alongside Leviathan and another protagonist – Rahab.

In these passages, the mythological elements are understood as poetic imagery. The prophet Isaiah places them more in a historic context by connecting them to the subsequent story of humankind, and the future hope of redemption (Isa. 51:9–11). The myth also becomes representative of eschatological expectation. God did not defeat the monsters at the beginning of time; rather, it is an expressed hope of the future messianic age.

> On that day, the Lord with his hard and great and strong sword will punish Leviathan the fleeing serpent, Leviathan the twisting serpent, and he shall slay the dragon that is in the sea.
>
> (Isa. 27:1)

Rabbinic Judaism took over this use of the myth and enlarged upon it; the righteous will witness a contest between God and the two monsters: Leviathan and the great ox, Behemoth. Having defeated them, God will serve them up as food in a great feast to celebrate the end of days.[3] This is the theme for a medieval poem, *Akdamut*, recited in Ashkenazi[4] synagogues, on the festival of *Shavuot*. The rather florid Aramaic has been translated thus:

> Then shall Leviathan's enthralling sight
> Divert them, with Behemoth's might
> On mountains bred, fast twined in mortal fight.
> As Taurus' lofty horn to gore begins.
> See, leaping Draco parries with his fins:
> Till his Creator wields His wondrous sword –
> And so prepares the righteous' festive board.[5]

In the first creation story of Genesis, however, none of these creatures appears. The battle, be it primal or eschatological, is irrelevant to creation and God's ultimate purpose. Creation provides instead the framework for a new and totally original idea – that of God resting. This becomes the reason for the observance of *Shabbat* by the children of Israel.

> Remember the sabbath day to keep it holy. Six days shall you labour and do all your work; but the seventh day is a sabbath to the Lord your God . . . for in six days the Lord made heaven and earth, the sea, and all that is in them, and rested the seventh day; therefore the Lord blessed the sabbath day and hallowed it.
>
> (Exod. 20:8–11)

Creation itself is introduced within the framework of time. The seven days mark the beginning of time and, as such, are the first event in history. The Jewish year is calculated from the first day of creation – believed to have been the first of the month of *Tishri* (*Rosh Ha-Shanah*) five thousand seven hundred and fifty four years ago.

THE SECOND CREATION ACCOUNT: GENESIS 2:4B– 3:24

While the mythological elements in the first chapter of Genesis seem to have been pared away, those in the second creation account and the story of Adam and Eve in the garden of Eden have kept much more of their original colour. This has been explained as the result of differing editing processes at quite different periods of Jewish history, but it may also have something to do with the subjects they cover. Genesis 1 is about God – and the Israelite perception of God appears to have been unique in the Near East – while Genesis 2 and 3 are about humanity and the human predicament – an issue shared by all peoples. The barren plain watered by a mist, God forming humanity out of the earth, the miraculous garden, the source of the four rivers, all have their counterparts in Sumerian, Akkadian and Ugaritic mythology.

In the *Epic of Gilgamesh*, Enkidu is formed by the goddess Aruru out of clay, and lives among the animals until, initiated into love by a priestess of the god Gilgamesh, he is rejected by them. As he is now like a god, the priestess clothes him, and brings him to Gilgamesh in the city of Uruk. Gilgamesh subsequently sets out to find the herb of immortality. He enters a paradise of jewel-hung trees, owned by the goddess of wisdom, but continues until he finds the herb at the bottom of the sea. He returns with it but it is subsequently stolen by a serpent at a freshwater stream.

The *Myth of Adapa* describes how the son of the god of wisdom is advised by his father to refuse the food of the gods, as they are seeking to kill him. Anu, the king of heaven, hears of this conversation and offers Adapa the bread of immortality instead. However, Adapa, heeding his father's words, refuses the bread and so condemns himself to die like mortals.

But while echoes of these stories remain in the Genesis account, there are significant differences. The yearning for immortality is replaced by the quest for knowledge. It has been suggested that the two trees in the garden of Eden were originally the trees of life and death.[6] A warning by God against eating the tree of death makes for a simpler and less theologically challenging story – more in keeping with that of Adapa. But the myth as represented in the Bible introduces a moral element that becomes the foundation for its subsequent history.

Gardens of delight in mythology appear to have originally been ruled over by goddesses, and a serpent was invariably present.[7] At a later stage, according to Raphael Patai, male gods usurped them and reduced their status and power. In Eden, God is the only God, who walks alone in the garden he created. However, his creature, Adam, remains almost incidental to the story. The core event takes place between the serpent and Eve, and the subject of their discussion – the tree – can then be interpreted to be the acquisition of wisdom. The wise woman played a prominent part in Israelite society, her wisdom being related either to practical skills and diplomacy (2 Sam. 13:39–14:7, 20:16–22) or to a magic, esoteric knowledge (1 Sam. 28). However, in its later interpretations, it is humanity as represented by a man that becomes the subject of the piece. It is Adam who is told not to eat from the tree. It is his disobedience, not Eve's, that is noted by God, and it is not wisdom that he gains, but a sense of morality – of good and evil.

The reworking of the myth has one main object in mind: to provide a background for the history of the world in general and for the people of Israel in particular. By making the loss of innocence a moral issue – the result of disobedience – it explains the evils of the world not as the consequence of a mistake, or a trick as in its Near Eastern counterparts, but as the beginnings of a degeneration that is entirely humanity's own doing. Redemption is open to humanity through the same process: through moral action – from Noah, considered righteous in his generation, through Abraham, in his faith, and through subsequent history where kings are described as doing good or evil in the sight of the Lord. Along with the gods, the principle of evil as an external force is eradicated from the story, and the myth – focusing on the notion of moral choice – becomes a 'historical drama of human rebellion and sin'.[8]

THE PRE-HISTORY: GENESIS 4–11:9

The stories that follow – of Cain and Abel, of the 'sons of God', of Noah and the Tower of Babel – can be identified with myths and folk tales of the region in which they were composed. But they have been brought together and altered by the editors to present meanings that may not necessarily have been part of the original telling. In particular, after the perfection of the original creation, the story describes the descent of humanity into moral depravity in a series of retellings of the second creation myth. In each tale, it is again humankind's decision to do wrong that brings with it, not only changes in relation to the environment, but also in relation to God. Each cycle of creation and fall takes humanity further from God till, in Babel, God does not speak to the people at all.

But the myths do not remain disjointed. The whole process is historicised with the introduction of geneaologies. These occur from the beginning, linking the independent narratives, making unrelated characters part of the same family, and connecting unconnected events in terms of the changing but continuing relationship with God. Creation itself is seen as a historical process. The juxtaposition of heavens and earth in Genesis 2:4 serves to link the two creations and also to emphasise their difference – the first creation is of the universe, the second of the world. Two geneaologies precede the flood and two follow it. Each pair has a longer and shorter form. There are ten generations before Noah and ten after him, giving him a special place, as it were, at the halfway point in pre-history. This clearly is not factual history but theological history. That the geneaologies are not historically accurate is not important. They are history in that they reflect the forward motion of time, of change and development, and it is these geneaologies that link the mythology of the first chapters of Genesis with the family history that follows.

The patriarchs

As we enter the lives of the patriarchs, we encounter a very different mode. No longer does the biblical text deal with universal elements, but focuses in on the domestic lives of specific people. While Adam, Cain and Noah were also named individuals, they represented 'Everyman', and their experience was that of all human experience. Abraham, Isaac and Jacob, however, are significant for the opposite reason. They stand out as individuals distinct from the rest of humanity, they are called by God to follow an individual path.

While in the first chapters the events are interpreted theologically, the patriarchal narratives are interpreted historically. The former's interest in humanity's relationship with God is replaced in the main by the human concerns of progeny and land. With the story of Abraham we are at the beginning of the history of the Jews.

ABRAHAM

It cannot be proved whether Abraham actually existed as an individual. Archaeological evidence of names and places, legal and social situations described in Mesopotamian, Egyptian and Syrian documents seems to confirm the situations described in the stories relating to him. Vast migrations took place through the fertile crescent in the middle bronze age. To move from Ur, to Canaan, to Egypt and back was not uncommon – nor to marry one's half sister (Gen. 12:19), adopt a servant as one's heir (15:2) nor use a concubine as a surrogate mother (16). Moreover, there is evidence of power alliances of several kings combining forces against other kings during the period from 2000 to 1750 BCE (Gen. 14). This places Abraham very firmly within a known context at a known period in time and certainly suggests the veracity of much of the narrative.

However, other elements are clearly mythological: the angels visiting Abraham at his tent (18), the fate of Sodom (19), the saving of Ishmael (21). Both the historical and mythological, however, are transformed by the editor to present one overriding theme – that of exile and return. This theme dominates subsequent Jewish history and, it can be argued, the events related about Abraham's life are read back from the standpoint of the Exodus from Egypt.

The first chapter of the Abraham saga encapsulates all of Jewish history. Abraham is called to leave all he knows, to go to a new, strange and unspecified land, one that God will show him (12:1). Once in the land of Canaan his movement, from the north of the country to Shechem to the Negev, marks the boundaries of what will be the future nation's home. At Shechem, God promises that the land will be given to his descendants, a promise reiterated again and again to Abraham and his descendants. Then famine drives him to Egypt (12:10), just as famine will force Jacob to Egypt. Abraham returns after Pharaoh is afflicted with plague, apparently with great riches. In just the same circumstances, the children of Israel leave Egypt, and they ultimately settle in the land that once was settled by Abraham.

The rest of the saga expands this theme. The covenants (15:7–21 and 17:1–15) promise the land and progeny. The stories relating to Lot emphasise the land, its division (13) and its conquest by Abraham (14). Subsequent chapters concern the search for an heir: Eliezer (15), Ishmael (16), the promise of the birth of Isaac (18), the jeopardising of that promise in Gerar (20), Isaac's birth (21), and near sacrifice in the *akedah* or binding of Isaac (22). Finally, in the death of Sarah and the purchase of a burial plot (23), the subject returns to that of the land. All point to a very heavy editing of the original material to concentrate on this theme.

One of the most apparent changes occurs in the chapters concerning the visitation of the angels to Abraham and to Lot (18 and 19). It contains the familiar tale of hospitality rewarded – the childless couple get their child, the 'wicked' man loses all he has. However, Lot appears as hospitable as Abraham – it is the people of Sodom who flout the convention. Indeed, hospitality is not mentioned at all. The sin of Sodom is moral outrage, and it seems that Lot's punishment is because he chose to live in such evil surroundings. Moreover, dominating the whole sequence is the conversation of Abraham with God on the nature of justice. The tale has been altered as we have seen myths altered before – to emphasise a moral dilemma.

In Jewish tradition, Abraham has become important as the man of faith, the first Jew. Though the Bible gives no such indication, tradition has it that humanity descended into idolatry and the one true God was forgotten. Terah is pictured as a maker of idols, so the question arises, how did Abraham come to know God? Genesis 12:1 suggests a pre-history, and this, the *midrash* provides.[9] Abraham, observing his father making the idols, feels they cannot be gods. He then watches the moon, stars and sun, and worships them in turn as each appears to supplant the other. Finally, he feels that there must be some prime mover of all the heavenly bodies. Another *midrash* describes how Abraham smashed all his father's idols except the largest one and then told his father that the large idol got angry and destroyed the others. When Terah remonstrates, Abraham retorts – 'if you do not believe the idol can do this, how can you worship him as a god?'

Abraham, the first Jew, becomes the 'father' of all converts to Judaism who, to this day, adopt his name as their patronym. He is described as having spent his life converting others until a great many 'souls' follow him to Canaan (Gen. 12:5). There, many more are converted wherever he builds an altar and 'calls upon the name of the Lord'. Yet Abraham's faith is constantly being tested. Each incident related of him in the Bible is regarded as such a test, with the binding of Isaac as the greatest and last of them.

> With ten temptations was Abraham our father tempted, and he stood steadfast in them all, to show how great was the love of Abraham our father.
>
> (Mishnah, *Avot* 5:7)

ISAAC

In comparison to the Abraham saga, what we are told about Isaac is brief and inconsequential. There is only one chapter – chapter 26 – that narrates actions independent of either Isaac's father or of his sons. The relative insignificance of Isaac is neatly summarised in chapter 25:19: 'These are the descendants of Isaac, Abraham's son: Abraham was the father of Isaac . . .'. Moreover, most of what is recorded parallels the life of Abraham. His wife is barren for many years (25) before giving birth, and he too is faced with rival heirs. Like Abraham, he goes to Gerar at a time of famine (26), and passes his wife off as his sister, with the usual results. He has trouble with the Philistines over wells he dug, paralleling 21:25, and, like his father, makes a covenant with Abimelech, though the wording in Isaac's case is more reminiscent of Abraham's dealings with Melchizedek (14:18). Twice he receives God's blessing with the promise of land and progeny (26:3–5; 24), and, like his father, he builds an altar at Beer Sheva and 'calls upon the name of the Lord'.

It is his father's story in miniature. Isaac's wanderings never go beyond the Negev region in the south. Most of the parallels with Abraham occur in the one independent chapter, which opens with a prohibition against going to Egypt (26:2) – even Abraham's status as a precursor of the Exodus is denied him.

Yet Jewish tradition ranks him as equal to both his father and his son. Adonai is 'God of our fathers Abraham, Isaac, and Jacob'. God is *pahad Yitzhak* (31:42), translated as 'the fear of Isaac'. The prophet Amos uses 'the house of Isaac' rather than the more common 'house of Jacob' as a synonym for Israel (Amos 7:16). *Midrash* points out that because God named him, he is the only one of the patriarchs not to experience a name change. This reflects on his character, which is blameless. He is the perfect dutiful son; witness the *akedah*.

JACOB

His son, Jacob, however, has all the vibrancy, and full characterisation of Abraham. As in the case of his grandfather, the narrative surrounding Jacob appears made up of separate incidents – real or imaginary – that were related of the patriarch. The editor has linked them into a continuous narrative, again with the purpose of showing the pattern of exile and return, and of setting the scene for the descent into Egypt. Central again are two blessings, promising progeny and the land. Jacob's movements again confirm the extent of the land. He leaves his father in the south, and moves northward via Bethel to Padan Aram, where he later establishes a border with Laban (31:51). He settles in Shechem and ends his days in Egypt, thus travelling almost to the extent of his grandfather's journeys. But the emphasis in the text is more on the progeny than the land, for here, for the first time, it appears the promise may come true. Each of thirteen children's births and namings is mentioned, and significant events in their lives are described. These stories may well also have been independent traditions, recording the leaders of clans or tribal groups, but they have been brought into the Jacob saga to provide the narrative of one large family – the early history of the people Israel.

This approach seems to vary from that of the narratives described earlier. The two very dramatic theophanies that are described, of the ladder at Bethel (28:10–17) and of the wrestling bout at the Jabbok ford (32:22–32), probably owe their origin to earlier mythic religious experiences. Unlike other such incidents we have encountered, they are not moralised or placed into a theological context. Each takes place at a moment of crisis in Jacob's life, and clearly they have a great impact on his own development, but what this is, is not spelt out.

The rivalry between Jacob and Esau harks back to that of Cain and Abel, and may well have the same mythological root. Yet it becomes in the Bible a recurring theme that appears again in the life of his son, Judah (38:27–30), which, in turn, becomes a blueprint for the events of the book of Ruth. A new element is introduced then, linking the concerns of progeny and land to the establishment of the future kingdom under the rule of the ideal king – David.

In the stories of the patriarchs we see ancient history and myth combined to form a new history. S.H. Hooke[10] sees, underlying these stories, the earliest movements of ancient peoples. Abraham, the 'Hebrew' (possibly part of the 'Hapiru' mentioned in literature of the period), demonstrates the movement from Ur to the land around Hebron. Jacob, the 'wandering Aramean' – also known as Israel – settled in Shechem. Isaac may represent a third people who lived an independent, settled, agricultural life around Gerar. Each patriarch is associated with a different epithet for God: the God of Abraham, the Fear of Isaac, the Champion of Jacob. Each patriarch is seen as choosing God for himself; each is blessed independently by God. It is possible, therefore, that each group had its own tribal god which, when later the nation of Israel emerged, combined to form the God of Abraham, Isaac and Jacob.[11]

In order to maintain the unity of the nation once formed (the books of Judges and Kings suggest it was at times a very precarious unity) the individual ancestors were also combined into a family – a family with clear limits of exclusion and inclusion, so only one child of each generation becomes part of the chosen destiny. In this way the patriarchs can be seen to have historical origins – though somewhat different ones from those described in the narrative. Yet, to the Jewish tradition, such speculation is irrelevant. Without the patriarchs, there would be no Jewish people. The history of Israel begins here in the lives of three individuals and their actions echo on down the generations.

It is noteworthy that, despite the length given over in Genesis to the Joseph story, Joseph is not considered a patriarch. Though he becomes the ancestor of two tribes, he is only one of the sons of Israel – all of whom have an equal share in the promise.

Moses

In all of the history of Israel, the Jews and Judaism, the figure that dominates is that of Moses. Prince and prophet; shepherd and showman; leader and lawgiver; Moses alone was responsible for the formation of the nation Israel, and the foundation of the Jewish faith. Yet there is no evidence that he ever existed.

Archaeology has confirmed that there were Semitic groups in Egypt, some of which moved northwest towards Canaan. Under the Hyksos, foreigners (like Joseph) attained high office; when the Hyksos were thrown out such foreigners were not likely to be kindly treated by the new dynasty. Furthermore, there are accounts of runaway slaves seeking asylum in other countries. The cities of Pithom and Ramses have been identified – built in the time of Ramses II in the thirteenth century. The Merneptah Stele, *c.* 1220 BCE, describes the nation Israel defeated in Canaan. The name Moses seems clearly Egyptian despite the etymology given in Exodus 2:10. All this gives great credibility to the story, and historians tend to date the events described in Exodus to the thirteenth century, with Ramses II as the pharaoh of the oppression and Merneptah as the pharaoh of the Exodus. But of Moses the man, or of a mass exodus of Hebrew slaves, there is no evidence at all. To the Jewish believer, such doubts are unthinkable. The Exodus and the Theophany at Sinai are absolutely central to belief. This is history that really happened – perhaps not entirely in the form given in the Bible – but it happened nevertheless.

While many of the stories in Moses' life can be seen as coming from the general pool of folklore and myth, the Exodus and the revelation of law on Mount Sinai are absolutely unique. Moreover Moses, despite the birth stories, his miraculous abilities and the success of his mission, never develops into a full-blooded hero type. He does not end up as king or conqueror but remains a shy stutterer, reluctant to fulfil his required role, and dependent throughout his life on the help of his brother Aaron, his father-in-law and the elders of Israel. Moreover, he dies before the people enter the promised land and so never sees the fulfilment of his mission. Such a person, the argument runs, would not have been invented – nor would such humble origins for the nation. Moreover, the Exodus event is so strongly imprinted upon the psyche of the Jew that the question of proof becomes irrelevant. It is in relation to this one event that the Jewish people are defined; all previous and subsequent history is interpreted in its light.

MOSES' EARLY LIFE

Moses was born to Israelite slaves in Egypt at a time of intense oppression (Exod. 1:8–22), and experiences a rescue from death and an upbringing incognito, common to many a mythological hero. After killing an Egyptian, Moses is forced to flee to Midian (2:11), where he first encounters God, and his mission to rescue his people from the cruelty of Egypt is made clear. Moses returns to Egypt and approaches Pharaoh, who, after falling victim to ten plagues sent by God, agrees to let the people go (5–12). The Israelites leave, but Pharaoh changes his mind and chases after them (13:17). They finally escape when a sea of reeds– *yam suf* – miraculously divides and lets them pass to the other side, while the pursuing Egyptians are drowned in pursuit (14:15–50).

The geneaology at the beginning of the book of Exodus (1:1–7), as in Genesis, links the narrative into the continuing historical line. With the description of the population explosion in Egypt, God's original promise to Abraham is seen to be half fulfilled. When Moses is called on Mount Horeb and God identifies himself as the 'God of your fathers, God of Abraham, God of Isaac and God of Jacob' (3:6), the indication is that he is now about to fulfil the second half of that promise. Yet it takes another four biblical books and another generation before this actually comes to pass. While the biblical editor is using the Exodus in the general context of exile and return, the event as described here and in subsequent history quite clearly had an independent life of its own.

Many of the events recorded of Moses' early life are the stuff of legend. The rescue from the water is reminiscent of several other birth stories, while Moses' magic staff, the plagues and the miracles have parallels the world over. However, the leaving of Egypt and the emergence into freedom of a nation of slaves, is particular to Israel, and records the precise moment in history when the nation was born.

THE EXODUS

Form critics suggest that the narratives of the book of Exodus fall into two parts, relating to specific cultic celebrations at two different sanctuaries.[12] The first section covers Exodus 1–15 and includes stories regarding the birth, growth and call of Moses as well as the events surrounding the leaving of Egypt itself, while the second concerns the events leading up to the revelation on Mount Sinai and a celebration of the covenant of law. These originally localised festivities now find their universal application in the festivals of *Pesach* and *Shavuot*.

The Exodus itself begins with the preparations before the last plague (12) – preparations that could well reflect the cultic observance of some event. God commands that the children of Israel select a lamb whose blood will be used to smear the doorposts of their houses and which will then be eaten just before they leave. This later becomes the *Pesach*, the paschal sacrifice offered in the Temple. But there is also evidence of another observance in this chapter – that relating to the feast of unleavened bread or *Hag Hamatzot*. Scholars suggest that two originally independent festivals are recorded here, one agricultural and one nomadic – both spring festivals but neither necessarily of Israelite origin. The nomadic *Pesach* later became specifically Israelite by linking it to the historical event of the Exodus; while *Hag Hamatzot* – possibly adopted once Israel had settled in Canaan – continued roughly in its original form. It is hard to say when the feasts were connected; biblical evidence suggests that the observance of *Pesach* was spasmodic at least until the time of Josiah (2 Kgs. 23:21–23), but it is likely that the popular harvest festivals would have been celebrated in their appropriate seasons.

The Exodus as a supremely significant event emerged in Babylon at the time of another exile, where the dreams of a return to the promised land shaped much of the history related in Torah. The return and restoration of the Temple saw a new observance: a lamb eaten at home to the accompaniment of Psalms and the telling of the Exodus story.

As Israel suffered further defeats and humiliations at the hands of foreign enemies, the Exodus experience intensified as the symbol of nationalistic hopes till, under Roman occupation, the passage from slavery to freedom took on an intense metaphysical as well as a political form. It is then that the Exodus became mythologised in the *seder* and its accompanying service book, the *Haggadah*. Though the form of the meal follows that of a Roman symposium, the intention is to recreate the last meal eaten in Egypt.

> In every generation each person is obliged to consider themselves as if they had personally come out of Egypt. As it is said: 'and you shall tell your children on that day, saying, "This is because of what the Lord did for me when I went out of Egypt."' (Ex 13:8) Not only our ancestors alone did the Holy One, blessed be He, redeem, but he redeemed us also with them, as it is written: 'And he took us out from there in order to bring us here to give us the land which he swore to our ancestors.'[13]
>
> (Deut. 6:23)

Much of the *Haggadah* is concerned with telling of the events that took place in Egypt leading up to the Exodus, but with distinctive differences from the biblical account. Moses is not mentioned at all. Instead, all the credit and glory go to God, and the narration is punctuated with elaborate songs of praise and thanks to God,

> 'who brought us out of Egypt with a mighty hand and outstretched arm, with great terror and with signs and wonders'.
>
> (Deut. 26:8)

Yet the events take on a wider spiritual significance. The four cups of wine drunk are symbolic of the fourfold promise of God to Moses (Exod. 6:6–7):

> I am the Lord, and I will bring you out from under the burden of the Egyptians; and I will rescue you from slavery; and I will redeem you with an outstretched arm and with great judgments; and I will take you to me from my people . . .

But there is another promise symbolised in the fifth cup of wine:

> and I will be to you God.

This cup is not drunk, but saved for Elijah, who will return heralding the Messiah and the End of Days. The introduction of the messianic theme adds another veneer to the story. The biblical subject of slavery and freedom, which becomes in Babylonian exile interpreted as exile and return and under the Roman yoke as occupation and liberation, is turned into the idea of the spiritual redemption that will come with the reparation of the world.

THE PARTING OF THE SEA

The crossing of the *yam suf* marks the final escape of Israel from the Egyptians. The story is told relatively simply in chapter 14, how God 'hardened Pharaoh's heart', who then set off in pursuit of his former slaves. The Israelites complain when they find themselves caught literally between the 'devil' and the deep blue sea, asking 'Were there not enough graves in Egypt that you had to take us into the wilderness to die?' (14:11). The way the story is written, its purpose appears to be to demonstrate God's saving power so that the Israelites will believe in him. Thus the last verse explains,

> And Israel saw the great work which the Lord did against the Egyptians; and the people feared the Lord; and they believed in the Lord and in his servant Moses.
>
> (14:31)

But the sheer drama of the event has meant its use in many other contexts – most notably in the Psalms.

> When the waters saw thee, O God,
>   when the waters saw thee, they were afraid,
>   yea the deep trembled.
> The clouds poured out water;
> the skies gave forth thunder;
> thy arrows flashed on every side.
> The crash of thy thunder was in the whirlwind;
>   thy lightnings lighted up the world;
>   the earth trembled and shook.

> Thy way was through the sea,
> thy path through the great waters;
> yet thy footprints were unseen.
> Thou didst lead thy people like a flock
> by the hand of Moses and Aaron.
>
> (Ps. 77.16–20.)

The personification of the sea as an adversary, and God's use of lightning and thunder, make this passage an echo of the Ugaritic myths.[14] It is God, once more facing chaos and subduing it.

In the famous song of the sea which follows the actual event (Exod. 15), similar themes are used. Though the enemy remains Egypt, and the sea God's agent rather than adversary, God is still described as a warrior, and the reward for victory is that he shall reign for ever in the abode he has built (15:17–18).[15] The song has clear references back to the Genesis account of creation. God's intentions are activated by his *ruah* – his breath – and again it appears that he is dividing the waters.

> At the blast of thy nostrils the waters piled up,
> the floods stood up in a heap;
> the deeps congealed in the heart of the sea.
>
> (Exod. 15:8)

Today, the central feature of the service on the seventh day of *Pesach* is the singing of the song at the sea. Some Hasidic sects re-enact the event also in a special dance, where water is poured on the ground and crossed; others will go down to the sea shore and recite specific Psalms. But in the main, Judaism today does not make as much of the event as it could.

There is every likelihood that in the past, the crossing of the *yam suf* was the most important feature of the Exodus story. It after all concludes the event. It is the climax, the most impressive of all the miracles and only at the very end of the story are the Israelites safely away from Egypt. Moreover, the crossing of the sea is deeply symbolic, reflecting a new creation, re-birth or baptism. It is here that the slaves become a nation. Yet in today's ritual, the first night of *Pesach* eclipses the last. The emphasis lies in Egypt with the oppression of the slaves and the retribution of the plagues. This reflects the reality of Jewish suffering under persecution down the ages. Jews are all, as it were, still in Egypt – occasionally sharing the triumph of a temporary respite as after a plague – but not yet having achieved the complete liberation experienced by crossing the sea.

REVELATION AT SINAI

The second cultic cycle takes the Israelites through the desert to the mountain of God where Moses and all the people of Israel are bound in a covenant relating to God's law. As with the Exodus narrative, the miraculous elements abound. There is God's providence along the way (Exod. 16), there is the battle with the new adversary – Amalek (17:8–13) and the great thunder when God descends upon the mountain (19:16–19). As with the Exodus narrative, there are what appear to be cultic preparations before the great event. In chapter 19:10–25 bounds are set around the mountain, the people wash and get ready for Moses' ascent.

Yet the actual event is of far shorter duration. God descends upon the mountain top amidst thunder and lightning, smoke and blasts of the *shofar*. He then proclaims the ten commandments in the hearing of all the people. There are further laws (20:22ff.), the incident with the golden calf and its repercussions (32–4), and the erection of the tabernacle, but it is that first theophany at Sinai that has become the significant event. And again, despite the miraculous overlay, the event seems to record an actual historical happening of such magnitude as to be everlastingly imprinted upon the nation's mind. This is the event that gave the people its identity. It became the nation of God, forged into a special covenant of which perhaps only later generations could properly see the significance. Something happened at Sinai – exactly what, cannot be said – but some religious experience so powerful and involving so many of the people that all subsequent religious experiences seem somehow to have emerged there and all subsequent generations shared in that experience. This feature is central to Orthodox Jewish theology.

> 'And God spoke all these words saying' (Ex 20:1). R. Isaac said: The prophets received from Sinai the messages they were to prophesy to subsequent generations; for Moses told Israel, 'Nor is it with you only

> that I make this sworn covenant, but with him who is not here with us this day' etc. (Deut 29:14) . . . Although they did not yet exist, still each one received his share.
>
> (*Shemot Rabbah* 28:6)

And similarly with rabbinic revelation.

> When God revealed himself at Sinai to give the Torah to Israel, he communicated it to Moses in order; Bible, Mishnah, Talmud and aggadah as it says, 'And God spoke all these words' (Ex 20:1). Even the question a pupil asks his teacher God told Moses at this time.
>
> (*Shemot Rabbah* 47:1)

In a sense then, history stopped at Sinai. All that followed is the fulfilment of prophecy. Yet in another sense, it is the beginning of history. The nation defining itself in terms of a relationship with God is a nation centred on the observance of his law. How many of the laws recorded in the rest of the Pentateuch are actually of mosaic origin is hard to tell, but again in religious terms this is not relevant. What is important is that the Torah became the blueprint for all action – religious, civil, and personal. The Mishnah, written about 200 CE, expands and interprets the laws of Torah in the light of Palestinian living at the time of the second Temple. The *Gemara* (which, with the Mishnah makes up the Talmud) comments on the Mishnah laws for the benefit of Jews living in Babylonia four centuries later. The process continues to this day. *Halakhah* is the term given to this constant interpretation of Torah into practical application – a word derived from the verb 'to walk', signalling a persistent movement, or change, or progression – yet Torah remains at the source and is never distanced by the process.

The revelation at Sinai is also the point where Reform, or Progressive, Judaism differs from its mainstream opponent. For the various non-Orthodox movements, Sinai was the first revelation of God and so the most important, but nevertheless limited by its time and place. The prophets had their own individual revelations of God relevant to the people and circumstances of their time, as did the later *rabbis* in theirs. This is termed 'progressive revelation' and demands a rather different understanding of the historical process within Judaism. For the Orthodox, the rabbinic saying, 'there is no before or after in Torah', holds sway. Chronology is irrelevant – the law all-important. For the Progressive Jew, chronology and an appreciation of history in general become more important than the laws.

The book of Joshua (8:30) describes a re-enactment of the events on Mount Sinai when, after the initial victories, Joshua assembles the entire nation to Mount Ebal where he records Moses' words on tablets of stone and initiates a series of blessings and curses in response to Deuteronomy 27:11. Today the celebration that takes place at *Shavuot* is less dramatic. In synagogue, the events of Exodus 19 and 20 are read from the Torah scroll but this is not seen as a reconstruction of the revelation in the way that the *seder* commemorates the Exodus. *Shavuot*, like *Pesach*, probably started out as a non-Israelite agricultural festival upon which the people overlaid a historical event. The same happened to *Sukkot* – an autumn feast which now commemorates the wilderness wanderings of the children of Israel. This is emulated by the 'dwelling in booths' – not skin tents as were used in the wilderness, but huts decorated with leaves and fruit which clearly did not grow in the desert but which celebrate the richness of a successful harvest.

Towards the end of time

The books that follow Torah in the Hebrew Bible – namely, the Prophets – are largely historical in their approach. They trace the ongoing adventures of the Israelites from their first step across into the promised land, through their conquest of Canaan, the tribal rivalries and allegiances, their unification under the monarchy, the capture of Jerusalem and consolidation of territory, to the division of the kingdom into two, their ultimate defeats and destruction causing the disappearance of tribes and exile of leaders. As we move forward in history, it becomes easier to demonstrate the actual existence of the main characters and to validate their actions through external documentation and archaeological finds. But the history as written in the Bible is theological history. The events as they occur are less important than the interpretation put upon them. David's sons squabble because of his 'sin' with Bathsheba (2 Sam 12:11–12). The kingdom is divided because of Solomon's idolatry (1 Kgs. 11:9–13) and so on. This becomes most clear in the treatment given in the Bible and in later literature to the figure of Amalek.

AMALEK

Amalek is first encountered in the wilderness by the Israelites just after their escape from Egypt (Exod. 17:8–15). The battle that ensues is decisively won by Joshua, with miraculous help from Moses. There then follows this passage, surprising in its vehemence:

> And the Lord said to Moses, 'Write this as a memorial in a book and recite it in the ears of Joshua, that I will utterly blot out the remembrance of Amalek from under heaven.' And Moses built an altar and called the name of it, The Lord is my banner, saying, 'A hand upon the banner of the Lord! The Lord will have war with Amalek from generation to generation'.
>
> (Exod. 17:14–16)

The decisive battle with the Amalekites came in the reign of Saul (1 Sam. 15). God remembers what Amalek had done to Israel in the desert and instructs Saul to finish off the nation:

> '. . . utterly destroy all they have; do not spare them, but kill both man and woman, infant and suckling, ox and sheep, camel and ass.'
>
> (1 Sam. 15:3)

But Saul disobeys. He takes the livestock as booty, and though killing every other Amalekite, makes King Agag his prisoner. The prophet Samuel, when he hears of Saul's actions, is furious and personally kills Agag. Historically, we know that the Amalekites were not totally destroyed. They are mentioned again in Saul's reign (1 Sam. 30:13) and presumably remained as a nation for some time after this. But tradition has another story: Agag, while imprisoned by Saul, sired a child and so his line was saved; in subsequent generations, wherever an enemy arose dedicated to the destruction of Israel, that enemy was sure to be a descendant of Agag.

The most well-known example is that cited in the book of Esther, where the evil advisor, Haman, is described as an 'Agagite' (Esther 3:1). The story, possibly based upon actual historical events that took place in the Persian empire, has a more universal significance in Judaism as portraying the primal battle between good and evil.

Haman represents Amalek, upon whom 'the Lord will have war'; Esther – a form of the Hebrew 'Hester', meaning 'hidden' – represents God. There is no direct mention of God in the story and this is interpreted to mean that God has 'hidden his face' (cf., Ps. 89:46; Ezek. 39:29). At times when Israel sins, rabbinic interpretation explains, God hides, or withdraws from the world. This allows for all manner of evil to emerge and punish the nation before God once again takes control.

In the story of Esther, a Jewish woman risks her life to save her people and her courage is rewarded, while the enemy Haman and all his sons are killed. This is celebrated today in the feast of *Purim*, where the story is read out, and at each mention of Haman's name, as much noise as possible is made with rattles and the stamping of feet, in order to 'blot out the name' and the 'remembrance of Amalek from under heaven'. The hanging of Haman's sons means, according to the story, that the centuries' old enmity is finally at an end. But tradition has it that the line did continue. Thus rabbinic literature describes Rome as Amalek, and late medieval commentaries attributed the lineage to Torquemada, the leader of the Spanish Inquisition. In our own time Hitler was the 'Agagite'. Under the Third Reich it really did seem as if God had withdrawn completely from the world.

While the battle between Israel and Amalek is seen as ongoing throughout history, history itself does move forward towards an end-point – the last days when all the world will be judged, the world will return to its former perfection – as in Eden – and all peoples will enjoy the delights of the messianic age. The harbingers of this age, however, are regarded as historical figures whose appearance in the past assures of their presence in the future.

ELIJAH

The Elijah of the Bible is a prophet of great and uncompromising zeal. Prophet during the reign of Ahab (ninth century BCE), he wages war on the idolatrous gods of Baal and Asherah, killing four hundred and fifty of their prophets (1 Kgs. 18:40). His stance led him into direct conflict with the ruling house, which depended on good diplomatic relations – and marriages – with the neighbouring pagan kingdoms to survive.

This made Elijah one of the great heroes of the Maccabean period (1 Macc. 2:58), where his example is set alongside that of Phinehas (Num. 25:6–15), and both seem to have been emulated by Mattathias in his slaughter of those worshipping the statue of Antiochus (1 Macc. 2:23–25). Yet, after the destruction of the Temple in 70 CE, the leader of the Jewish people was a completely contrasting character. Rabbi Johanan ben Zakkai was a pacifist who, according to legend, was smuggled out of besieged Jerusalem in a coffin. He then approached the general (soon to be emperor), Vespasian, and made his peace with him. As a result of this new leadership image, the perception of Elijah underwent a transformation. His battles with Ahab and Jezebel are so interpreted as to make him the champion of the ordinary people against the might and wealth of the ruling class (1 Kgs. 20). Much of Jewish folklore has Elijah wandering the earth in the disguise of a beggar who rewards those who are kind and charitable and brings punishment on those who cheat the poor. Above all, the prophet who killed four hundred and fifty prophets of Baal, is portrayed as a man of peace.

One of the most dramatic biblical stories is the account of how Elijah was translated to heaven in a fiery chariot (2 Kgs. 2:1–11). This gives way to the notion that he never died, and returns to earth from time to time, to help rabbinic students get out of their difficulties when studying the Talmud, or to relieve oppression and right wrongs. But the most enduring belief is that of his return at the end of days. This has its basis in the Bible itself.

> Behold I will send you Elijah the prophet before the great and terrible day of the Lord comes. And he will turn the hearts of fathers to their children and the hearts of children to their fathers, lest I come and smite the land with a curse.
>
> (Mal. 4:5)

Elijah becomes the forerunner of the Messiah, the announcer of the end of days, the proclaimer of the reign of peace and perfection. Thus it is that his company is sought in a great variety of Jewish rituals. It is in 'Elijah's chair' that a boy is circumcised. Elijah is one of the guests who enter the *sukkah*, and he is expected at every *seder* meal. His return is requested in the grace said after meals, and every

Shabbat, at the close of the day, the ceremony of *havdalah* concludes with a song enjoining him to come quickly.

Elijah the prophet, Elijah the Tishbite, Elijah the Gileadite.
Speedily in our days, let him come to us
With the Messiah, the son of David.

DAVID

Of all the characters described in the Bible, more is written of David than anyone else. Undoubtedly a historical figure, much of his life is embellished with legend, inevitable for a character whose youth and attractiveness, and brave deeds, would make him an obvious national hero. But the biblical account stays away from the miraculous. David is deeply religious, and his actions are motivated by a desire to serve God, but God does not 'act' in his story in quite the same way as he did for Moses.

A shrewd politician and diplomat, as well as military leader of unquestioned ability, his conquests brought Israel vast tracts of land way beyond the boundaries promised to Abraham, bringing under Israelite suzerainty many of the surrounding nations. But David's most significant achievement was to unite the different tribes more or less successfully under his leadership. He did this by capturing Jerusalem – a Jebusite city that was not part of the original division of the land – and so excited no tribal claim (2 Sam. 5:6–10). This he made his capital, and centralised all administration so that tribal leaders and officials would be obliged to reside there. He then divided the land into twelve districts, but districts that did not correspond with the original apportioning of the land to the twelve tribes. He made Jerusalem the home of the tabernacle (2 Sam. 6:1–15), and prepared to build a temple there, thus centralising the cult. Finally, he made the High Priest subject to him, and the Levitical priests, who operated throughout the land, his agents.

To aid this policy, the 'myth' of Jerusalem as the city of God was actively encouraged. We see it reflected where David decides to build a temple: 'See now, I dwell in a house of cedar, but the ark of God dwells in a tent (2 Sam. 7:2). In a dream, God tells David that he will not build the temple but that his son will.

> When your days are fulfilled and you lie down with your fathers, I will raise up your offspring after you, who shall come forth from your body and I will establish his kingdom. He shall build a house for my name, and I will establish the throne of his kingdom for ever. I will be his father and he shall be my son.
>
> (2 Sam. 7:12–14)

A link is made here between Jerusalem as God's house, and the Davidic line, established 'forever'. This is made even more explicit in Psalm 132, which describes the bringing of the ark to Jerusalem (cf., 2 Sam. 6).

> For the Lord has chosen Zion;
> he has desired it for his habitation:
> 'This is my resting place for ever;
> here I will dwell, for I have desired it.
> I will abundantly bless her provisions;
> I will satisfy her poor with bread.
> Her priests I will clothe with salvation,
> and her saints will shout for joy.
> There I will make a horn to sprout for David;
> I have prepared a lamp for my anointed.
> His enemies I will clothe with shame,
> but upon himself his crown will shed its lustre.'
>
> (Ps. 132:13–18)

It receives its classic formulation on the completion of the Temple building.

> . . . 'I have heard your prayer and your supplication, which you have made before me; I have consecrated this house which you have built, and put my name there for ever; my eyes and my heart will be there for all time. And as for you, if you will walk before me, as David your father walked, with integrity of heart and uprightness, doing according to all that I have commanded you, and keeping my statutes and my ordinances, then I will establish your royal throne over Israel for ever.'
>
> (1 Kgs. 9:3–5)

But despite the assurances of eternity intended to boost David's position, the tribal rivalries soon overcame the central monarchy.

After Solomon's death, the vast Davidic empire, stretching from the Euphrates to Egypt, was divided and eroded till the northern kingdom was no more.

The descriptions of David's eternal greatness were reinterpreted into the hope that one day, in the future, his descendants would once more rule over a united Israel:

> 'In that day I will raise up
>   the booth of David that is fallen
> and repair its branches,
>   and raise up its ruins,
>   and rebuild it as in the days of old;
> that they may possess the remnant of Edom
>   and all the nations who are called by my name',
>   says the Lord who does this.
>
> (Amos 9:11–12)

At the same time, a shift in emphasis is perceived, from the emphasis on the eternity of the dynasty to the character of the future king.

> Of the increase of his government and of peace
>   there shall be no end,
> upon the throne of David, and over his kingdom,
>   to establish it, and to uphold it
> with justice and with righteousness
>   from this time forth and for evermore.
>
> (Is. 9:7)

On the return from Babylonian exile, the Temple was rebuilt, but the Davidic dynasty was never restored to the throne.

When the Hasmonean leader, Aristobulus, took upon himself the kingship (104 BCE), and when the Romans dispensed with the monarchy and destroyed the Temple (70 CE), the motif of kingship and Jerusalem, exile and return, had developed an eschatological as well as political side. As one of the pseudepigraphical Psalms of Solomon says:

> Behold, O Lord and raise up unto them their king, the son of David,
> At the time in the which Thou seest, O God, that he may reign over
>   Israel Thy servant.

And that he may purge Jerusalem from nations that trample her down to destruction . . .
And he shall gather together a holy people, whom he shall lead in righteousness
And he shall judge the tribes of the people that has been sanctified by the Lord his God.
And he shall not suffer unrighteousness to lodge any more in their midst,
Nor shall there dwell with them any man that knoweth wickedness
For he shall know them, that they are all sons of their God.

(17:23–25).

The king of David's line has become the Messiah, the Anointed of God. His role in rabbinic literature is various. He will do battle against Israel's enemies and win. He will gather the exiled of Israel back to the land and restore each tribe to its original inheritance (the very inheritance that the original David tried to downplay). The Messiah will also, it seems, act as judge alongside God, and he will establish the rule of justice and peace, and reign over a perfected world till the end of time.

The belief in a messiah who would come and restore Israel and the world in this manner has kept Jews alive in hope at times of the deepest persecution. During the Holocaust, the words of Moses Maimonides' twelfth article of faith became a watchword for those in concentration camps: 'I believe with perfect faith in the coming of the Messiah; and though he tarry, yet will I wait daily for his coming' (Authorised Daily Prayer Book, p. 255). With the establishment of the State of Israel in 1948, Jews once more were in possession of the land of Israel, and the ingathering of the exiles – from the camps of Europe, from North Africa and the Yemen – began. The messianic age seemed to some to have arrived. Yet many religious leaders were against the establishment of the State on the grounds that the Messiah had not yet come and that to settle in Israel before then would be a blasphemy. Such a view is now a minority one, and most people distinguish between the Jewish state and the messianic kingdom which is to be established from on high.

The Lubavitch Hasidim are convinced that the Messiah is here and living at this moment in the person of their leader, Rabbi Shneerson. Their posters announce his imminent arrival as 'King Messiah' but this depends upon the penitence of all Jews living today. Thus messianic belief is today as strong as it has ever been.

Jerusalem is once again in Jewish hands, but the reign of peace and love is not yet at hand. So Jews today express their longing at *Pesach* – no longer in the traditional wish, 'Next Year in Jerusalem', but in the extended 'Next year in Jerusalem rebuilt', demonstrating their hope for a new David to dance once more with the ark to Zion.

THE END OF TIME

The ingathering of the exiles is not necessarily the end. Judaism looks beyond to a point where time itself ends. Beliefs abound that when the Messiah comes there will be cosmic turmoil, a general resurrection, a judgement, and ultimately a time when all live in perfect peace and harmony.

Much of Judaism's eschatology is hazy and contradictory. Its ideas stem from Babylonian influences but these have never been made their own in the way that so much of earlier mythology had been. Perhaps it is that Jews are better at looking back than looking forward, and of seeing life in the context of time rather than beyond it.

Jewish history and hope are ultimately summed up in Zechariah, who looks back to creation as well as forward to the end of time when all humanity is once again unified in its obedience to God:

> And there shall be continuous day, not day and not night, for at evening time there shall be light.
> On that day, the living waters shall flow from Jerusalem, half of them to the eastern sea and half of them to the western sea; it shall continue in summer as in winter.
> And the Lord will become king over all the earth; on that day the Lord will be one and his name one.
>
> (Zech. 14:7–9)

NOTES

1. Heschel, Abraham Joshua (1955) *God in Search of Man*, New York, Scribners, p. 206.
2. Epic recounting the triumph and kingship of the god Marduk over the

first gods of the primordial waters recited at the Babylonian New Year Festival.
3. Babylonian Talmud, *Bava Bathra* 75a, *Leviticus Rabba* 13:3, 22:10.
4. Jewish communities that originate in Germany or Eastern Europe.
5. Translated by Raphael Loewe in *Service of the Synagogue*, London, Routledge & Kegan Paul, 1954.
6. Gaster, Theodore H. (1969) *Myth Legend and Custom in the Old Testament*, New York, Harper & Rowe, p. 32.
7. Graves, Robert and Patai, Raphael (1964) *Hebrew Myths*, London, Cassell, p. 80.
8. Kaufman, Yehezkiel (1972) *The Religion of Israel*, New York, Schocken, p. 295.
9. *Bereshit Rabba*, 38:13.
10. Hooke, S.H. (1963) *Middle Eastern Mythology*, London, Penguin.
11. Albright, W.F. (1957) *From Stone Age to Christianity*, New York, Anchor.
12. Rad, Von (1965) *Old Testament Theology*, Edinburgh, Oliver & Boyde.
13. 'The Passover Haggadali'. For a good translation and commentary see Raphael, Chaim (1972) *A Feast of History*, London, Wiedenfield & Nicholson.
14. See also Isaiah 51:9–11.
15. Compare Marduk and Baal, p. 121.

FURTHER READING

Childs, B.S. (1959) *Myth and Reality in the Old Testament*, London, SCM.
Freedman, H. and Simon, M. (eds) (1977) *The Midrash Rabbah*, London, Soncino.
Gaster, Theodore, H. (1969) *Myth, Legend and Custom in the Old Testament*, New York, Harper & Rowe.
Ginsberg, Louis (1968) *Legends of the Jews*, Philadelphia, Jewish Publication Society.
Graves, Robert and Patai, Raphael (1964) *Hebrew Myths*, London, Cassell.
Hooke, S.H. (1963) *Middle Eastern Mythology*, London, Penguin.
Nicholson, E.W. (1973) *Exodus and Sinai in History and Tradition*, Oxford, Basil Blackwell.
Seters, J. van (1983) *Abraham in History and Tradition*, New Haven, Yale University Press.
Scholem, G. (1971) *The Messianic Idea in Judaism*, New York, Schocken.
Roth, Cecil (ed.) (1972) *Encyclopedia Judaica*, Jerusalem.

6. Sikhism

Beryl Dhanjal

Sikhs would almost certainly deny that there are any Sikh myths, assuming the popular use of the word, to mean something that is untrue. However, the homeland of Sikhism is India so the myths and folk tales of Hinduism, Buddhism, Jainism and Islam are the backdrop to the development of the religion. There are some (mostly Victorian) collections of folk tales and myths of the Panjab but no modern studies.

The anthropologist, Malinowski (1963: 261),[1] considered myth to be a social charter, an instrument manipulated by the holders of power, privilege and property. In this sense, Sikhism does have myths which explain the existing social order in historical terms and justify it by providing a moral basis, presenting it as a system based on right. Such stories tell of the first performance of acts which are now repeated as ritual, such as the initiation ceremony, and they show how the Gurū Granth Sāhib was installed, and the ritual behaviour which is enjoined towards it. They offer the effective precedent of a glorified past for repetitive actions in the present.

Myths that confirm the dominant position of a particular group are usually the most significant of all. Sikh writings could be looked at in this light, especially with regard to the position of the *Khālsā*, and the development of historiography by the Singh Sabha and the Akālīs. The picture is further coloured by the activities of the British and the process described by Hobsbawm[2] as the 'invention of tradition' and the effect that this had on views of history. The emphasis given to various elements in the story shows contests for power among groups, and also shows the evolution of the community over time. There has, unfortunately, been little written about these matters.

This approach to myth would explain the reason for the loss in popularity of many of the ancient stories, the folk tales and myths of Panjab. They were sung by bards who were employed at the courts of local grandees to sing of heroes and warlike feats of valour. The bards would include the genealogy of the family they were serving and accounts of its feats, showing them in a suitably heroic light and as socially powerful.

There were priestly bards who sang sacred legends of Hinduism on festive occasions, and there were wandering minstrels who had attached themselves to a holy man and who collected alms in his name as they went about, singing of his prowess and, more importantly, of his powers. There were people of particular *jatī*s (castes) who had their own heroes to sing about. In the case of the lower castes, these tales are now being translated into separate religious identites (*Balmik*s, *Ravi Dāsi*s etc.). Balmik is the local way of saying Valmiki, the poet who wrote a version of the *Ramāyāna*, and he is revered as God by some devotees. Rav Das has poems included in the Gurū Granth Sāhib. His devotees have a quasi-Sikh identity.

The songs of the common people were regarded with contempt by the literati as early as the Victorian era (Temple 1884).[3] Times were changing, and as the old order changed so did the myths. Modern, progressive, western-educated, scientifically minded people no longer wanted to hear about mythical heroes and battles with demons.

Many of these myths are referred to, and quoted, in Sikh sources as they are part of a common Panjabi heritage which cut across religious affiliations. They reflect the values and traditions of pre-modern, undivided Panjab. The fact that they are less known now reflects a situation of which it has been remarked that there are no Panjabis any more, only Hindus, Muslims, and Sikhs (Nayar 1984: Preface).[4]

Yet the heart of the pre-modern Panjabi material has survived. The romances, the tales of *Sassi* and *Punnu*, *Sohni* and *Mahinval*, and above all the tale of *Hir* and *Ranjha*, remain popular. They were used as metaphors, with the heroine (the soul) suffering in separation from her Lord. Because this was so, these tales provided a rich source of imagery, for Panjabi poets are appreciated by all Panjabis regardless of religious affiliation.

The other interesting development that has preserved these tales is the popularity of the *qissa*, which is a narrative poem and which has universal acceptance, significantly due to the tale having been secularised. These important parts of the common Panjabi culture are therefore still accessible to Sikhs.

Elsewhere, where values have remained unaltered but times have changed, legends and themes have been re-worked. Soldier-saints are an adaptable topic and an ancient theme. The duty of a soldier to act in accordance with his *dharma* is an ancient theme in Hinduism, and in Islam military service is expected from the able-bodied. To take one small, individual example, Ghazi Salar was supposed to have been a nephew of Mahmud of Ghazna. He was killed fighting for the cause in 1033, at the age of nineteen, on his wedding night. Apart from a Sikh preoccupation with the notion of soldier-saints, Ghazi Salar reappeared as 'the Patron Saint of the inhabitants of the British cantonments of Northern India' (Temple: 1884).

Although 'myth' had been used in a technical sense by scholars, such techniques were not applied to Sikhism until recently. The pioneering efforts of W.H. McLeod (1968, 1980) to apply an understanding of myth as a 'construct of human imagination, developing out of an actual situation or seeking to give meaning to that situation', to the *janam sākhī*s have proved controversial. Some Sikhs have been unable to understand and accept the purpose of such a study. The fundamental questions being dealt with by McLeod concern the functional utility of his sources and not questions of historical truth. From the point of view of some Sikhs, the sources represent absolute historical truth, and they feel that there is no room to question either the purposes of writers or the functions of their writings. So this is a sensitive area. Yet historical writings relate to the age they were written in, and can be understood only in the context of their times.

The recycling of myth is not a tidy process – traditional myths do not die immediately and nor does anything change overnight. Traditions overlap each other. Rival groups produce rival history. In the example of the *janam sākhī*s, the various accounts can be related to sectarian groups.

From the time of Guru Nanak there were musicians associated with Gurūs. There are three verses associated with Guru Nanak's companion, Mardana, in the Gurū Granth Sāhib. Subsequently, when the Sikh Gurūs developed as earthly princes, there were resident bards at court. The Gurū Granth Sāhib contains the *Vār* of Satta and Balwand and the writings of *bhaṭṭ*s (a caste of bards and genealogists). Surjit Hans (1988: 178) has observed that the writings of Satta and Balwand and those of Bhai Gurdas may be seen as reflecting 'the great tradition of the reflective few', as against the *janam sākhīs*, representing the 'little tradition of the unreflective many'. The distinction enabled Hans to analyse the differing functions and to differentiate between what he calls the 'orthodox' and 'unorthodox' *janam sākhīs*. The writers sing of the spiritual paramountcy of Guru Nanak. These writings emphasise the uniqueness of Guru Nanak and his oneness with his successors. The inclusion of the writings in the Gurū Granth Sāhib gives them a divine sanction.

The importance of court poets, the bards and genealogists is evident from the period of Guru Govind Singh, for the works in the *Dasam Granth* are either by the Gurū or by his court poets. The bards were to tell and retell the legends of heroes and warriors and the genealogy and valour of the family. The *Dasam Granth* bears evidence of their concerns. The traditional tales of warriors and battles, the demon-slaying goddess, and Kṛṣṇa, are the backdrop to the history of the *Bedīs* (the ancestors of Guru Nanak) and *Sodhīs* (ancestors of Govind Singh) and the mission of Guru Nanak. These are the stage setting against which the *Bachitar Nāṭak* – the wondrous, miraculous drama which was Govind Singh – is played out.

The *janam sākhīs*

Many pre-modern values, concerns, beliefs, and styles were used in the writings called the *janam sākhīs*. All the sources are part of the common matter, the traditions of the Panjab. The traditions included elements of Hindu myths and legends, the epics and *purāṇas*, *Nāth Jogi* and Ṣūfī tales, and even the Buddhist *jātakas*. Some tales also emerge from the poems and teachings of the Gurū.

The earliest writings about the Gurūs are the *Vārs* of Bhai Gurdas, which differ from *janam sākhīs* in that Gurdas wrote poetry and the *janam sākhīs* are prose. *Vār I* offers only a few brief incidents in the life of Guru Nanak. Gurdas was a theologian and is known as the 'key' to the Gurū Granth Sāhib. Bhai Gurdas equates the Gurū with God, and since Guru Nanak appointed a successor, the Sikh became the Gurū and the Gurū the Sikh. As Hans has pointed out, Bhai Gurdas called the *saṅgat* the abode of God. Carrying water for it therefore becomes a valued task. Many Sikh ideas and institutions were in place from the beginning.

Bhai Gurdas used strong language to condemn opponents to the successors of Guru Nanak. Hans (1988: 185) has observed that his preoccupation with them may be a measure of the gravity of the situation. The *janam sākhīs* give further evidence of their ideas.

The charismatic figure of the first Gurū clearly fascinated people. Soon after Nanak died, tales began to be told about him and these were eventually collected together. In South Asia it is common for there to be such collections of tales – hagiographies – about holy men.

The *janam sākhīs* have been classified into various traditions and described by McLeod (1968, 1980). The most popular account is the *Bala* tradition, reputed to have been the work of one Bala Sandhu, who accompanied Guru Nanak on his travels. The account is very confusing and at times incoherent. It begins with Guru Angad asking about Guru Nanak's horoscope but turns into a lengthy account of the life and travels of the Gurū. The *Bala janam sākhī* is associated with a heretical group called the Hindalis, followers of a contemporary of Guru Hargovind.

A better organised *janam sākhī* is a work associated with Sodhi Miharban, who was the son of a rival claimant to the Guruship. His *sākhīs* are more learned and the stories are used as vehicles for exegesis. Miharban remained faithful to the spiritual message of Guru Nanak. The tradition has been added to throughout the years, for the text was produced over several generations. The original may have been written by Miharban but later additions show the concerns of the non-*khālsā saṅgat*s, following the spiritual teachings of Nanak during the eighteenth century.

Another tradition is known as the *Gyān Ratnāvalī*. According to Hans (1988: 207), this tradition is associated with Udāsīs (a sect associated with one of Guru Nanak's sons, Sri Cand), and is aimed at the legitimation of Sikh rule, claiming recognition for Udāsīs. It is clear then, that *janam sākhīs* were produced by groups with conflicting interests.

Janam sākhīs are presented in a roughly chronological sequence, starting with the birth (accompanied by the usual miraculous signs), childhood, and the life and travels of the Gurū. Some tales may have a basis of historical truth. Some are miracle stories. Some tales are attached to poems, teachings, or places. In most stories, the Gurū and Mardana are travelling, encounter a third party, have a discussion or argument which is won by the Gurū, and the defeated person falls at his feet and opens a *dharamsālā* (a place of worship). The most sophisticated traditions use the incidents as settings for quotations from *gurbāṇī* and offer further teaching.

PURPOSE

Yet the purpose of the *janam sākhī*s is not only to teach. The purpose is soteriological. Nanak insisted that the way forward was to hear the *śabad* (word) *Nām* uttered by the Gurū (God), but the words '*śabad*' and 'Gurū' rapidly acquired new meanings. McLeod (1980: 241) observed that

> the *guru* is no longer the inner voice of God, but the personal manifestation of that voice in Baba Nanak. From this, it follows that the divine Word must be identified with the actual utterances of Nanak, and so the term *śabad* (shabad) is almost exclusively used as a synonym for a *pada* or 'hymn' of Nanak.

The 'little tradition' *sākhī*s provide a way that ordinary people could have *darśan* (audience) with Guru Nanak even after he had died. By reading the *janam sākhī*s people could still have a meeting (in a sense) with the founder and take advantage of the route to liberation offered by him.

The *janam sākhī*s have always been popular. The fact that this is so demonstrates the enduring strength of their message. The stories are simple and told in such a lively, jolly way that they are instantly memorable! They are stories for telling and retelling aloud. The words linger in one's head.

They are not a scripture as such, though many devout people view the *janam sākhī*s as sources of information on the life of the Gurū – as biographies. In fact, the stories usually date from about the seventeenth and early eighteenth centuries. The world they describe is the Panjab of that time. They are a valuable resource because they are pre-*khālsā* writings, dating from a period which is looked at with post-*khālsā* assumptions. There is much information that can be gleaned. They tell us about the people who followed, and Guru Nanak's heritage. McLeod (1980: 245) has written of the function of the *janam sākhīs*, and of how they maintained communal cohesion in the pre-*khālsā* period. They became less important as the eighteenth century 'created new needs which they were ill suited to serve'. During the Singh Sabha reform movement of the late nineteenth century, they recovered some of their popularity. As McLeod observed: 'New needs demand new ideals and new vehicles for those ideals'.

In the eighteenth century there was turmoil in the Panjab. The situation caused a radical change in Sikh identity. After 1708, there was no longer a living Sikh Gurū, and the Moghul empire, which had been comparatively peaceful, had dwindled in power. There were many invasions from Afghanistan, and these came to be seen in the terms of conflict between Muslims and Sikhs. There had also been, as has often been observed, the recruitment of a substantial number of *jaṭ*s into the Sikh *panth*. *Jaṭ*s are a social group found in northern India. They are often described as a caste, but are actually more tribal in structure. There were new needs, and McLeod (1980: 247; 1989a: 43) has described how the needs were met by recourse to distinctively *jaṭ* patterns, and to institutions which distinguished the Sikh from the Muslim. From these elements evolved the *rahit*, the code of discipline. There also evolved a distinctive style of myth-history, a way of retelling the past to provide legitimacy for present action.

The *Gur Śobhā* and *Gurbilās Dasvīn Patśāhī*

As the *panth* evolved during the eighteenth century, so did the style of writing. In Malinowski's terms, there were new holders of power, and the social charter needed renewal. This period was to be viewed with hindsight as a heroic period. It was a period when power was vested in Sikh warlords and their bands, and for them, it was no longer a *janam sākhī* world.

The new approach involved producing works about the splendour of the Gurūs. Courage and prowess in battle were highlighted. (Naturally, this centred upon Gurus Hargovind and Govind Singh, who were warriors.) This was not a sudden departure, for inspiration came from the *Dasam Granth*, from *Bachitar Nāṭak*, and the *Śastar Nām Mālā* (the Inventory of Weapons), and all the works about mythical battles which were the culture of the court.

Guru Govind Singh himself had written, or perhaps had inspired others to write, of his mission and the battles he had fought, his heroism and his destiny. As was the case with *janam sākhīs*, the new writings of the eighteenth century, the *Gur Bilās* tradition (Splendour of the Gurūs), tell more about the period in which they were written than they tell about the Gurūs they describe.

Surjit Hans (1988) has described some of these writings. The earliest of these works is called *Gur Śobhā* (Radiance of the Gurū), and one possible date suggested for it is 1711, just three years after the death of Guru Govind Singh. Others date it around 1745. Either date places it in the immediate post-Gurū era.

The purpose of *Gur Śobhā* is redemption through reading *Gur Śobhā* and through participation in the *Khālsā*. It was traditional to specify the purpose of a piece of writing, and with most early writing, the avowed purpose is liberation. *Gur Śobhā* is a denunciation of *masaṅds*, local organisers who had been appointed by the Gurūs but who were prone to abandoning the Gurūs' cause and diverting resources to their own purposes. By this stage, Sikh theology had reached the point of identifying the Gurū as God himself. It is difficult to think of a firmer basis for a charter for action.

The strongest image in the *Gur Śobhā* is that of the Gurū in the field of battle, an echo of the *Bachitar Nāṭak*. The battle scenes described both in writings of the *Dasam Granth* and writings of this period are horrific. There is carnage – appalling bloodshed – on battlefields inhabited by supernatural forces.

> Vultures croak, foul spirits belch.
> There Kali and other dreadful spectres shriek and roar.
> Here heroes and ghosts stagger about
> There carrion-eating demon spirits laugh . . .
> They care for nothing
> But only shout Kill, Kill! . . .
>
> One has a limb cut off,
> Another, his long hair pulled out by the roots.
> Another has his flesh in shreds,
> While another falls, hacked to pieces . . .
>
> (*Bachitar Nāṭak*)

Though such images may be upsetting today, there was clearly an appeal to warriors in reading matter of this kind: 'When the poet sings of warfare the warriors are filled with joy'.

In *Gur Śobhā*, the *Khālsā* is given prime importance theologically, thus entering its claim for social recognition. The *Khālsā* is spiritual enlightenment. He who remembers God joins the *Khālsā*. Deceitful, self-willed, deluded individuals do not join the *Khālsā*, so the *Khālsā* is redemption. The *Khālsā* is a body of warriors and also the body of the Gurū. In *Gur Śobhā* the *Gurū-Khālsā* doctrine was made explicit by the Gurū:

> The Khalsa is my physical form;
> I am one with the Khalsa.
> To all eternity I shall be manifest in the Khalsa.
> They whose hearts are purged of falsehood shall be known as the true Khalsa;
> And the Khalsa, freed from error and illusion will be my true Guru.
>
> (Sainapati, *Gur Śobhā*: 8)

As Gurūs had been indistinguishable from each other, so the position was extended to the *Khālsā*. Later in history a tradition was to develop that after Guru Govind Singh had initiated the first five beloved ones at Anandpur in 1699, he had had them initiate him in return. The Gurū became the disciple and the disciple the Gurū, as indeed, Bhai Gurdas had said of the appointment of Guru Angad by Guru Nanak. By having himself initiated by the *Khālsā*, the *Khālsā* was made the legitimate source of authority. Five members of the *Khālsā* could henceforth initiate others. And that ritual is re-enacted to this day.

Hans (1988) has said that *Gur Śobhā* was a *de facto* manifesto for Sikh rule in the eighteenth century. It showed Govind Singh as the 'paragon of fighting spirit', as a ruler and it invested the *Khālsā* with Guruship, giving it the legacy of independent rule. *Gur Śobhā* was also the first of a line, for the tradition of such works continued through into the nineteenth century.

There are several other works of this genre. One dating from the end of the heroic period, 1797, is Sukha Singh's *Gurbilās Dasvīn Patśāhī*. Hans (1988) says that it is associated with the Udāsīs, the group associated with Guru Nanak's son, Sri Cand. Udāsīs can still be found in Panjab. Perhaps their importance has been overlooked. Their *akharas*, or religious centres, often have images of Sri Cand

and their own *mahaṅts*, or chief officiants, and they worship the deities of Panjabi Hinduism. The Udāsīs were often in charge of shrines until the 1920s, when the Akālīs challenged their position. But Udāsīs are said to have fought for Guru Govind Singh. In putting forth the claims of the Udāsīs, Sukha Singh goes into explicit detail concerning the historical implications of Guru Nanak's vision. He claimed that the *kalyug* (the evil age we live in, the last of the four ages of Hindu mythology) had disrupted caste and that Muslim dynasties were polluting the world. This was written at a time when anti-Muslim *rahit nāmā*s were produced. While Nanak is often presented in *janam sākhī*s as having a mission of reconciliation, and writings from the time of Ranjit Singh needed to draw different religious groups together, during the invasions of the eighteenth century there was little doubt about who was seen as the enemy.

According to *Gurbilās Dasvīn Patśāhī*, there was no longer a Hindu *dharam* and the universe, right down to mythical bull which supports the earth, was shaken. There were no *kśatriya*s, no warriors any more, so the Sikhs became the *kśatriya*. Guru Govind Singh, living in the *Khālsā*, assumed the role. The Sikh Gurūs were *Panjabi Khatri*s (a mercantile caste but one tracing mythical origins back to the *kśatriya*). A process of caste mobility similar to that described by Srinivas (1980) as sanskritisation seems to have been operating. Myth-history is a necessary component, providing the socially mobile with historic legitimation for their claims.

A further element in the eighteenth-century Panjab which was important in the development of *Khālsā* ideas was the influence of *śaktism*. Guru Hargovind and his successors had spent some time in the Śivalik hills where *śakti* beliefs were powerful, and their influence can be detected in some writings. Sukha Singh therefore claims that the *Khālsā* was born out of God, the sword, and Devi the goddess. The climax of the divinity of the *Khālsā* was reached when Guru Govind Singh asked for *amrit* (immortality) at the hands of the *Khālsā*. The Gurū became included within the *Khālsā*.

Gurbilās continued to be produced during the nineteenth century. Some of these writings give good indications of Sikh practice and beliefs of the times. During the reign of Maharaja Ranjit Singh, needs changed again, and writings reflect the altered state. Writings present a somewhat Hinduised portrayal of the Gurū, and show him in conversation with *Qazī*s, concluding that Sikhism and Islam are not very different from each other. This is a period when the authority of the Gurū Granth Sāhib is more pronounced than the notion of authority being vested in the *Khālsā*. These writings reflect a time when there was a need for Ranjit Singh to create stability and rule.

There are immense problems in the interpretation of Panjabi and Sikh history – *khālsā* and non-*khālsā* sources. *Khālsā* ideals, historiography and mythology are strongly established. It is probably impossible to estimate the relative strength of the *Khālsā* or that of other non-*khālsā* groups at most periods of history. Even now, there are discussions as to who is a Sikh and who is not, and the positions of various groups. Certainly, not everyone joined the *Khālsā*. There always were peaceful groups, *Sahajdhāri*s (people in bliss from meditating on the Name), concentrating on the path of the Name, though the term *sahajdhāri* has usually been used to mean non-members of the *Khālsā*, people who were 'slow to adopt' the Singh identity. Being initiated as a Singh has come to be considered a superior position by many. The British used Singh and Sikh interchangeably. Often, this is still done. McLeod (1989a, 1989b), Fox (1985) and many others have written at length about the development of Sikh identity.

During the eighteenth century a varied collection of writings was being produced – *Rahit nāmā*s, *janam sākhī*s and the *gurbilās* writings. The variety of writings shows that there were widely differing groups and opinions abroad. Each writer appeals to the past, and to religious sanction, to validate their present and future.

The variety of writings is evidence of the multiplicity of groups. Alongside these more militant writings, the peaceful *janam sākhī* world had not faded away. The B40 *janam sākhī* dates from 1733, making it contemporary with *Gur Śobhā*. As McLeod (1980: 45) has pointed out, the B40 *janam sākhī* offers evidence of a *Nanak-paṅthi* group living somewhere around Gujrat or Gujranwala in 1733. There is no hint of *Khālsā* awareness or of military activity. Indeed, there is no hint of the *Khālsā* code since one episode involves an impoverished Sikh cutting off his hair to pay for food for the Gurū.

Other interest groups: Gurūs' families and Brahmans

There are writings by many interest groups. Each evoked the past to justify the future. One example is the *Mahima Prakaś* of Sarup Das Bhalla, a descendant of Guru Amar Das, who felt that descendants of the Gurūs should be honoured and that the families had sanctity of some kind for which they should be recognised.

Another displaced group who wrote were the Chibber family, brahmans and servants of the Gurūs. Such people, on the margins of Sikhism, offer startling insights into the development of Sikh institutions and ideas. Eighteenth-century writings are very varied, and this is important, because they represent the efforts of an assortment of groups to lay claim to the heritage of the Gurūs, to use the religion, myth and history as the basis of their own claims.

Writings developed to cover problem areas

Bachitar Nāṭak discourses on the histories of the *Bedi*s and *Sodhi*s, to answer criticism about the Guruship becoming a family matter, but by the eighteenth century a story is commonly told that Bibi Bhani (the mother of Guru Arjan) asked for the *gaddī* (throne) to remain in the family and that persecution and trouble were a consequence. The theory was also developed that after the Gurū Granth Sāhib was compiled and sealed, Gurūs no longer wrote *gurbāṇī*.

Nineteenth-century *khālsā* historiography

By the mid-nineteenth century, further development was evident. In 1841, Rattan Singh Bhangu completed his *Prācin Panth Prakāś*, a history of the *Khālsā*, concentrating on battles and heroism, and the *Khālsā* and its destiny. Rattan Singh's own grandfather was one of the heroes.

It was a theme which was to recur. Works by Gian Singh, published between 1891 and 1919, give a very lengthy and popular history of the *Khālsā*. These works begin with an account of Guru Nanak and his successors, but in the major part of the work, the writing focuses on forts, defenders, battles and enemies. The names of some of the enemies are still not forgotten, and are mentioned as examples of evil to be fought against, should similar people ever arise again – in the same way as the name of Hitler is mentioned in Europe. The writings record massacres, horrible atrocities, persecutions and tortures. There are many stories of the bravery and sacrifices of individual heroes and martyrs. One of the most popular martyrs is Baba Dip Singh, and pictures of him fighting, holding his decapitated head in one hand and spouting blood, are very popular, as is the shrine to him in Amritsar. Legend has it that he continued to fight the enemy, clutching his decapitated head in his hand. The daily *Ardās* briefly sums up:

> Those loyal members of the Khalsa who gave their heads for their faith; who were hacked limb from limb, scalped, broken on the wheel, sawn asunder, who sacrificed their lives . . . .

The very words of *Ardās* are drawn from eighteenth-century sources, showing how powerful the imagery and writing of the era were and what a spell they cast.

The works of Rattan Singh and Gian Singh are taken very seriously and are much consulted, and they add a particular flavour to subsequent re-workings of Sikh history. They have to be taken into account to understand modern beliefs and views, for it was while they were being written that the modern doctrines, *rahit*, identity, orthodoxy, crystallised. They have been used extensively in writing histories, sometimes without much attention being paid to their context and times. They are the sources and models of *khālsā* myth and history.

Family histories

Rattan Singh Bhangu was not the only writer with family connections; others had reasons to create individual family mythical histories. Jassa Singh Ahluwalia's descendants, who became the rulers of the state of Kapurthala, commissioned works on family history. One of them, the *Jassa Singh Binod*, dates from about 1831. It begins with an evocation of Gaṇeśa and Kṛṣṇa, traces the genealogy of the Ahluwalias from Brahmā, invokes the Royal house of Jaisalmer as a connection, names the Muslim kings of Hindustan and gives a brief history of the Gurūs. This takes up about one sixth of the manuscript. The remainder is devoted to the eighteenth-century politics of Panjab, with special reference to Jassa Singh Ahluwalia. The emphasis is on seeking to show the Ahluwalia family with an elevated lineage. The work was written during the reign of Ranjit Singh when the family had lost power. They were showing their ancestor as a major leader, and their family as overlords to the family of Ranjit Singh who was now all-powerful.

There are many works which eulogise Maharaja Ranjit Singh who ruled Panjab from 1799 to 1839. There are also historical sources such as the state archives of the various Sikh rulers.

Western interest

At the end of the eighteenth century western scholars began to take an interest in the Sikhs, their customs, beliefs and history. Some people believe that western scholarly interest led to the creation of neo-Sikhism – 'Sikhism' or even 'Singhism' in its modern form. Certainly, western writings feed back into Sikhism and affect it. British activity in Panjab led to change: Fox (1985) has considered the effect of the introduction of a capitalist economy and the importance of recruitment, and of British military recruitment policies and how these affected Sikhism.

The British came to India, however, with myths of their own, the intellectual baggage which they took with them. Their explanations of the social order, and of their own position within it changed several times during the period of British contact with India, but by the time the British were ruling Panjab, the empire was at its zenith and the background to the imperial myth was the theory of biological determinism – the idea that races have inbred qualities. Crudely, it might be called racism. White, western society was seen as most 'evolved', and other races as less so. Racialism is the term given to acting upon racist belief.

The Panjab School of Administration was paternalistic. The District Officer rode about dispensing justice and being the father and mother of all. The Army Recruiting Officer also rode about, with a firm idea in his mind, which was enunciated in his 'Handbook', as to precisely which type of Sikh he wanted to recruit. The recruiting manuals tabulate the districts of Panjab, commenting on their 'relative value' as recruiting grounds. The British saw the recruits as having inbred qualities, though in the case of the Sikhs, religion was also held to have an effect.

Cunningham's *History of the Sikhs* (1848) was the standard work on Sikhism for a hundred years. It is still reprinted and sold, as are the army recruitment 'Handbooks'. Cunningham wrote about the Gurūs and the eighteenth century, describing Sikh society, which he called theocratic confederate feudalism. He covered the period of Ranjit Singh and his successors down to the Anglo–Sikh war. He was criticised for being an apologist for the Sikhs, writing more or less from a Sikh point of view, and for taking their side in the matter of the war with the British. But he was also criticised for his sympathy for, and appreciation of, their religion.

Cunningham interpreted Sikhism as the birth of a nation. This nation had been created by a historical process in which race and religion were dominant factors: 'The characteristics of race and religion are everywhere of greater importance than the accidents of position or the achievements of contemporary genius'. For Cunningham, the significant factors were racial – the *jaṭs* (often referred to as a caste but closer to being tribal in social structure) were, according to Cunningham and many of his contemporaries, 'the finest rural population in India'. He made the somewhat startling claim that Sikhism altered people physically. The effect of Sikhism was, according to Cunningham, to make Sikh *jaṭs* substantially different from Hindu and Muslims *jaṭs*. It distinguished them from 'all other peoples of India'.

For the British, race and religion were important factors to bear in mind in ruling Panjab. Blood, they believed, would out. As Europeans could 'go native' and ruin themselves, so Sikhs could 'go soft' by reverting to Hinduism. This curious British notion was expressed most fully by authorities like Lieutenant General Sir George MacMunn, KCB, KCSI in his book, *The Armies of India* (1911; repr. 1980, New Delhi, Gian). Most races of India, it was said, lacked martial aptitude and physical courage. The races classed as martial showed such qualities and were therefore suitable recruits for the Army. It therefore seems rather extraordinary that the same people could also be considered fine cultivating races and favoured by the Punjab Alienation of Land Act 1900.

There was another curious British myth visited upon India: that religion was strengthened by suffering and persecution. Macnicol (1934: 213)[5] says that Sikhism would have been re-absorbed into Hinduism had 'it not been that the spirit of religion was reinforced by the passion which persecution aroused'. Somewhat confusingly, he also claimed that the peaceful days of British rule, with the sword being replaced by the ploughshare, were having a similar effect to persecution, for 'nationalism and political ambition' were 'arousing the Sikh spirit from its stagnation and causing them to reaffirm their separation from Hinduism'.

The British were concerned with enumerating everything possible in their empire. This passion was also applied to religion in India. Were there more Sikhs or fewer Sikhs? The question might have been more sensibly posed had they ever defined what was meant by 'Sikh'. The Census of 1881 (Vol. 1: 140)[6] says that, 'In times of war converts to Sikhism are much more numerous than in times of peace'. This led to reformers teaching people to register as Sikhs. Because the government offered favours to the more numerous groups, numbers became a preoccupation which has never vanished.

The obsession with numbers and the idea that Sikhism is being absorbed has been a powerful and moving myth. Khushwant Singh, a moderate writer, concludes his *History of the Sikhs* (1966) with the call for a separate Sikh state. He also believes that persecution strengthens religion: 'no people can become a strong and great nation without learning to shed blood'.

English translation of the Gurū Granth Sāhib

The British were interested in the Gurū Granth Sāhib and arranged for a scholar, Dr Ernest Trumpp, to undertake a translation. However, the pieces he translated were inaccurate and the work was not a success. Max Arthur Macauliffe undertook a new translation, designed to counteract Trumpp's work. Macauliffe's six-volume *The Sikh Religion* (1909) was well received. Macauliffe's work is not just a translation of the Gurū Granth Sāhib. It also includes matter from the *janam sākhīs* and other sources. There are lives of all the Gurūs and selections from their writings, and in the final volume there are some lives and poems by the other writers included in the Gurū Granth Sāhib.

Macauliffe offered a neo-Sikh, reformist Singh Sabha style of Sikhism. The Singh Sabha was founded in the 1870s. Initially, it had problems because one section was made up of the traditional élite, members of the Gurūs' families and aristocrats from Amritsar who accepted the old mythology. This contrasted with a second Singh Sabha group who were Lahore businessmen and who differed in their approach. They were reformers who felt that Sikhism was on the verge of being swallowed up by Hinduism. With missionary zeal they set about propagating institutions, symbols and their own historiography – their own version of tradition and orthodoxy. Previously there had been other schools of interpretation but the Singh Sabha was to become orthodoxy.

Macauliffe's writings have been enormously influential. Sikhism presented as a separate race and religion led to scholarship designed to support and give substance to the new orthodoxy. Macauliffe hated *gyanis* (learned people) who could give different interpretations of almost every line of the sacred verse. His work was to be

> an exact presentation of the teaching of the Sikh Gurus and orthodox writers . . . and by no means a portrayal of the debased superstitions and heterodox social customs of Sikhs who have been led astray from their faith by external influences.
>
> (Macauliffe 1909, Vol. I: xvi)

One might wonder why an Englishman of that era should be so concerned, but Macauliffe's stated view was that Sikh orthodoxy was closely in tune with their loyalty to the crown. He observed that, 'In the present day an injunction is added at the time of baptism to be loyal to the British Government, which the neophytes solemnly promise' (Macauliffe 1909, Vol. V: 96). The English were even viewed as part of the mission. Macauliffe mentions prophecies concerning the British made by Guru Govind Singh, that the British and *Khālsā* united armies would be powerful, obtain prosperity, and that there would be wealth, happiness, learning and religion in every house. It is prophecies such as these, 'combined with monotheism, the absence of superstition, and restraint in the matter of food which have made the Sikhs among the bravest, the most loyal and devoted subjects of the British crown'.

Macauliffe never entertained any doubts. He was furious at the thought of a movement to declare the Sikhs Hindus and was beside himself when he met some descendants of the Gurūs who

> told me they were Hindus. . . . Whether the object of their tutors . . . was or was not to make them disloyal, such youths are ignorant of the Sikh religion . . .

It is astonishing to think that an Englishman took it upon himself to tell the Gurūs' descendants what to believe and how to interpret their own religion, but looked at in the light of the need to create the necessary social charter, Singh Sabha scholarship was confident and assertive. The reformers entertained no doubts.

Reform, history and the new élite

The processes which have taken place from the beginning of the story are complex and, as yet, not well understood. From a fairly simple chronological account, which has been the usual model for writings on Sikhism, it is now beginning to be appreciated that there are a wealth of complex reasons behind each situation and development. The sources described have often been regarded as true accounts of what happened in the past, rather than as evidence of what was happening at the time they were written.

Nineteenth-century Panjabi society was pluralistic. The élite had a pluralistic social vision – not a single Sikh identity. There were locality, caste, family, and there were holy men, living and dead, who were revered. There were numerous sects. Some of the sects are nowadays seen as reforming movements and others are seen as being beyond the pale. While the old views prevailed and the old élite ruled, religion was not of great importance in defining people in their own terms. It was a category that the British used.

Colonialism created a new élite. The traditional and the new élite had very different social visions. The new élite cut across the traditional areas in which people had operated: kin, neighbourhood and caste. Everything that had held society together changed: the economic basis of society, the opening of new lands, irrigation, power, employment, roads and railways, medicine, education, science, famine relief, flood control, notions on public morality and values. Perhaps the most important factor to create change in the modern age is communication. With modern transport people could move about and address meetings. As time passed, posts and telegraphs arrived. The written word was most important. The printing press was an essential part of the revolution. The Gurū Granth Sāhib was made available: it was printed. Not everyone could have a copy, but many could have a *guṭkā*, a little prayer book, or a *nit nem*, a daily rule, a book of daily readings.

There is not a simple explanation of what did happen during the British period. Fox (1985) has written of changes in the economy and how a section of the trading castes were initially attracted to the Arya Samaj, but when Aryas attacked Sikh traditions, the people who subscribed to those traditions left. For Fox, the army and recruitment were a major influence in the development of the Singh identity. The British created Sikh regiments and soldiers followed the rules of prescribed orthodoxy. This identity was taken up by the discontented members of the trading castes. McLeod (1989b: 77) disagrees with Fox, saying that there were other traditions within Sikhism, but he feels that the *Khālsā* was the strongest. The *Khālsā* certainly became more coherent during the reform period.

To the reformers, the many ways of being Sikh, the fellow travellers on one path, were not acceptable if the ideal was a demarcated religious community. There was a struggle as the ideal was put in place. The new institutions which replaced the old élite were western – committees ruled, and they still do. The model and concerns were modern and somewhat western. The Singh Sabha reformers were prolific writers. They were intent on creating the casteless, egalitarian society which they felt was intended by the Gurūs. To this end, they used missionary activity, preaching, education, social reform and literature.

There was scholarly writing, and in view of the topics that had been central to Sikh writings of the past, the new scholarship naturally centred on religion and history. Whereas in the earliest period, authors like Bhai Gurdas began their writings by mentioning the history of the known world, giving an inventory of Hinduism and Islam in order to place Guru Nanak on the pinnacle of world religious development, later writers began by invoking deities. Since the final reform phase, books have started confidently, 'Guru Nanak was born in 1469', and, having claimed this authority, have proceeded through the 'history' chronologically. In doing so, they stake a claim to legitimacy and, having done so, introduce their own cause.

Scholarship

It would be wrong to suggest that modern writings are mere propaganda. There are many scholarly works too. In the area of scriptural commentary, the first major work is known as the *Faridkot Tika* ('Faridkot commentary') because it was commissioned and published by the Maharaja of Faridkot. Principal Teja Singh, Bhai Vir Singh and Sahib Singh have also produced works of distinction, those of the last two being published in the 1960s. Some of the works produced are invaluable and are in use today. No one would contemplate serious study of Sikhism without a copy of the *Guruśabad Ratanākar Mahān Koś* (the 'Great Dictionary') (1931) by Kahan Singh of Nabha. It is an enormous encyclopaedia of literature, religion, and seemingly just about everything one might ever want to know about Sikhs and Sikhism. Unfortunately, it is not translated. Another of his books stands out. It is called *Ham Hindū Nahīṅ* ('We are not Hindus') (1898). According to Kahan Singh, Sikhism was distinct from Hinduism. In saying this, he brought almost four centuries of tradition to an end, for the Sikhs had shown little interest in distinguishing themselves from Hindus before. This first charter of Sikh separatism was published in Hindi. But the movement was not confined to intellectuals. Hundreds of newspapers and journals, pamphlets and leaflets were produced. Christian missionaries began to produce Panjabi tracts, often retelling Bible stories. These were popular, especially stories like that of Ruth and Naomi, which have values with a wide appeal.

The Khalsa Tract Society was founded and the first Panjabi novel, '*Sundarī*', was produced in 1898. Each chapter was published as a tract, in serial form, so there is a great cliffhanger at the end of every chapter. It is the stirring tale of a heroic Sikh girl in the 1740s, when the *Khālsā* faced persecution and danger. The heroine faces threats of a fate worse than death and conversion to Islam in most chapters. This novel was one of a trilogy. Thus myth-history was re-worked into a newly introduced western literary form – the novel. The author was Bhai Vir Singh who, apart from writing scriptural comment, was a novelist, poet and genuine renaissance man. Significantly, the Panjabi language was the chosen vehicle. This was also Singh Sabha policy. Hitherto, Panjabi was not much used for literature except by some Muslims, the outstanding example being Varis Shah's *Hir* (1766). Panjabi was usually regarded as a crude, rustic vernacular.

As time passed, political agitation began which was to remove the old élite. There were court cases which hinged on the point of whether Sikhs were Hindus or not. The Sikh Gurdwaras Act 1925 was the first to define a Sikh in legal terms and specify which shrines in Panjab belonged to the Sikhs. The heritage from the struggles was that Sikhism became politicised, the largest and longest lived of Sikh political parties being the *Akālī Dāl* (Army of Immortals). *Akālī* was the name chosen by those fighting to gain control of shrines during the early years of this century, in conscious imitation of the eighteenth-century warriors.

This century has not been peaceful for Panjab. In 1947 there was much suffering when India and Pakistan were created. There have been many subsequent problems. There have been many grievances, real and imagined, afflicting the Sikhs. The genuine problems involve farming, water, economics, employment, industrialisation. Although there has been much unhappiness, it is to be hoped that the future will be brighter.

NOTES

1. Malinowski, B. (1963) *Sex, Culture and Myth*, London, Hart Davis.
2. Hobsbawm, E.J. and Ranger, T. (eds) (1984) *Invention of Tradition*, Cambridge, Cambridge University Press.
3. Temple, R.C. (1884) *The Legends of the Panjab*, Islamabad, Institute of Folk Heritage (repr. 1981).
4. Nayar, K. and Singh, K. (1984) *Tragedy of Punjab: Operation Bluestar and After*, New Delhi, Vision Books.
5. Macnicol, N. (1934) *The Living Religions of the Indian People, Wilde Lectures 1932–34*, London, SCM Press.
6. The Census of India, 1881, Punjab Vol. 1, Calcutta, Government Printing Press.

FURTHER READING

Cunningham, J.D. (1848) *A History of the Sikhs from the Origin of the Nation to the Battles of the Sutlej* (repr. 1981), Delhi, S. Chand.

Fox, Richard G. (1985) *Lions of the Punjab: Culture in the Making*, Berkeley, University of California.

Hans, Surjit (1988) *A Reconstruction of Sikh History From Sikh Literature*, Jalandhar, ABS Publications.

Khushwant Singh (1966) *A History of the Sikhs*, Oxford, Oxford University Press.

Macauliffe, M.A. (1909) *The Sikh Religion*, Oxford, Clarendon Press. Reprinted 1985, New Delhi, S. Chand.

McLeod, W.H. (1968) *Guru Nanak and the Sikh Religion*, Oxford, Clarendon Press.

McLeod, W.H. (1980) *Early Sikh Tradition*, Oxford, Clarendon Press.

McLeod, W.H. (1989a) *The Sikhs: History, Religion and Society*, New York, Columbia University Press.

McLeod, W.H. (1989b) *Who is a Sikh?*, Oxford, Clarendon Press.

Srinivas, M.N. (1980) *India: Social Structure*, Delhi, Hindustan Publishing Corporation.

7. Chinese Religions

Xinzhong Yao

The role of myth in Chinese civilisation is weaker than that in many other civilisations. Chinese myth perhaps never gained a position independent of historical records. According to the traditional orthodox ideology, its main functions would be nothing more than filling the gaps where the historians have no materials available, and stimulating the imagination of poets and literary scholars. Though some scholars may well believe that myth had once flourished in China and been popular, its popularity waned during the long history, and only a small part survived. The pieces of ancient myths are scattered in tens of hundreds of philosophical, literary and historical works, and mythologists today have to work very hard to put these casual references and fragmentary pieces in sequence and to find the mythological meaning in abstract metaphors, vivid poems, religious parables and popular stories.

Sources of Chinese myth

Compared with Chinese civilisation, the mythological records which have come down to us appeared quite late, and some of the comparatively systematic myths were recorded only in works dated around or after the period of the Warring States (403–221 BCE). Of the works which preserve mythological materials for us, three types are of most significance. First there are historical books, such as the *Book of History*, which is one of the Confucian classics, and the *Records of History* by Ssu Ma-chien (135–? BCE), the father of Chinese historians. In books of this kind, the myths were historicised as a part of, or a complementary illustration to, the historical chronicles. Then we have philosophical books, such as the *Chuang*

Tzu, the *Hsun Tzu*, the *Han Fei Tzu* of the period of the Warring States; and the *Huai Nan Tzu*, the *Lie Tzu* of the Han Dynasties (206 BCE–220 CE). In these works, the ancient myths were abstracted or reformed into philosophical or religious parables. Thirdly, we see literary works and collections of ancient folklore, such as the *Songs of Chu* of the fourth century BCE (which is believed to be the richest storehouse of the Chou mythological lore), the *Shan Hai Ching* (*The Book of Mountains and Seas*) of the second century BCE, *San-wu Li-chi* (*Records of Cycles in Three and Five*) and *Fen-su Tung-yi* (*Comprehensive Interpretation of Customs*) of the third century CE, and *Shi-i Chi* (*Records of Strange Events*) of the sixth century CE and so on. Generally speaking, these works recorded the myths more faithfully than any other kinds of books and are therefore the most reliable sources of our knowledge of ancient myths.

The reasons why Chinese mythology was under-developed have been explored by various writers, and they range from the nature of the ancient Chinese who lived on agriculture and therefore lacked enough imaginative ability to complete a system of mythology, to the humanist world-view which unifies the spiritual world and the human world. However, the most plausible explanation is perhaps the double effect of Confucian domination in politics and history and its tendency to humanism in religion and philosophy, and the powerful influence of Taoism in the popular culture. Confucians, by their nature, are hostile to the so-called fantasies and occultism of mythology. Confucius is said, in the *Analects*, to have 'never talked about the strange things, physical exploits, disorder and spiritual beings', which are exactly the topics of mythology. Furthermore, he boldly changed the ancient myths in the light of his own moral view, as in the case when he was asked why the Yellow Emperor (2698–2598 BCE) was said in the myth to have had four faces; his explanation was that the Yellow Emperor sent four governors to the four directions. When he was asked whether it was true that the Emperor had lived for three hundred years, Confucius explained that the Emperor actually lived only for one hundred years. For one hundred years after his death his people showed reverence for his spirit and for the next one hundred years they continued to follow his teaching, and that was how the mention of three hundred years in the myth came into being. His explanations fit perfectly with his moral and political principles. Following his example, later

Confucian historians and literary scholars tended to get rid of, or change, everything of the ancient legends which was not consistent with Confucian ideals of morality and history. This resulted in the loss of many ancient myths, confusions in identifying mythological references and a distorted relation between history and myth.

In contrast to Confucian dislike of myth, Taoists embraced most topics of mythology, and derived nourishment from those sacred or spiritual stories. If we say that in Confucianism historicisation and moralisation are the two basic attitudes towards mythology, then in Taoism, 'philosophisation' and 'immortalisation' are the two fundamental contributions that classical Taoism and religious Taoism made to mythology. For instance, in mythology, the original state of the world, *hun-tun*, was chaos, in which no distinction or shape existed. However, in the famous parable in the *Chuang Tzu*, *hun-tun* was imaged as the central god, who took no shape or form. Because he was so nice to other gods, they were eager to repay him for his kindness. They decided to 'help' him to dig out seven holes in his face. Each hole took a day to dig out and seven days later *hun-tun* died. Chuang Tzu (369–286 BCE) used this myth to illustrate his philosophy that intelligence did not mean the same as happiness. As soon as intelligence began to be used, the natural and taoist life was stopped. Later, along with the rise of religious Taoism, Taoists tended to rephrase or revise mythical stories in the light of their special conceptions, and they gave their myths connotations of immortality. Thus they created a huge number of immortality legends which almost devoured all the existing myths and paved the way for another 'history' which was quite different, not only from that of Confucian historians, but also from the narratives related by the ancient myths.

Two-way traffic of myth and history

A good explanation of the relationship between myth and history depends upon a proper understanding of what is history and what is myth. Though 'history' usually is used in two senses, 'as the narratives of the events of the past and as the whole of these events themselves' (Ricoeur 1987: 274), in this chapter we have to concentrate on its first meaning since there is no way for us to trace and check the events narrated in the myths of the far remote ages. In this sense, the history related by Chinese myth and the myth recorded in the writings of the historian are so closely intertwined that we may well say that they actually constituted a two-way traffic on the road of cultural evolution in China. In order to illustrate the interaction between myth and history in China, we should examine it in the light of 'myth in history', 'myth about history' and 'mythical history'.

What is meant by 'myth in history' is that the appearance of myths in history formed a string of 'historical' records. In Chinese literature, as far as we know, the first mythical story was recorded in the *Shih Ching*, or the *Book of Poetry*, at the beginning of the Chou dynasty (1122–221 BCE), and is a myth about a flood. Another great myth which has come down to us appeared during the period of Spring and Autumn (770 BCE–476 BCE) in a book known as *Kuo Yu*, or *Narratives of the States*, and is a myth about 'Separation between Heaven and Earth' or 'Separation between the spiritual world and the human world'. Then in the later Chou dynasty, we see a myth about the Archer Yi and his shooting at the suns. Myth entered a glorious age in the Chin (221–202 BCE) and the Han dynasties, flourishing in almost every kind of book. Narratives about ancient heroes and strange experiences, were repeated and chanted so that they were believed to have been real historical events. Examining these myths which have appeared in different stages of history, we find that the earlier a myth was formed, the simpler it was, and most of the great myths were developed out of the comparatively simple records of earlier ages.

'Myth in history', though meaningful for historians, appears not to be very attractive for mythologists because the connections between these myths are loose and illogical. Therefore, we have to explore further those myths which 'talk' about history. According to the definition in the *Oxford Dictionary of English*, myth is 'a pure fictitious narrative usually involving supernatural persons, actions, or events, and embodying some popular idea concerning natural or historical phenomena'. However, in China, myth which talks about human civilisation is in the mainstream of mythology, and constitutes a glorified history of cultural heroes whose starting point has been universally regarded as the first human sovereign, Fu Hsi (2852–2738 BCE). This kind of myth deals with almost every cultural invention, from agriculture to language, from abstract philosophical ideas to the composition of music. We cannot deny that the contribution of historians in the development of such myths as these has been tremendous; by them great inventions and cultural progress were attributed to the legendary emperors, and intentionally revised and changed into a sequence of historical chronicle. The sequence of historicised myths replaced the narratives of mythological storytelling and became the true 'history'. The most obvious example of this is that Ssu Ma-chien, when writing his *Records of History*, borrowed or used a lot of mythological materials as the lost links of the cultural history. The stories of gods or half-gods were pure myth no longer. Some of them were taken as true history, not only by the historians but also by the philosophers and the common people. Here, however, we should remind readers that there is still an argument between historians and mythologists as to whether myth or history came first. The former hold a theory called the 'historicisation of myth': myths are translated and changed into recorded history, while the latter have developed a theory called the 'mythologisation of history': myth is an imagined evolution from the true historical events. In fact, this two-way traffic co-existed for a long time. Real events appeared in mythical forms, while the imaginative myths also forced their way into historical records. This fact requires us to be very careful when we examine these 'myths about history'. As far as the relationship between myth and history is concerned, we should not take all 'myths about history' as true historical events, nor must we dismiss them all as works of the imagination. Archaeological excavations have helped to support the historicity of some mythical stories. For example, the Great Yu, the founder of the Hsia dynasty (2205–1776 BCE), was believed in the myth to have been the conqueror of the flood. Though we are still not sure when the flood happened and whether it was conquered by some hero called Yu or not, there is evidence that there was indeed a disastrous flood in ancient China, and some remains of apparent attempts to control the flood are also an indication of the presence of humans.

Besides 'myth in history' and 'myth about history', the interaction between myth and history is often influenced by so-called 'mythical history', a history forged by the logic of myths. In this sense, the contents of fragmentary Chinese myths can be divided historically into three stages. The first stage contains what are called the 'earliest' myths. The reason why we call this kind of myth the 'earliest' is not that they were the first created but that their authority in explaining prehistory is unchallenged. They deal with primary events, answering such questions as: How did the universe come into being? Why was it presented in such a diverse manner? What or who was the creator of human beings? They are, perhaps, the remains from the first civilised imaginings of these 'events' of prehistory. When later historians tried to trace history back to these events, they had either to adopt faithfully the stories which the myths told them, or to leave them alone and make no comment at all.

In the second stage, the myths are stories about human culture and human civilisation. As stated above, this was an epic age. Heroes, sages and kings played a central role in the myths. In the third stage, Chinese myths degenerated into local legends and popular fantasies under the strong influence of religious Taoism (and in some sense also of Buddhism), and were heavily permeated by the ideas of these religions, especially those of Taoist immortality. These myths may be called, in Henri Maspero's term, 'modern mythology' (1981: 77). The divine stories of this kind, though not constituting a separate 'narrative', gave a rich colour to mythology, and to religions as well as to history. History, in these mythological stories, was extended, changed and enriched, and this kind of history, in turn, exerted a great influence on Chinese religious theories, political ideals and mythological ideas.

Chronology of mythical history

In order to discover the essence of Chinese myth and the interaction between myth and history in China, it is necessary for us to explore the chronology of Chinese mythical history. The logical beginning of mythological history lies in the myth of creation. In any great civilisation, the topic of creation is always the privileged field of myth. This is not only because the creation is beyond any historical exploration, but also because it is the basis and starting point of religions. In China, there are several pieces of mythology which can be identified with creation. Among them, the most interesting and representative is that called Pan-gu Opening Heaven and Earth.

According to this myth, the original state of the universe, that is, before there were heaven and earth, was imagined as a *hun-tun*, which was described as a chicken's egg, and as a state of complete darkness with no distinction. From this dark *hun-tun*, Pan-gu the cosmic giant emerged. After 18,000 years, he woke up and felt very bored with this darkness and chaos. So he split it with one stroke, and *hun-tun* was separated into two parts: what was bright and light ascended and thus formed the heaven, and what was dark and heavy descended and thus formed the earth. Thereafter, during another 18,000 years, the heaven daily increased ten feet in height, the earth daily increased ten feet in thickness, and Pan-gu, between the two, also daily increased ten feet in size.

Pan-gu, by now, was still only an opener of the cosmos. However, by his death he became a creator of the myriad things of the universe. After Pan-gu was sure that the heaven was separated from the earth far enough that they could never combine into a dark chaos again, he lay down on the earth, rested and died. His death marked the creation of the universe. His breath became the winds and clouds, his voice changed to the thunder, and his eyesight evolved into the lightning; his head became mountains, his eyes turned out to be the sun and moon, and the flow of his blood was transformed into the rivers. His flesh became the soil, the hair of his body grew on as the flowers and trees, and his bones and teeth became stones and metals. In other stories, it is also said that Pan-gu's happiness formed the clear weather, while his angry mood formed the cloudy and stormy climate.

According to one story, it was after the creation of heaven, earth, the sun and moon, the ocean and mountains, the planets and climates through the transformation of the body of Pan-gu that 'the parasites on his body, impregnated by the wind, became human beings' (Girardot, 1974: 194). However, this myth did not appeal because in it human beings were regarded as on a level with parasites. Fortunately, there is another myth of the creation of human beings which tells us that many years had passed since the creation by Pan-gu, and the earth, though with myriads of creatures, remained in its original state, unchanged. The great goddess Nu Wa, who is said to possess a human head and a dragon body, was distressed with this weary and lonely land and decided to make some creature who would enrich and beautify the world. She took a lump of yellow clay (this is why the Chinese are yellow people) and made it into a creature with a head like her own and put two arms and two legs on it. When she put down this new creature on the land and puffed her breath into it, the first human came into being. She worked very hard to make as many such creatures as she could so that the world would be full of their activities. However, she was still worried about their destiny: they could not live for ever, nor did she wish to perpetuate her creative function in the same way. So the goddess put men and women together and instituted the rite of marriage. Thereafter, human beings began to reproduce themselves.

From the creators of the universe and human beings, the attention of Chinese mythology turned to the cultural heroes who were regarded as gods or half-gods. Though there are many myths which tell us about these gods (and in these mythical stories we can see that it was recorded history that 'stole' materials from the myths), recorded history began to exploit these myths in explaining their meaning. Since the myths and historical records are relating the same events in different ways, we have to look at their differences carefully. Formal Chinese history is believed to have started with the 'Three Sovereigns and Five Emperors', of whom the first is Fu Hsi. In history, Fu Hsi is generally regarded as the first sovereign of China, and is credited with many cultural inventions. Before his day the people are said to have lived like beasts, clothing themselves in leaves or skins, eating raw meat with its hair and blood, knowing their mothers but not their fathers, and pairing without decency. Fu Hsi taught them to cook their food, to sow and reap, and to make musical instruments with spun silk, and to record events using symbols rather than knotted cords. These descriptions presented Fu Hsi as a cultural hero and the founder of Chinese civilisation. However, myths tell us a quite different story: he was miraculously conceived, his mother becoming pregnant by the inspiration of Heaven, and his gestation lasting twelve years; his invention of the eight trigrams representing heaven, earth, fire, water, thunder, wind, mountain and lake did not come by his observing the movements of heaven and the principles of earth, as recorded in the *Book of Change* and other historical books, but was divinely revealed to him on the back of a dragon-horse, which appeared to him from the Yellow River. He was the husband of the goddess Nu Wa, and later they were worshipped as the god and goddess of marriage. In the bas-reliefs of tombs of the Han Dynasty, the pictures show Fu Hsi and Nu Wa as deities, with human heads and entwined snake-tails.

After Fu Hsi, the most important historic figure is Huang Ti, the Yellow Emperor (2698–2598 BCE), who is believed to be a true ancestor of the Chinese people. The historical books recorded that he invented wheeled vehicles, armour, ships, pottery, the calendar, and so on. Among his marvellous performances as a ruler, the most memorable is his battle with, and conquest of, the rebellion of aboriginal *Miao* tribes under their chief, Chih Yu. About this battle, however, the myth tells us another story: Huang Ti was a god. When he was informed that there were rebellions in the land, he descended from heaven to set earth in order. Chih Yu was a monster who had a bull's head on a serpent's body. Against Chih Yu, who had invented the weapons, Huang Ti marshalled armies of fierce beasts – bears, panthers, tigers, and the Winged Dragon. When Chih Yu summoned to his aid the spirits of the wind and the rain, Huang Ti had to make his daughter Pa, the goddess of drought, who had eyes in the top of her head, come down from heaven against them. At last Chih Yu was overcome and killed. The goddess Pa, perhaps because she had been contaminated by earthly evil, could not go back up to heaven, and was banished to the wilderness where she was transformed into deserts. After that, wherever there was a drought, the people first must make a sacrifice to this goddess and appeal to her compassion.

After another two sovereigns came the sage king, Yao (2357–2256 BCE). Yao was succeeded upon his death, not by his son, but by his minister Shun (2255–2206 BCE), who, due to his extreme filial piety to his parents and kindness to his evil brother, had obtained the respect of the people and was trusted by the ruler. During this time, we hear of two major events in Chinese mythology, involving the Archer Yi and Yu the Great, who were, respectively, the heroes of the myth of the sun and the myth of the flood.

In ancient times, there were ten suns, who were said to be ten sons of Shang Ti, the Sovereign on High, and whose duty was to travel in the sky from the east to the west every day. Each morning one of them had to climb up the giant tree, *Fu-sang*, on which they rested in the night, and ride in the chariot pulled by six dragons, to begin his tour. Some time during the reign of Yao the ten of them, perhaps bored by this routine, suddenly appeared in the sky together. The world was soon scorched and burnt, grains and trees died of overheating and the people tried to save themselves from this disaster by every means they could find, such as offering sacrifices to the goddess of drought, forcing a sorceress to dance in the sun until death, in order to get the gods' pity. However, all these measures failed to stop the burning heat of the suns, and the people were desperate. Upon hearing their complaints of unbearable heat and the prayers of Yao, the ruler of the earth, the ruler of Heaven, Shang Ti, sent his warrior, the Archer Yi, down to earth to help Yao restore the natural order. Yi shot down nine of these suns whose spirits turned out to be three-legged golden crows, leaving the single one which, as the sun, brings light and warmth to the earth. The people once again enjoyed a happy life and the ruler Yao reigned peacefully.

The myth of the flood and the historical account of Yu the Great contain similar variations. In the myth, it was said that, during the reign of Shun, a disaster again threatened the peace and order of the whole of China. Shang Ti, having been disappointed by the people's wickedness and evil ways, decided to punish them by sending down endless rains. Flood overwhelmed the dwelling places, rose above the hills and devoured everything that grew on the land. The grandson of Shang Ti, Kun, felt grief at seeing the miseries of the people, and besought his grandfather to withdraw the flood. When he realised that Shang Ti could not be moved by his words and tears, Kun stole the 'swelling mould or living soil' (*hsi rang*) from heaven and brought it to earth to build dykes and dams. Shang Ti was angered at his disobedience and had him executed at Feather Mountain. There Kun's body remained for three years, with no hint of decomposition, breeding his son in his body, so that when it was cut, Yu emerged from Kun's belly, and continued his father's work. Yu split the hills and mountains which blocked the waterways, dug the channels and built the embankments of the rivers, so that the flood could flow from the west to the seas of the east. However, in the history related by Confucians and Mohists, Yu appeared as a great hero. He was praised as selfless, brave and happy to benefit humankind. Being appointed by Shun as the successor of his father, Kun, who failed to control the flood by damning it with dykes, Yu led the people, digging out the watercourses for thirteen years and three times passing his home without entering it. At last he succeeded, the flood went down and the people again enjoyed a peaceful life. Yu the Great became the ruler after Shun's death, and the founder of the first dynasty, the Hsia.

Integration between legends and history

As time passed, the integration of myth and history continued. In the three dynasties, the Hsia, the Shang and the Chou, which covered a period between about the twenty-first century BCE and the third century BCE, the importance of myths was emphasised because they could support the legitimation of each dynasty and each ruler. The secular authority was believed to be sacred through the mythological connection between the clans and the spiritual world. Marvellous lives and experiences of the ancestors, and achievements and glories of the founders of dynasties were believed to be not only truly historical events but also an essential part of mythical stories, in which the ancestors and founders were endowed with a divine power by Heaven, the Chinese God.

Starting from the period of the Warring States, however, there was another factor which influenced Chinese mythology, that is, Taoist ideas and ideals of immortality. Myths began to deal with longevity, the elixirs of never-dying, and alchemy. The figures in the ancient myths, such as the Yellow Emperor, appeared as heavenly immortals. The stories of immortals, flying up to the heavens, of the transformation from mortals to immortals, and of practices relating to longevity, became the stuff of this kind of myth. On the one hand, these new ideas made the ancient myths more colourful, on the other, they carried on a 'history' formed by ancient mythological narratives. Since then, history and legend seem never to have been completely separated and the earlier tendency of integrating myth and history was faithfully continued by later generations. Every new dynasty and every great figure left behind not only a chronicle of historical events, but also a rich and fascinating storehouse of mythical stories. This tendency contributes colour to the history, but it can also provide a breeding ground for personal cult, especially in the field of politics. This tradition was so strong that even the modern Communists, who claimed to be the most atheist in the history of China, created a new mythical story through the modern media. The personal cult dominated the whole country for several decades and the deified leader was worshipped as the 'red sun', the 'saviour of the people', with a life of ten-thousand and ten-thousand years. The narratives about him were intertwined with modern China's history. His words, statues and even pictures were invested with magical power which could get rid of 'sin' (selfishness) and enable people to create miracles. The majority of the Chinese people did not realise or critically examine, until very recently, this kind of negative effect of the integration of legend and history.

Finally, we have to mention the relationship between myth and religions. Though many of the ideas of Chinese myth were borrowed or used by later religions, especially Taoism, its influence on these institutional religions was much more limited than on the popular religions. As stated above, Confucianism rejected the mythological explanation of the universe, the spiritual world and human society, and Taoism either philosophised myths or turned them into stories about immortality. Only in the popular religions did the ancient and modern myths find a stage for their presentation. In this sense, Chinese myth is always closely connected with legends, folklore and non-orthodox history, which are essential parts of the common people's religious life.

FURTHER READING

Birch, Cyril (1961) *Chinese Myths and Fantasies*, London, Oxford University Press.

Bodde, Derk (1961) 'Myths of Ancient China' in Samuel N. Kramer (ed.) *Mythologies of the Ancient World*, New York, Doubleday, pp. 357–408.

Chiu, Milton M. (1984) *The Tao of Chinese Religion*, Lanham, University Press of America.

Girardot, N.J. (1974) *Myth and Meaning in Early Taoism*, Berkeley, University of California Press.

Maspero, Henri (1981) 'The Mythology of Modern China' in *Taoism and Chinese Religion*, Amherst, University of Massachusetts Press.

Ricoeur, Paul (1987) 'Myth and History' in Mircea Eliade (ed.) *Encyclopedia of Religion*, vol. 10, New York, Macmillan.

Werner, Edward T.C. (1922) *Myths and Legends of China*, London, Harrap.

Yu, David C. (1981) 'The Creation Myth and its Symbolism in Classical Taoism' in *Philosophy East and West* 31: 479–500.

8. Japanese Religions

Ian Reader

Introduction: myth and fictive history in Japan

In order to understand fully the nature and role of myth and history, and to comprehend the relevance of myth, in the development and nature of Japanese religion, it is important to contextualise what is meant in Japanese terms by the notion of myth and to outline what the general Japanese religious perceptions of the nature and uses of history tend to be. Myth in Japanese terms is only part of a far wider tradition of stories that express and narrate religious ideas and that create accounts of mythic or legendary events with religious messages and meanings. This tradition includes not only myths (*shinwa*), but legends (*densetsu*), foundation stories, especially of temples, shrines and other holy sites (*engi*), miracle stories (*reigenki*), and tales of miraculous events and deeds that contain a moral meaning (*setsuwa*). These categories and the types of story contained within them (especially the last four mentioned) are often very similar and it is not always possible to differentiate them clearly.

The first term (*shinwa*), which is most closely associated with the Shinto religious tradition, more specifically relates to the deeds, actions and realms of deities, and often occurs in non-human realms such as heavens and hells; the rest, reflecting the vast impact in Japanese religion of Buddhism and its fusions with the folk religious tradition, relate more closely to the actions of holy figures such as wandering saints and *buddhas*, and their interactions with the human world. They centre on actions and events that are linked to locations in the present, physical world, and to 'historical' time; even if the time of their reputed occurrence is imprecise and swathed in legend, it is nonetheless posited as occurring within the framework of human history rather than, as with the deeds of gods outlined in myths, somewhere beyond it.

All of these categories, which will be discussed more fully later, have appeared throughout the ages in Japan, in religious texts and oral transmissions, and have been used by religious preachers and political authorities to create and legitimate a religious (and, indeed, social and political) history pregnant with meanings. Legends and myths have imbued people, places and representations of the sacred (such as statues and religious buildings) with holy power, showing them to be affiliated not just to the mundane, human world but to the realms of the spiritual. They have therefore encouraged the development of cults of faith, and created religious traditions in their wake. In political terms, too, such stories and fictive histories have served to create and reinforce social and political views of the structure of power and lineage. The 'history' thus formulated by these varieties of story, all of which purport to narrate events that 'happened', is not of the factual or empirically based form, but of one that might best be described as fictive history, which expresses what are considered to be religious understandings of the nature of the world and of human life.

While it would be inaccurate to say that there is one single, specific Japanese understanding of what history is or should be, or even what a Japanese religious construction of history is, it is nonetheless reasonable to say that for religious and political authorities, history, and hence the past, has been a fluid entity that can be moulded for the purposes of the present. History therefore has largely been regarded not primarily as a means of understanding the past and its cultural influences on the present, but as a means of creating and shaping a past that has relevance to the present, presenting it with messages that legitimate present world views, and furthering the teaching and understanding of religious messages relevant to the present. This idea is found in the Shinto myths of creation to be discussed below, which underpin and express a specifically Japanese-centred view of the world and posit a special relationship between Japan, the Japanese and their indigenous deities. It is also deeply embedded in the Buddhism that flourished in Japan, which generally considers history to be valid for what it can 'teach' the present about the meaning of Buddhism, and for the uses it can have in persuading people to follow Buddhist teachings. In such terms, myth and legend are legitimate expressions of 'history', and the 'past' can act as a form of myth (or as a mythic or fictive reality) devised to provide religious truths and meanings for the present. Hence the past need not be an empirically verifiable past but an imagined, or imaginative, one; history is not, therefore, just or primarily what empirically happened but what 'ought' to have done. This is not a deliberately misleading creation, however, for its intent is not to mislead people but to guide them to realities that transcend such mundane things as 'factual history', and to provide them with cultural understandings of the world around them.

A good example of this can be found in the *Nihon Ryoiki*, one of the most important collections of *setsuwa*, or miracle stories with a moral undertone. This text was very widely used by preachers and teachers of Buddhism as a means of preaching the graces and salvific powers of Buddhism to the masses, and its content will be discussed more fully later. Written in the ninth century CE by the Buddhist monk Kyokai of the temple Yakushiji in Nara, it reports various miracle stories he had collected. Kyokai was concerned to emphasise issues of karmic reward and retribution, and to preach the immanent and salvific powers of the *buddhas*; thus his stories report occurrences of reward, often in the form of miraculous cures, for those who perform good deeds of faith and virtue, and punishment (usually, like the rewards, immediate and direct) for those who insult Buddhist figures or transgress against Buddhist teachings (Nakamura 1973: 33–44). It is clear that Kyokai's underlying religious purpose in reporting the events described in the *Ryoiki* has coloured its content. To ask whether they 'actually' happened, whether Kyokai reported them accurately, or whether he embellished them and wrote in a miraculous dimension, is to miss the point. Their relevance and intent express a religious world-view commonly held in ninth-century Japan (one that is not uncommon today) about the influence of the spiritual realms on the physical world. In the understanding of Kyokai and his contemporaries, and of the preachers who in later years used Kyokai's text as a means of enhancing their message, miracles could happen and spiritual rewards and punishments could be experienced directly and immediately, and need not be subjected to 'rational' questioning. As such they served as proofs of the salvific powers and intercessionary grace of the *buddhas* and as moral lessons showing people how they would benefit by good, and suffer by bad, behaviour. Thus they could be used by later preachers to spread the faith and develop an understanding of religious reality that was not fettered by the shackles of 'mere' history.

Shinwa: myth, meaning and identity in Shinto

Shinwa is the Japanese word most closely approximating to the English word 'myth'. It consists of two ideograms, *shin*, which is also read as *kami* and means deity or god,[1] and *wa*, tale or story. *Shinwa* are thus stories about the actions of the *kami*, the indigenous Japanese gods venerated in the Shinto tradition, and they are usually set in the space and time of the gods. They are clearly mythical stories in the sense of being ahistorical and not being located (even in fictive terms) in the human realm.

Probably the most pervasive of all such myths are those that recount the creation of the islands of Japan, their relationship to the *kami* or Japanese gods, and the emergence of the Japanese people and their imperial family. This series of myths has been set down in two eighth-century CE texts, the *Nihon Shoki* and the *Kojiki*,[2] which codified them for both religious and, more importantly, political purposes. These texts narrate a series of interrelated myths; the *Nihon Shoki* presents an account of the earliest Japanese emperors that purports to be historical but in reality narrates a mythical history, while the *Kojiki* sets out a cycle of myths in which deities procreate, giving birth to further deities who then produce the islands of Japan, followed by other deities who give life to the land, and finally followed by an imperial line that descends from the deities to rule, with their blessing, over this land.

In these myths two deities, the male Izanagi and the female Izanami, themselves the descendants of earlier deities, combine to give birth to the Japanese archipelago and numerous deities, until Izanami dies while giving birth to the god of fire. Izanagi, raging and demented, enters the world of the dead in order to see his wife again, but is shocked by finding her in a maggot-infested and decaying state. At the sight (reflecting basic human horror at the confrontation with death) he flees the underworld, only to be chased by Izanami, who seeks to retain his company by dragging him into the underworld for good. He escapes by drawing a boulder across the boundary between this world and the world of the dead, by asserting, in an argument with her, the primacy of life over death, and by subsequently bathing in a stream to purify himself. Not only does this wash away the pollutions of death and spiritually purify him, it also causes him, in this restored state, to bring forth further deities, including Amaterasu, the Sun Goddess, to whom Izanagi then bequeaths hegemony. Amaterasu's grandson, Ninigi, is subsequently commanded to descend to earth (i.e., to Japan) as its ruler and is entrusted with various items of imperial regalia including a sacred mirror that represents Amaterasu on earth. According to Shinto belief, this sacred mirror is enshrined at Ise, the most important of all Shinto shrines. Ninigi's great-grandson, Jimmu, is entrusted with guarding the imperial regalia and the sacred mirror, and becomes the first emperor of Japan. Subsequent legends and lineages (often themselves fictive) show that all subsequent emperors have descended from Jimmu, who in turn descended from Amaterasu. This myth thus means that the Japanese emperor and imperial family are direct descendants of Amaterasu, and therefore are at least potentially divine.

The myths thus underpin the political reality of imperial rule, and were written down in these texts in the eighth century CE for such a purpose. As such, they reflect what has been described as 'mythistory' (Ebersole 1989: 3–16), a use of mythical images to develop a history that fitted the needs of those who wrote it. The myths (of which the events told here are but a small part of the overall cycle[3]) express many issues of importance in terms of political power and structure, in terms of understanding Japanese cultural identity, and in terms of indigenous orientations of Shinto.

Politically, the myths have long legitimated the position of the emperor and imperial household, and for ardent nationalists even today they may be seen not so much as myth but as plausible history. In times of extreme Japanese nationalism, such as the decades leading up to 1945, the myths could be used as a bulwark of nationalistic Shinto, as a means of elevating the emperor to the status of a deity (which, as a mythical descendant of Amaterasu, he was in terms of the mythistory of the *Kojiki*) and forcing all to venerate him as a national symbol, and as a legitimation for Japanese expansionism. Political realities and constitutional necessities have nowadays blunted such extremism, but there remain those who venerate the emperor and consider that there is a direct line of descent between the gods and the Japanese.

Certainly the myths affirm the innate sanctity of the land of Japan as a sacred construct[4] and, by setting out the mythical relationship between the country, the people and their gods, they serve to underline a continuing sense of Japanese identity permeated by an implicit sense of uniqueness, for the myths relate to the Japanese and *their* gods alone. This sense of cultural self-identity has been a major factor in Japanese self-perception over the centuries and has played an important part in contemporary Japanese views of themselves and the world around them, especially providing a means of self-esteem and cultural strength in the face of increasing cultural encroachments from abroad in recent years.

The themes espoused in the myths, from this innate relationship between the gods and the Japanese, to the more explicitly religious elements within them, have formed the basis of the Shinto religion and of many basic Japanese religious perceptions. The humanesque and often capricious behaviour of the gods (who thus need to be placated and humoured, after which they may grant wishes and benefits) is displayed frequently throughout the myths, and points to the importance of religious rituals as a means of entertaining, placating and gaining assistance from the gods. The pollutions of death, and the dangers accompanying the recently dead, are reflected in the complex and extensive rites that follow death,[5] while the life-creating power of acts of purification, as expressed in Izanagi's bathing, are recurrent themes in Shinto practice.[6]

Densetsu, *engi*, *reigenki* and *setsuwa*: legends, miracle stories and the dynamics of folk Buddhism

Although *shinwa* such as those recounted in the Izanami–Izanagi–Amaterasu cycle provide powerful messages and meanings in religious, cultural and political terms, and have been important in formulating and expressing many of the themes of indigenous Japanese religion, they have perhaps not been as comprehensively influential in the construction of religious histories and meanings as has been the vast corpus of tales and legends covered by the terms *densetsu*, *engi*, *setsuwa* and *reigenki*. Since these categories overlap extensively, sharing similar themes and transmitting similar messages, they will be treated as one broad genre of religious story here. All these forms of story have contributed to the production and dissemination of a popular religious culture in which

Buddhist teachings and cults of veneration of Buddhist figures of worship have merged with folk religious ideas and concepts to create a culture in which teachings about salvation, morality and religious awareness have been expressed in simple and accessible forms for the ordinary person.

Such stories, which largely focus on the acts and deeds of holy figures, Buddhist monks, mountain ascetics, *bodhisattva*s and *buddha*s, show how these can bring mercy, salvation and retribution to the masses, performing miracles to reward the faithful and bringing instant judgement on the unfaithful. The stories have also served to underpin the development of sacred sites such as temples and shrines by showing how miraculous deeds have been performed, oracles received, and signs of the holy perceived in specific locations, thereby laying mythical foundations for such centres of worship. Stories such as *engi*, *setsuwa* and the like have therefore been important in the creation and legitimation of a sacred geography. While the *shinwa* narrated in the *Kojiki* have served to sanctify the whole of Japan as a divine land, the legends and tales produced by folk and Buddhist preachers and storytellers have served to mark out specific places as specially holy.[7]

Densetsu (legends) are literally, in the meaning conveyed by their ideograms, 'explanations of tradition', and narrate deeds involving, or carried out by, figures with some historical basis to them. They typically involve holy men who have attained special powers through religious practice and awareness (almost invariably in the Buddhist tradition, and often related also to mountain asceticism) and who use these powers to reward the virtuous and to improve the lives of ordinary people through the performance of miracles, or to punish people for bad deeds. *Densetsu* relate person, place and time in a manner that says that at some (imprecise and undefined) time, a holy figure performed a miraculous deed in a particular location. That they are told about specific places and holy figures does not mean they cannot be transposed elsewhere; the same *densetsu* can be found in numerous locations and be superimposed on the fictive holy lives of numerous religious figures, and a huge corpus of regionalised *densetsu* exists to explain the formation of geographical features, local customs and popular beliefs.

Probably the most extensive set of *densetsu* in Japan are the *Kobo densetsu*, legends about the wandering miracle worker and Buddhist saint, Kobo Daishi. Kobo Daishi ('the great teacher who spread the law of Buddhism') is the posthumous name of Kukai, a ninth-century Buddhist monk and religious leader who is perhaps the most inspirational figure in Japanese religious history. According to legends that began to develop among his followers in the decades after his death, Kobo Daishi transcended death and lived on in order to save humanity and to spread the word of Buddhism. Preachers from Mount Koya, the religious centre he founded, began to travel around Japan, using the figure of Kobo Daishi as a means of propagating a simple Buddhist faith; stories of him appearing as a wandering pilgrim-like figure, performing miracles, healing the sick and dispensing grace, began to spread across Japan.

Among the most common *Kobo densetsu* are stories of Kobo Daishi as a wandering pilgrim entering a village and making a request for water. In one version of the story, there is little water available there but the old woman he asks goes off a long way to fetch him some; as a reward he strikes his staff on the earth and clear spring water gushes forth. In another, the woman refuses to help him although there is abundant water in the vicinity, and as a result he condemns the area to go dry. Another version of the legend has him asking for a potato and being refused, at which all the potatoes in the region turn to stone. Although such legends are commonly told throughout Japan to 'explain' why places have good or bad water, etc., and on this level are little more than aspects of regional lore, they also contain the implicit theme of a test of people's inner being; the disguised saint, by asking for something, is really testing their spiritual character, and the stories articulate the basic Buddhist views that one should help others, and reinforce the basic Japanese folk custom of hospitality to strangers.

Among the religious devotions spread by the tales preached about Kobo Daishi was the Shikoku pilgrimage, one of Japan's most commonly followed pilgrimages, which goes around the island of Kukai's birth and in which pilgrims are believed to walk under the guidance of the saint. The pilgrimage originally developed from the travels of ascetics to sites connected with Kukai's life and gradually it extended into a large-scale popular religious activity. As it did so, various legends focusing on Kobo Daishi's grace emerged to promote the merits of the pilgrimage, including collections of miracle tales in which Kobo Daishi heals the sick and grants the requests of the virtuous. The earliest of these collections was compiled in 1689 by the ascetic, Shinnen, in order to encourage people to go on the pilgrimage and devote themselves to the veneration of Kobo Daishi.

Before that, however, many other legends had emerged, including the legend that Kukai (i.e., Kobo Daishi) himself established the pilgrimage in 815 CE. This is an historical impossibility, for there are extant records to show that Kukai was not in Shikoku in that year, and the pilgrimage did not develop until several centuries later, but the story that he had founded and walked the route has become written into most accounts and guidebooks of Shikoku, and has become part of the pilgrim's perception of the pilgrimage. Another equally important legend, which remains one of the most commonly told mythic stories in Shikoku, is the legend of Emon Saburo. Emon is, according to the story (which is usually located in the ninth century CE), the richest and meanest man in Shikoku. Kobo Daishi comes, disguised, to his door to beg alms but Emon, meanly, drives him away with insults. As a result of this sin, Emon's eight sons die one after another and, realising that through his meanness he has lost everything, Emon sets out to find Kobo and seek forgiveness. He walks the island twenty times (on the way establishing the eighty-eight temples the pilgrim visits) before falling, dying, on his twenty-first circuit. At this point Kobo Daishi appears before him to grant him absolution and Emon dies content.

The story offers some salient messages: through the pilgrimage one can gain absolution and release from one's sins; in ardently following the route one can meet Kobo Daishi face to face; and, perhaps, most pertinently for the fifteenth-century pilgrims among whom this legend appears to have first been created, it encourages the practice of giving alms to pilgrims! It is thus no wonder that it has assumed a major position in pilgrimage lore, and has been used as a moral tale by generations of religious teachers.[8]

When such legends tell a moral tale, they are often also referred to as *setsuwa* ('explanatory tales'), and an extensive literature of this sort has developed in Japan. Many *setsuwa* texts, such as the *Nihon Ryoiki*, provide teachings and explanations of Buddhist ideas, and give examples of what happens when one behaves correctly, and what happens when one does not. The *Ryoiki*'s tales have titles such as 'On an evil man who was negligent in filial piety to his mother and gained an immediate penalty of violent death' and 'On attaining a great fortune immediately owing to devotion to Kannon and praying for a share of benefits' (Nakamura 1973: 96), and so the collection reinforces aspects of popular morality and social custom as well as preaching religious devotion. Among other examples of *setsuwa* literature (which often also contain secular tales, although as a rule the bulk of tales are of a Buddhist nature) are the *Konjaku Monogatari* of the twelfth-century and the *Uji Shui Monogatari* of the thirteenth-century.[9]

Besides *setsuwa* and *densetsu*, further bodies of legendary stories that narrate the portents that sacralise particular places and religious sites (*engi*) and stories of miraculous intercessions by deities and statues of *buddhas* and *bodhisattvas* (*reigenki*) have also added to the wealth of such literature in Japan. Most temples and shrines have their own *engi*, or foundation legends, which narrate how an apparition or sacred sign marked the spot out as holy, thereby giving religious sanction and legitimation to the temple built on the spot.[10]

Reigenki are, in general, collections of miracles said to have been performed by figures of worship at particular temples; thus the *Hasedera Kannon Genki* is a thirteenth-century compilation of tales of miracles said to have been performed by the statue of Kannon enshrined at the Hase temple near the old capital of Nara, in which the miracles range from cures of illness to obtaining salvation through the grace of Kannon for oneself or one's parents (Dykstra 1976: 117). The titles of stories in this collection are not dissimilar to those found in the *Ryoiki* or indeed in the *Kobo densetsu* mentioned above, as is demonstrated by story titles such as 'A story about praying for a child and receiving a filial daughter' and 'How a poor woman dedicated a poem to Kannon and was instantly blessed with a fortune'. Such tales of miracles and foundation legends were often used by preachers to extol the virtues of particular temples, so as to encourage popular cults of devotion to them. That most *engi*, *reigenki*, *densetsu* and *setsuwa* occurred in the (fictive) past does not mean that the tradition has not continued. Temples continue to promote their *engi* as a means of encouraging visitors and faith, and collections of contemporary miracle tales continue to appear, such as the *Shikoku hachijuhakksho reigenki*, stories gathered on the Shikoku pilgrimage and published in 1984 to demonstrate the continuing efficacies of the pilgrimage.

One of the stories in the *Shikoku hachijuhakksho reigenki* tells of Mizutani Shigeji and his wife Shizu, both devout followers of Kobo Daishi and ardent Shikoku pilgrims. In 1964 Shizu was so ill that both feared that she might soon die, so they went to Shikoku for (in their words) a 'last pilgrimage'. *En route*, at one of the sites, Shizu suddenly had an awakening in which all her pain disappeared and she was cured. Mizutani's account goes on to narrate how this miracle fired them to deepen their faith, perform more pilgrimages and encourage others to do likewise. Besides the published version,[11] this story has been widely recounted among Shikoku pilgrims, with additional embellishments about the couple's faith in Kobo Daishi and the intercession of the Buddha of Healing, Yakushi. In my interviews with Shikoku pilgrims I have heard it narrated by several different people, each with their own additions about the miraculous nature of the event. In one of the latest versions, Mizutani later passed on a talisman for good fortune to a third person. This person carried Mizutani's talisman in his pocket. One day while working, he inadvertently cut through an electric mains cable with his shovel. There was a flash and the man was flung far down an embankment and into some bushes. His workmates thought he must be dead, but he emerged unscathed – except for the charred talisman, which had absorbed the blast, in his pocket. The story of the original miracle, which promotes faith in the pilgrimage, now sanctifies Mizutani and transforms him, an ordinary pilgrim, into a holy figure. No doubt in time the legend may develop further, and from a simple event with a plausibly rational explanation (by visiting a temple and praying to the Buddha of Healing, the wife attained a sense of peace and hence felt better), a full-blown course of miraculous events has emerged in oral tradition to inspire others.

Behind these various stories lies what might be described as 'belief-centred reality'. If the stories may be inventions or elaborations of tales passed on to the authors, they nonetheless reflect underlying Japanese religious beliefs and hence are, within this view, innately feasible. Though few people will believe that Kobo Daishi 'actually' stopped by in a particular village and made water come out of the ground or turned the potatoes into stone, or that being unpleasant to one's mother will bring immediate and unpleasant death, the realities that the stories express – that one should be good and generous, and that doing ill to others, especially one's parents whom one should respect, will have repercussions on one's life – are immediate and real. Hence, the stories, even if fictive, inform people of 'how things should be', and represent a reality that transcends any quirks in the way things work out in practice.

Legends, legitimation and the formation of cults: the example of pilgrimage

Legends, of course, often serve to legitimate practices after they have developed. Clear examples can be seen in the ways that various legends and stories have been used to promote and give religious legitimation to some of Japan's most popular pilgrimages. As has been mentioned above, the vast corpus of legends surrounding the figure of Kobo Daishi was especially important in framing the Shikoku pilgrimage, in giving meaning to it and in encouraging people to give help to pilgrims.

A further case is shown by the Saikoku pilgrimage dedicated to the Bodhisattva of Mercy, Kannon, which goes around the Kansai (western region) of Japan, visiting thirty-three temples. This pilgrimage developed gradually from around the twelfth to the fifteenth centuries as a form of popular religious devotion, and was inspired by various miracle tales that pointed to Kannon's over-arching grace. In time, too, the pilgrimage developed its own foundation tales and legends, which came to be narrated by pilgrims and preachers alike, and which endowed the pilgrimage with legitimation and with a sacred message that encouraged people to perform it. The legend starts with a Buddhist ascetic, Tokudo, who in the eighth century founded Hasedera, one of the temples on the route. In this story, Tokudo was summoned into hell by Emma, the Lord of Hell, who showed Tokudo the endless numbers of people falling into hell and instructed Tokudo on how he could save them from so doing. Emma then told Tokudo of a course of thirty-three temples established by Kannon, and said that those who travelled this route would be saved from falling into hell. After Tokudo's pilgrimage, however, the route remained hidden until the Emperor Kazan abdicated the throne in 986 CE to become a monk. When he did so, Kazan received an oracle telling him of Emma's teaching to Tokudo and instructing him to perform the pilgrimage. Kazan did so, formally establishing the pilgrimage in 987 CE.

This historically impossible story emerged as a legend somewhere around the fifteenth century (the era when the pilgrimage itself really had begun to attract large numbers of pilgrims) as a means of giving status to the pilgrimage, by linking it to the imperial line, and in order to transmit messages about its efficacy and encourage pilgrims. Its influence remains strong; the belief that performing the pilgrimage will eradicate all the pilgrim's sins and lead him or her to the Pure Land after death remains a popularly held belief that motivates many contemporary Saikoku pilgrims. The clearly fictional foundation date of 987 continues also to carry resonance in the histories of the pilgrimage, and in 1987 the Saikoku pilgrimage temples celebrated the 1,000th anniversary of its founding by Kazan, with numerous religious ceremonies, events and publicity. Just as Shikoku guidebooks continue to use the fictive foundation date of 815 CE for that pilgrimage, the date 987 is often inscribed in Saikoku pilgrimage guidebooks and has become the 'belief-centred reality' of the pilgrimage.

New religions and the development of contemporary myths

Myths continue to be developed for religious purposes and with underlying religious meanings, especially among the new religious movements. Many of the new religions which have developed because of the charismatic powers of particular founder-figures, have produced hagiographic accounts of their founders that show all the signs of evolving into miraculous and legendary stories. In addition, many new religions have developed copious sets of myths that, while incorporating themes found in traditional Japanese myths and legends, also absorb and enlarge on myths from beyond Japan. An example of this can be found in the myths of the Lost Continent of Mu, a continent said to have existed many thousands of years ago as the fount of civilisation before disappearing beneath the ocean some 15,000 years ago. Myths surrounding Mu and the advanced civilisation it was supposed to have produced, often coupled with legends that Mu would rise again to bring about a new, paradisal civilisation, have appeared in much twentieth-century western occultist, Theosophist and New Age literature. Such myths have also appeared in a number of Japanese new religions, especially in Mahikari, which has identified Mu with Japan, and has used the myth of the advanced culture of Mu and of its future rising again to teach that Japan is the emergent centre of a new-world civilisation based on the culture of Mu, with Mahikari as its driving force.

Further amendments to this myth have been found in other new religions, such as Megami no Umi, a small religious group headed by the shamaness, Fujita Himiko, who weaves into the mythic background of her religion and the Mu legends various other Japanese folkloric myths and legends concerning a miraculous underwater realm, its ruler the Dragon King (who in the myths is depicted as the rightful ruler of the earth, who had been displaced by Amaterasu, the Sun Goddess) and his daughter, the Dragon princess, Ryugu Otohime. The myths associated with Ryugu Otohime (with whom Fujita for long identified herself), as with Mu (which have also entered Megami no Umi's mythology) have very similar underlying meanings. In the Ryugu Otohime myth, she will return to Japan to assert control over, and spiritually renew, an increasingly unhappy world; in the Mu myth as developed by Mahikari, a similar process of world renewal will occur through the re-emergence of the civilisation of Mu in the form of Japan, spiritually led by the Mahikari religion. Both religions, then, utilise these myths as a means of showing that they have a message of renewal pertinent to the modern world, and as a way of giving themselves a sense of legitimacy and spiritual power.[12]

Such myths are by no means peripheral to the underlying patterns of contemporary Japanese religions, which have seen a great surge of interest in new religious cults that look back to a mythical and pristine Japanese past that will rise again to reassert Japanese (and through it, world) spiritual and cultural power and make Japan into a world leader, not so much in the economic as in the spiritual sense. Their innate themes strongly affirm that Japan is the centre of its universe and that the Japanese themselves, as descendants of Mu and as associates of the Dragon princess who will renew the world, are a chosen, special people. These mythically expressed themes are thus in many respects not dissimilar to those found in the early Shinto myths recounted in the *Kojiki* (see above) which emphasise the sacred and central nature of Japan and affirm Japanese cultural and religious identity.

Conclusions: stories and religious propagation in Japan

A major factor in the development of myths and legends, and in their application as religious teachings, has been the manner in which they have been endlessly recounted and narrated over the centuries, both as oral stories and in textual forms. Myths and legends have not just provided background religious (and, as in the case of the *Kojiki*, political) messages; they have been at the forefront of the dissemination of religious ideas and the propagation of faith. The messages of the *Kojiki* and *Nihon Shoki* have framed Shinto perceptions of the world in political, cultural and religious terms, while the messages contained within *setsuwa*, *densetsu* and *engi* have been at the forefront of popular Buddhism and have been perhaps the main vehicle through which a popular folk Buddhism has become widely disseminated in Japan. Much of this dissemination (and indeed, much of the dramatic effect upon which the ability to make people believe in the messages is transmitted) has been due to the skills of preachers who narrated miracle tales and legends about Kobo Daishi in order to propagate religious faith and the Shikoku pilgrimage, or who used the *setsuwa* from collections such as the *Nihon Ryoiki* to infuse the populace with a sense of devotion and morality. Similar talents are important today in extending the scope of such myths; as Young points out, Fujita Himiko may not be innovative (the myths of Megami no Umi are generally recycled from other sources) but she is 'an outstanding story-teller' (1989: 38).

It has largely been through such skilful narration and expression of myths, legends and stories, from *shinwa* to *densetsu* and *setsuwa*, that religious teachings have been spread in Japan. The continuing oral traditions of story-telling, backed by various textual compilations, have continually provided a source of religious dynamism and development. As the cases of myth formation in the new religions mentioned above seem to suggest, this process continues to be important in Japanese religion. Indeed, it would be reasonable to say that it is through myths, legends and other stories which create a fictive and living history, rather than through erudite philosophical commentaries and the production of sophisticated religious texts, that religious messages, particularly those of Buddhism, have been spread at popular levels in Japan. As a rule, doctrine has occupied a far less prominent place than have practical tales of efficacy such as *setsuwa*, and it is probably no exaggeration to say that, whereas most Japanese, even in today's highly educated society, are largely unaware of Buddhist philosophy and doctrine, few are unaware of some of the folk tales, legends and parables that constitute popular Buddhism's history and narrate its inner messages in Japan.

NOTES

1. It is important also to realise that, for the most part, the term *kami* relates to indigenous Japanese deities, and to understand that Shinto has innumerable *kami*, and that the word 'god' is only a very rough approximation of the meaning of the Japanese concept.
2. The chapter on Japanese religions in the volume *Sacred Writings* in this series deals at some length with these texts and their religious motifs.
3. A complete translation of the *Kojiki* is available in Philippi (1968).
4. See the chapter on Japanese religions in the volume *Sacred Place* in this series.
5. See the chapter on Japanese religions in the volume *Rites of Passage* in this series.
6. All these issues have been discussed at length in Reader (1991: 23–8). See also Reader, Andreasen and Stefansson (1993: 69–76) which takes the reader through the cycle of myths with a commentary and selected passages from the text.
7. See the chapter on Japanese religions in the volume *Sacred Place* in this series for a more extensive discussion of these points.
8. In Oliver Statler's fictionalised account of the Shikoku pilgrimage there is a description (again fictional, but based on various textual accounts) of a holy man narrating this story in order to fire up villagers with faith and enthusiasm (Statler 1984: 168–72).
9. Mills (1970: 5–45) provides a general outline of the developments of *setsuwa* literature and some of the issues associated with it.
10. See Reader (1991: 141–7) for a fuller discussion of *engi* and the development of sacred sites.
11. This is given in Mizutani, S. (1984) 'Kumo no ue ni wa taiyo ga kagayaite iru' in Shikoku Hachijuhakkasho Reijokai (ed.), *Shikoku hachijuhakksho reigenki*, Sakaide, Shikoku Hachijuhakkasho Reijokai Honbu Jimusho, pp. 49–54.
12. For fuller discussions of these myths, see Young (1989) on Megami no Umi, and Davis (1980: 67–84) on Mahikari. The myths of both religions have also, in a typical case of Japanese syncretism, managed to absorb the figure of Jesus as a Japanese deity or religious figure.

FURTHER READING

Davis, W. (1980) *Dojo: Magic and Exorcism in Modern Japan*, Stanford, Cal., Stanford University Press.

Dykstra, Y.K. (1976) 'Tales of the Compassionate Kannon: The *Hasedera Kannon Genki*' in *Monumenta Nipponica* 31/2: 113–43.

Ebersole, G.L. (1989) *Ritual Poetry and the Politics of Death in Early Japan*, Princeton, NJ, Princeton University Press.

Mills, D.E. (1970) *A Collection of Tales from Uji: A Study and Translation of the Uji Shui Monogatari*, Cambridge, Cambridge University Press.

Nakamura, K.M. (1973) (trans. with an introduction) *Miraculous Tales from the Japanese Buddhist Tradition: The Nihon Ryoiki of the Monk Kyokai*, Cambridge, Mass., Harvard University Press.

Philippi, D. (trans.) (1968) *Kojiki*, Tokyo, University of Tokyo Press.

Reader, I. (1991) *Religion in Contemporary Japan*, Basingstoke, Macmillan.

Reader, I., Andreasen, E. and Stefansson, F. (1993) *Japanese Religions: Past and Present*, Folkestone, Japan Library Ltd.

Statler, O. (1984) *Japanese Pilgrimage*, London, Picador.

Young, R.F. (1989) 'The Little-Lad Deity and the Dragon Princess: Jesus in a New World Renewal Movement' in *Monumenta Nipponica* 44/1: 31–44.

Index